TURNING TOWARD HOME

TURNING
TOWARD HOME

A Sojourn of Hope

JOYCE HOLLYDAY

1817

Harper & Row, Publishers, San Francisco

New York, Grand Rapids, Philadelphia, St. Louis,
London, Singapore, Sydney, Tokyo

FIRST EDITION

Library of Congress Cataloging-in-Publication Data

Hollyday, Joyce.
  Turning toward home.

  1. Hollyday, Joyce. 2. Christian biography—United
States. I. Title.
BR1725.H637A3 1989   209'.2'4 [B]   88-45984
ISBN 0-06-064002-2

---

89 90 91 92 93 HAD 10 9 8 7 6 5 4 3 2 1

To Arthur M. Brown

Contents

Foreword

Joyce Hollyday's book, things being otherwise, life leading her elsewhere, might have been entitled *Memoirs of a Protestant Girlhood—and Sequel.* The "otherwise," the "elsewhere," are the marvel. They enable her, led as she was, to write neither a roman à clef nor a disenchanted diary.

Everything in place, everything operating in her favor. Her childhood was a tale still told here and there, where money and family take their stint at plugging the raging dike of the times. She was lucky indeed, a mysterious fall of the cards known as Providence.

Another advantage. Through the world 'round and home to her spouse and community, she met extraordinary people. People who inspired, offered ideals in action, made goodness attractive.

And the timing! The right person seemed to cross her path at precisely the right moment, when, one thinks, she was neither numbed nor outwitted by "the world, the way it goes." Life proceeded as a kind of stately minuet celebrating uprightness, intelligence, good sense, the perdurance of style—a dance to the tune of a twentieth-century WASP concerto.

The theme, a few notes that govern all, is quite humble and often taken for granted. It is the secret of Bach, a kind of Protestant secret; which all said, is a Christian secret. It is played out ever so discreetly, in lives as diverse as Bonhoeffer and Merton and Dorothy Day and the suffering servants Joyce encounters across the world, all those who have the primary notes by heart. And at length discover to their delight that they echo the music of the spheres.

Once the theme is firm, Joyce may improvise: outreach, political imagination, a voice for the inarticulate and victimized.

The music cannot be subsumed under some sterile rubric like *activism*, a cliché coined by media, stopped in their tracks by an unexplainable melody of persistence and sweetness. The music issues from an opposite pole, inward, a center.

The feat is something like the placing of a piling that allows for a stupendous cantilever. It implies, requires, rewards discipline. That which, etymologically, makes, creates, the disciple.

Another word for the secret music is prayer. I lost count, or forgot to take count, of the occasions when in Joyce Hollyday's life, she had recourse to prayer. Natural as air it seemed, or the breathing of air. Daily, hourly, minute by minute, defining a day, a season, a year.

Then another kind of prayer. Passionate, beleaguered, a kind of last-ditch recourse. Prayer sustaining her in the inferno of the world, whether Harlem (the place of her first awakening, a cruel macadam garden of experience) or Central America, or Southern Africa or, hardest and hottest of all, the fervently stoked capital hell of Washington.

Against such as she, and those she stands with, the world indeed strikes hard; peacetime triage, warehoused neighborhoods, the courts, the bridge of sighs joining expendable lives to strategic next-door jails. And then across the world, straight-faced American chicanery, war upon war, a glut of weapons that chokes the gorge of Mars.

Why keep going on, when against every effort a new field of dragon's teeth is sown, a new harvest of warriors springs up?

One keeps on because there is no other way of being human. No other vocation than this; choices, being chosen. So William Stringfellow said, in his laconic way. So said a stricken teacher she knew in New York. So said others in their own way. And finally, her community.

It goes this way. She meets a friend and takes a step, and

the step leads further, in no predictable direction. It is all one, it is all mysterious.

Then the metaphors and incidents, so bright and clear and blessed at the start, grow ominous. Shortly there are stalemates and precipices and high-wire acts to be coped with. And now and then the choices are narrowed to the scope of a gimlet or gunsight, as though she were a Nicaraguan peasant surrounded by contras. She is forced to witness or hear of unutterable horrors; she must keep going or die.

Thus her story unfolds; no pilgrim's progress made easy, a middle-class child on track, family to college to job to marriage to suburb. Something terribly other. The pilgrim's stalemate, the pilgrim's detour, the seizure of the pilgrim, the pilgrim jailed, death surrounding the pilgrim, the pilgrim crying out in the night.

Joyce is—I risk a cliché—the story of all of us. At least in ricochet, in longing. (And in recoiling from?) The story we wish were ours, the story we fear might be ours. The life we pray for (and against), the life we know we are called to (at least in metaphor, and according to circumstance), the life we wish could happen, or wish could never happen, to us. Admiration and fear, that uneasy mix.

And then the world. And prayer. She meets the one, armed with the other, and with that strength beyond strength, the love of good friends.

For this we thank her. And because she insists in so gentle and candid a way (her book a loving glance in our direction): "So can you keep on."

Daniel Berrigan

Acknowledgments

This book was written over a period of about four years, from Detroit to Block Island, Rhode Island; from Roque Bluffs, Maine, to three corners of Pennsylvania. I want to thank first of all those who offered me the quiet spaces in which to write: my parents, Ann and Robert Hollyday; my in-laws, Phyllis and James Wallis; Daniel Berrigan; Nancy Moorehead; Robert Raines and friends at Kirkridge; and Joan Chittister and the always welcoming Benedictine sisters of Mount St. Benedict in Erie, Pennsylvania.

I am grateful to my editors at Harper & Row: Roy Carlisle, who from the beginning encouraged me to dream about and undertake this project, and Rebecca Laird, who saw it through to completion.

Much logistical support was offered along the way from staff members of *Sojourners* magazine, including Barbara Ryan, Mark Honeywell, Karen JonesWaddell, Suzanne St. Yves, Steve McKindley-Ward, and Karen Vernon-Young.

A few days before the catalog announcing this book was set to go to press, an author's worst fear came true: the title I had been working with for almost four years (*The Way Home*) was discovered on another book of considerably different perspective. I want to thank Brian Jaudon, Joe Lynch, and Jim Rice for sacrificing an afternoon on short notice to help me come up with a new title (even though they did say *Turning Toward Home* sounds like what horses do at a racetrack and offered alternatives like *There's No Place Like Home; Home, Home on the Range;* and *I Am the Way Home, the Truth, and the Life*).

I want to extend my appreciation to everyone on the staff of *Sojourners* for their patience and support, especially Martha

Keys Barker, who offered valuable suggestions on the manuscript, and Karen Lattea, who gave me continual encouragement to keep going and graciously shouldered extra burdens at the magazine to make it possible.

I also thank all my sisters and brothers of Sojourners Community—marvelous companions on this journey—who offered encouragement, prayers, and chocolate when they were needed the most.

Special thanks go to Jim Wallis—my husband and best friend—who at a critical juncture in my life took hold of my hand and, through many years of joy and otherwise, never let go. Without his unwavering faith in me and this project, his persistent encouragement and tireless support, this book would have remained merely an idea.

The book is dedicated to Art Brown, who many years ago dared to take a bunch of college students into Harlem, changing the life of at least one of them. Today Art struggles in the lonely prison of infirmity. But he offers to all who know and love him a most important reminder: that the one who made us requires only that we do justice, love mercy, and walk humbly—even as we sometimes stumble—with our God.

1. Homeless

The knock at the church door came at three o'clock in the morning. It was late November, and the city was wrapped in a blanket of frigid air that signaled the beginning of a long winter.

Sixty homeless men had finally settled down in the huge social room off the church's kitchen for a short winter's nap; some would awaken in just a few hours to go stand in long lines in the bitter cold, waiting for an unemployment check, a doctor, or a chance for a job. The clamorous dinnertime was over; the sleeping mats were all arranged, one against the other. And for a moment all was quiet but for some snoring and an occasional wheeze.

Then came the knock. I opened the door a crack to find two young Hispanic women on the stoop, clutching three babies and two garbage bags full of possessions. They told me in Spanish that they had been sent by the police and needed a place to spend the night.

"But there's no room—and we can't take children in here with all these men." My Spanish was awkward.

Their weary eyes pleaded for rest as another gust of bone-chilling air rushed in from outside where they stood. One by one the babies started to cry.

"OK."

Three other children appeared from behind them as I ushered the small parade through the snores and back to the kitchen, where I had planned to grab some sleep. I lifted my sleeping bag off the kitchen floor and spread it in the basket of the large dishwasher to make a bed for the six-month-old twins.

"¿Hay leche?" Yes, there was milk. I hunted through the

kitchen for a pan and some matches and began to heat the milk. The babies quieted and drank hungrily.

I went in search of blankets and returned with several. We found spaces between the cabinets, under the tables, in front of the refrigerators, for everyone. All were soon sound asleep. All except one.

Four-year-old María climbed into my lap and whimpered softly as I stroked her hair. Sitting on a blanket on the concrete floor, I cradled her and rocked until she fell asleep. Then I leaned back against the refrigerator and tried to sleep myself.

Efforts at sleep were overpowered by a rush of thoughts. "This is no place for children as precious as these," I whispered to myself as I gazed at María asleep in my arms. And I wondered what it would be like to have a childhood without a home.

Home was something I had thought about often in the month since I had arrived in Washington, D.C. I was on a journey that made me wonder if I would ever again find a home. I knew that my first home would never be home in the same way again. And yet it had a power over me, that place that held all my memories of eighteen years of growing up.

I had felt an odd sense of loss when, just weeks before, my parents told me they had decided to put our home in Hershey, Pennsylvania, up for sale; they had begun plans for a new house on a piece of farmland thirteen miles out of town. The night before coming to Washington, I had decided to take one last, long walk down the familiar streets of my hometown.

It was a brisk, late-October night, and I turned up the collar of my ski parka against the blasts of wind that sent dark leaves swirling in circles in the street. The family dog walked beside me, her breath coming out in white clouds as she panted in the cold.

We walked slowly together down the dark, deserted, and Halloween-expectant streets. Homemade goblins danced on every front door, and smiling jack-o'-lanterns sat in windows—

the children who created them now tucked safely away in bed, dreaming of costumes and candy.

I remembered a Halloween years past, one I hadn't thought of in a decade. My family had entered the local Halloween parade. Dad had made a huge float from an old wagon. The theme of our float was a line from a famous poem: "When the frost is on the pumpkin, and the corn is in the shock." Who wrote it? I couldn't remember.

We made a corn shock from stalks in our garden. And we found a big pumpkin, which my younger sister, Debra, sat on. Yes—she was "Jack Frost," dressed in a glittery white costume with an icicle nose. And Mom and Dad were farmers and pulled the float. And I was a pumpkin.

We made a huge sphere out of coat hangers that reached from my neck to my knees, covered it with sheets, and spray-painted it orange. I poked my arms out of the sides to wave at children and shake their hands.

Kay. What was my older sister? A scarecrow? Maybe. I couldn't recall—but I think this was her idea. A picture of us made the front page of the local paper. I laughed as I remembered it. It was a night just like this.

Halloween—what a great town Hershey is to be in when it comes, I thought. Easter, too. Chocolate holidays, celebrated in the town that chocolate built. I kept on wandering, shuffling through fallen leaves and feeling the sting of a light rain that began to fall.

I walked the streets where Deb and I had a paper route one year—trudging up and down in deep snow as it grew dark during winter and delivering the papers in half the time on roller skates in summer. I passed the store where I got my first "viola" in fourth grade—actually a three-quarter-size violin with viola strings and strips of adhesive tape to show me where to place my fingers.

I went by a friend's home where we had an all-night party on the night of our high school graduation, eating a ten-foot-long salami-and-cheese submarine sandwich and then sneaking out to the fountain in Hershey's square and dumping in a large box of bubbling soap. I passed by another friend's house, where in sixth grade we had rehearsed our parts in "The Cuckoo Clock Song" from *The Sound of Music*. I followed the route that our church youth fellowship had taken Christmas caroling on a cold, snowy night each year, recalling the homes where we had been invited in for cookies and hot chocolate.

The field where my grandfather and I one spring had discovered a nest of young geese on the bank of the stream came into view, the same field to which I escaped almost daily in later years when I wanted to be alone and undisturbed. There I watched autumn sunsets, walked in winter snowdrifts, gathered bouquets of wild violets in spring, and witnessed a shower of falling stars one summer.

And then I found myself on the path home from school—a route I had walked hundreds of times before. As I walked, a story came back to me, and I laughed aloud as I thought of it.

When I was in second grade, our class planned to take a field trip to a turkey farm. (It was quite a special treat at the time.) When the big day arrived, I was sick with a cold. Hoping that I had forgotten, and knowing that I would be terribly disappointed to miss it, Mom told Kay not to mention it when she said good-bye on her way to school. Trying to make me feel better, Kay came in and said, "Good-bye, Joyce. Don't worry that you're sick today; your class isn't going to a turkey farm or anything." I cried half that day; and I laughed hard now as I remembered it.

Then I became very quiet as I thought about Kay, who was living in Kentucky and carrying the child that the following summer would make me an aunt. Deb was even farther away in Colorado. Their distance from me made the emptiness in Hershey seem even greater.

I felt unprepared for all the changes that were taking place. I longed for old securities and tried to fathom all the changes that were inevitably part of the passage of time: the death of my grandfather; the marriages of sisters and friends; the building of a new home by my parents as they looked forward to retirement—a peaceful place that would be "perfect for the grandchildren."

But I was also overcome with gratitude for a past graced with so many special moments. I was thankful to have a history filled with places that hold my secrets and people who hold my love. Everyone needs a town and a street and a home—more special to them than any other place—that is their memory's own.

It must have been midnight when I turned the last corner and caught a glimpse of home. There was a warm glow from the porch light, which was on—as it had always been through the years—to welcome me.

It would always be home. But it would never again be the same. I went into the kitchen and heated up some hot chocolate, trying to make a windblown, rainswept, tear-stained, nostalgic twenty-three-year-old kid feel better.

María stirred slightly as I ended these memories; she sighed, then settled more deeply into sleep. As I watched her dream, I wondered what memories of home would be part of her life, what past she would have upon which to build her dreams.

She was so vulnerable, and there seemed, despite our embrace, to be such a distance between us. Somehow I felt that understanding María and her vulnerability was a key for my future.

The twins woke up hungry just as the first light of day peeked through the tiny window overhead, and my musings got swallowed up in the need to warm up more milk and make oatmeal for the men in the next room.

I had never cooked for sixty before, and my first effort was not hailed as a great success. As I dropped a blob of oatmeal the consistency of mortar into the bowl of a toothless, whiskered old gentleman wearing three coats, he looked at me and said, "I hope you're not planning on getting married."

After breakfast, María's mother explained to me that she was going to hitchhike with her sister and all their children to San Antonio, Texas. When I asked her if she knew how long that might take, she answered, "I don't know. I'm not sure how many towns there are between here and there." I arranged a ride for them to Travelers' Aid, an agency designed to help people in their predicament.

As I opened the church door to let them out, another blast of bitter air rushed inside, reminding us that winter was here to stay for a while. I wondered how long I would stay. It was a long way from Hershey, Pennsylvania.

2. Chocolatetown U.S.A.

The first snowfall hit in early December, blanketing the city in sparkling beauty by day and a soft hush at night. More snow fell on our heads that winter of 1977 than Washington had seen in a very long time. The children were ecstatic, reveling in "snow days" off from school and the chance to throw snowballs and push stranded cars out of the huge snowbanks that put in a rare appearance in our inner-city neighborhood.

It was alien territory for me, and the children were the first neighbors to offer a welcome. They had been the first to greet Sojourners Community, which I had come to join, when the small band of people moved from Chicago to Washington two years before.

The first members of the community to arrive found their new house piled high with garbage and old mattresses. Several children, who had observed their arrival from neighboring stoops, joined in the task of cleaning it out, dragging the mattresses back to the alley behind the house.

Many of the children were part of a family of thirteen, who later moved into a community household when they were evicted from their home. The boys spent hours tumbling on the old mattresses, dubbed themselves "The Afrobats," and years later won several trophies in citywide gymnastics tournaments.

The first snowfall brought a temporary end to gymnastics season in the alley and the arrival of a snowball-slinging gang on the front stoop of one of our Sojourners households. From across the street, I watched amusedly as they knocked on the door and then retreated to assume positions in the street from which to pelt the house.

Before long, members of the household were out on the

porch firing back. They seemed to be winning; the snowballs from the street kept sailing high over the heads of the targets on the porch. The strategy became clear when one of the kids fired the critical-mass snowball that shook loose the huge layer of snow from the house's roof, burying the Sojourners in an avalanche.

Everybody came up laughing, with the laughs in the street being the loudest. The snow was something to revel in that year.

For as long as I could remember, I had reveled in snow, and the abundance of it that winter made me nostalgic for Maine, where during my college years I often took off on a pair of cross-country skis for the quiet and solitude of the woods. I thought even more about Hershey, about Kay and Deb and a game we used to play called "Wagon Wheel"—a version of tag played in the snow.

Thoughts about Hershey became an anchor during my first weeks in Washington, a means of getting perspective on where I had been. Understanding Hershey helped me to understand why I had come to Washington.

Hershey, Pennsylvania. "Chocolatetown U.S.A." A quiet little town brought to birth at the turn of the century by a chocolate entrepreneur, who had envisioned more than the usual company town.

Milton Hershey converted Pennsylvania cornfields into a land flowing with milk and sugar. Cows were brought to the rich central Pennsylvania farmland, and sugar poured in from South America and the Caribbean. When cocoa beans began to arrive from tropical countries all over the world, the formula was complete for a taste treat new to America: "milk chocolate."

The early chocolate confectionaries, in the shapes of bicycles, cigars, and lobsters, were immensely popular, and the town thrived under the wealth generated by the chocolate sensation. As soon as schools and churches were in place, Mr. Hershey began designing the town's golf course, amusement park, and zoo.

Half a century later, when I arrived on the scene, the town was well known not only for its chocolate—celebrated with such touches as streetlight domes in the shape of Hershey's kisses along Chocolate Avenue, the town's main street—but also its large amusement park, spacious convention facilities, twenty-three-acre rose garden, and five golf courses (giving it, according to the promotional literature, "more golf per square foot than any other place in the world").

The adjective *pleasant* seems designed to describe Hershey, the word bringing to mind broad, tree-lined streets and children peacefully at play. At the center of town, on the four corners created by the intersection of Chocolate and Cocoa avenues, stood the community center, which held the library and theater; the bank; the Cocoa Inn; and the drugstore, where you could buy cherry- or chocolate-flavored Cokes on hot summer days. On most days, and particularly on cloudy ones, the sweet smell of chocolate hung in the air.

On summer days Kay and Deb and I would often take a couple of dollars to the park to ride the wooden roller coaster known as "The Comet" and one of the oldest merry-go-rounds in the world. And on summer nights we fell asleep to the distant shriek of the "Dry Gulch Railroad" whistle as the train made its last loop through the park. When we got older, we fulfilled our duty as good children of Hershey by doing our summer stint selling waffles and ice cream or announcing dolphin shows (having applied too late for the coveted opportunity to wander the park in a box mimicking a Mr. Goodbar and waving at children).

And we were, for the most part, good children of Hershey. We saluted the flag, obeyed the Safety Patrol, and never darkened the door of the principal's office.

Like most children of Chocolatetown, Kay and Deb and I took frequent tours through the chocolate factory, which hosted several thousand tourists a day. When our fascination with huge vats of chocolate and conveyor belts carrying miles of cans of chocolate syrup waned, we discovered a way to cut the tour down to five minutes—by lining up with a group of tourists behind a Hershey-kiss-hatted guide and, at the appropriate moment, shortcutting and joining a tour just leaving the factory. Thus we could acquire several free Hershey bars a day, each being the reward at the end of a tour.

We often played in a large field bordering Cocoa Avenue. Occasionally tourists would call to us for directions to the chocolate factory, the park, or the hotel. One day, a bit tired of these intrusions on our play, I stepped forward to give a carload from New Jersey directions to the factory: "Make a U-turn, go a mile out of town, make a right, go past the golf course . . ." Kay and Deb were rather horrified and then laughed as they realized the car making the U-turn was on its way to the sewage treatment plant.

I lost sleep that night, so plagued was I with guilt for my misdeed and with a vision of a carload of New Jersey tourists wandering aimlessly for days through the Hershey countryside, asking everyone they encountered, "Have you seen the chocolate factory?" It was the only vaguely dishonest thing I remember doing as a child—apart from, of course, our conspiracy toward the inordinate acquisition of free candy bars. I think it could be said that, had I not lived in a town with a chocolate factory, I would have had a clean moral slate.

Honesty was a virtue stressed by my grandfather. A banker who had driven an ambulance during World War I, Grandpa Minnich was a granddaughter's delight. He lived with my grandmother in Gettysburg, Pennsylvania, and was an expert on the Civil War. He never tired of telling us—at dinnertime, at naptime, at bedtime—about how the Confederate soldiers came into Gettysburg looking for shoes, and how the terrible battle was won by the brave Union Army. And my sisters and I never tired of listening.

One of Grandpa's heroes was Abraham Lincoln, who, he

would joke, "also had a Gettysburg address." When I was six, on one of many visits to my grandparents' favorite cafeteria, I picked up a piece of butter for my bread and only discovered after the meal had been paid for that another one was inadvertently stuck to it. I mentioned my concern about it to Grandpa, and a few days later I got an envelope from him in the mail containing a receipt from the cafeteria for three cents and a note telling me how proud he was "to have a granddaughter as honest as Honest Abe."

I remember Grandpa's boxes full of treasures—relics of the war, Indian arrowheads, colorful marbles used for playing Chinese checkers, rings and cards for magic tricks, and old coins—among them his "special pennies," including one that had been flattened by a train and another that he had touched to President Dwight Eisenhower's pew in a Gettysburg church. By sending off self-addressed, stamped envelopes to postmasters all over the country with a request that they be mailed back, he had also acquired a delightful collection of postmarks from places such as Accident, Maryland, and Bird-in-Hand, Pennsylvania.

But my warmest and best memories are about the times when Grandpa and I—just the two of us—climbed into his two-tone green Studebaker, built the year I was born, and drove to what we always called "The Lot."

The Lot was a seven-acre piece of wooded land near Gettysburg with a stream and a rushing waterfall. Kay and Deb and I spent endless hours there as children climbing the rocks, floating sticks over the falls, and wading in the shallow, sunny pools filled with minnows.

A large rock overlooking the falls resembled a man's profile, and we dubbed it "Old Man of the Falls." In winter he looked cold and lonely, but in summer a patch of moss grew above his sharp nose, and it became an annual ritual to try to be the first to spot his "eyebrows."

The times when Grandpa and I went alone to The Lot began as soon as I was old enough to walk through snow with a handful of birdseed and place it safely on top of a large rock or in the hollow of a tree. Grandpa took it as his personal responsibility to see that the wild birds and small animals didn't starve in winter. Those days often brought the excitement of discovering a wild rabbit burrowed into snow or the tracks of a deer.

Our treks alone there were education for me, but also spiritual journey. I never got over being awed by the variety of God's good creatures, the delicateness of the wildflowers, the beauty of the sturdy trees. Grandpa taught me the kind of appreciation and trust for the Creator that comes from reveling in the creation.

He taught me how to identify trees by their leaves and bark, how to tell maple from oak. He showed me where to look for the mitten-leaved sassafras with its sweet-smelling bark, and the myrrh with a halo of seeds and a root that tasted like licorice. He uncovered the clean, white Indian pipes that grew buried under leaves and pointed out the mayapples on the underside of broad plants that looked like umbrellas.

Grandpa took care of his trees like he did his animals. He watched for vines that might choke young seedlings, for fallen branches and damage from lightning. He went through the woods with a can of black, tarry stuff that he said would heal the wounds and keep disease from creeping in. And when he got too old to climb the trees himself, he sent me up to gently paint the goo on wounded limbs.

Kay and Deb and I were also blessed with two grandmothers who took an interest in us. Grandmother Minnich greeted us every visit with fried chicken, strawberry custard, and banana bread just out of the oven; listened to stories of all our activities and accomplishments; and was particularly tolerant of the cacophony we created every time we tried to play viola, guitar, and flute together.

Grandmother Hollyday, a keeper of African violets, is the white-haired matriarch of a large Hollyday clan. A strong and faithful woman, she raised my father and four other sons during the depression and is gifted with a sense of humor that was probably her survival in those days. When I asked her recently about her new hearing aid, she said, "Well, it's really nothing to shout about."

My sisters and I were introduced to God at the First United Methodist Church on Chocolate Avenue. I remember celebrating my fifth birthday in Sunday school there. After blowing out candles on a plastic cake that was recycled for every birthday, I was allowed to choose a picture of Jesus to keep. The classic pictures were all awesome to me—Jesus knocking at the door, feeding the five thousand, preaching on the mountain, walking on the water.

But I knew immediately which picture I wanted: Jesus holding the lost lamb. I knew the story well—how the Good Shepherd had forsaken all the other sheep to go after the weak and wounded lamb.

At that time I faced the usual fears and insecurities that plague young children—plus a few that seemed uniquely mine. I drew mishaps like a magnet.

My most vivid memory is of the day I slid off the edge of a boat at age four and plunged into Lake Wallenpaupack in Pennsylvania's Pocono Mountains. (Kay—with legs much longer than mine—had been dangling her feet over the side in the water, and I thought it looked like fun.) I still remember the feel of the cold water rushing over my head and the fear. Dad jumped in and saved me, losing his wallet and camera in the process.

I had been born with my knees a bit cockeyed, which made my feet turn in (my knee bones being connected to my leg bones, being connected to my foot bones, and all that). I started school with elastic braces on my legs and orthopedic shoes. I will never forget the anguish I felt when a classmate threw me off a swing at school one day and yelled "Cripple!" in my face.

It was not a serious or long-term handicap. It was nothing compared to what many other children have to face. But I started my social life feeling different and insecure around my peers and often lonely—feelings that usually seem far behind me now but in some ways will always be part of me.

I was particularly conscious of them that day in September 1959. As I stood in front of the Sunday school class in my leg braces—just two weeks after I had started school—I pointed to the picture of Jesus with the lamb and whispered, "That one." In some childlike way, I knew I was that lamb, that I needed to be cradled and protected by this Good Shepherd.

I kept that picture by my bed, and I often turned to it and found comfort, trusting in the promise that, despite everything, Jesus loved me. That feeling, formed very early, is one that has lasted through a lifetime of fears and insecurities.

I am grateful now for some of the painful lessons of those days. I discovered what I could only years later articulate—that we are each a combination of woundedness and strength. I learned never to exploit other people's pain or hardship. I learned to tackle life as a challenge, to rely on my own resources when other people failed me, and, most of all, to trust the God who had given me life—and didn't let me lose it at the age of four at the bottom of Lake Wallenpaupack.

My sisters and I were as creative as most kids. We invented a game we called "corn shockey," a form of hockey played in the fall just when the corn stalks were about ready to be cut down and made into a large corn shock. Kay, Deb, and I—each armed with a corn stalk and defending one wing of our three-winged driveway—attempted to knock a whiffleball into one of the other corners for a score. The stalks broke of course with every other hit, and the challenge was to run back to the garden, pull another stalk out of the ground, and be back to defend your corner before a sister scored against you.

As soon as we could prove that we could tread water for ten minutes, we were taught to water-ski—I learned at age seven. Imagining ourselves the aqua-stars of Cypress Gardens (we had seen them perform at the 1964 World's Fair in New York), our attempts at piggyback skiing and several other feats we had seen only left us laughing and sputtering from various plunges into the Susquehanna River. One of the greatest accomplishments in my young life occurred the day four male cousins and I succeeded in skiing behind one boat at the same time one summer in Vermont.

Kay and Deb and I shared a love for and fascination with the ocean. As soon as Kay was old enough to drive, we made summer treks to the beach, leaving in the middle of the night in order to catch the sunrise over the waves and coming home late. We gathered a repertoire of stories and still reminisce about such adventures as the time Deb locked our beach clothes in the gas station ladies' room with the key inside at six o'clock in the morning.

As children of Chocolatetown, we had the unique opportunity of being guinea pigs for the chocolate corporation's marketing staff, bearing the burden of representing all the first-graders in America as we chose our favorite among six eye-catching wrappers for the latest Hershey product—a welcome interruption to reading class. In junior high we graduated to taste-testing, eating samples of chocolate interspersed with pieces of celery to remove the previous taste, thereby avoiding chocolate confusion. When the test was over, we cheered wildly for the sample we were told was Hershey's, giving the competitors' entries the appropriately overly dramatized "Yech!"

This, of course, was all part of our understanding that we were the very best. And indeed it was easy to believe that in Hershey, because we had the very best things. Our high school was considered the best in the area. Our high school football games were played in the same stadium that the Philadelphia Eagles used for training. Our small town was wealthy enough to have its own professional hockey team (originally called the Hershey Bars and later the Hershey Bears).

By the time I was a teenager, the chocolate corporation had accrued so much wealth that its executives decided to build a top medical center and school on the outskirts of town. Local wisdom has it that the president of the chocolate corporation called up the president of Pennsylvania State University and asked, "Are you interested in a medical school? We'll give you $50 million to get started." I had the privilege of being one of the first patients at the emergency room of the impressive new facility, brought there from high school basketball practice with a sprained ankle. (Unfortunately, some things didn't change with age.)

Hershey was clean and comfortable, its children competitive and clever. Each school year began with the football rivalry between Hershey High School and the Milton Hershey School, a private school established by the town's founder as an orphanage for boys. As the coveted Cocoa Bean Trophy (with its honest-to-goodness shellacked cocoa bean on top) was passed between the two schools from year to year, it stood as a kind of symbol of striving for the best in this town that chocolate built.

Hershey was quintessential middle America. It stood—and stands—as a monument to the good life, to the triumph of capitalism and competitiveness. It was born from the dream of one man and, a generation later, reflected the aspirations of an entire nation.

Heady with triumph after the Second World War, America set out to have its way in world politics and productivity, expanding the notion of hegemony and launching an unprecedented consumer era. Her foot soldiers came home from the war ready for the good life. In my home the foot soldier came home without his toes, sacrificed in the war effort to gangrene and frostbite on a battlefield in Germany.

My father, like many others, wanted above all else to provide the best materially for his young family. A generation that had grown up through the struggles and insecurities of the Great Depression and World War II worked to construct a world without struggle or insecurity, a world that promised a college education and the finer things in life to all its progeny.

And its progeny were grateful. We took piano lessons and played tennis and rode ten-speed bikes in junior high, became productive young actors and athletes and editors of the year-book (the *Choclatier*, of course) in high school.

But something changed for one of Hershey's children on April 4, 1968. I was thirteen years old when Martin Luther King, Jr., was assassinated.

Five years earlier, when a president was shot, we were given three days off school and sat glued to our TV sets; we watched the assassination over and over, and the funeral procession and John-John's salute, and heard the adults talk about how awful it was. I don't remember anyone in Hershey talking about the tragedy when Martin Luther King, Jr., was killed. And I, a young Hershey teenager, had no real idea who he was.

Then the race riots wracked Harrisburg, just thirteen miles from my home. There were rumors about race riots in Hershey, about how all the black people in Harrisburg were going to come to our town and tear down our park.

On television every night for days I watched the houses burning in Harrisburg, feeling a mixture of fascination and fear. I was puzzled by the desperation of people who burned down their own homes and by the fact that no one seemed to be able to explain to me why.

At the age of thirteen, I felt for the first time what I would feel several times again: that my world was turning upside down. The riots invaded my comfortable world. And though they eventually subsided from the headlines and TV news reports, they churned up in me a rash of questions that remained unanswered for a very long time.

I began to feel that there was something incomplete, something terribly wrong, about Hershey. I couldn't explain it. But somehow I felt I hadn't been given a true picture of life. Something was missing.

Four years later another tragedy put Harrisburg in the news. In June of 1972 Hurricane Agnes swept through central Pennsylvania.

For us in Hershey the great flood of '72 was mostly an inconvenience—even a bit of an adventure. The football field was severely flooded, and my high school graduation exercises had to be moved indoors. Hershey's water system was damaged, so every day Kay and Deb and I took five-gallon camping jugs and stood in line with hundreds of others behind Hershey milk-tank trucks where drinking water from a nearby town was rationed.

Hersheypark was also flooded, and the Hershey Fire and Rescue Squad carried its two dolphins by ambulance to the local swimming pool where I worked that summer, filled with salt water to accommodate Skipper and Dolly. The only lasting effect for me, I discovered a year later when I had to have my wisdom teeth removed, was that my dental records in my oral surgeon's Front Street office in Harrisburg had been swept away and were by then likely at home somewhere at the bottom of the Atlantic.

As soon as the water had subsided enough to make the streets passable again, Kay and Deb and I signed up for "flood relief work." It was not as glamorous as we had hoped—we were assigned to a Hershey beauty salon that had been flooded and spent most of three days trying to get mud out of hair curlers.

But for the residents of Harrisburg, the flood was a tragedy of the highest order. With no discrimination, the Susquehanna overflowed its banks and washed through the insurance companies and office buildings on Front Street and then swept away the ghetto behind them. From our safe and dry distance, we sat riveted to our TV sets, getting hourly reports on the flood stages of the river and watching rescue efforts. There were endless vivid pictures of suffering—cars and trees wrapped around bridges, families huddled on floating roofs as the homes beneath them were swept away from their foundations, a child helplessly calling after her dog as it lost its struggle and drowned in the swift water.

Hershey had the means to recover quickly from its minor damage. But for Harrisburg's poorest citizens, the damage was permanent. People who had so little lost everything. Their suffering raised new questions in me, this time with implied judgment toward a God who sent a hurricane's fury to a city's most vulnerable residents. The overarching question for me still was *why*.

Kay listened to me a lot in those days, as she does today, and together we dreamed of how we might "help poor people." She and my mother were models of compassion for me, Mom having given herself through the years to all types of church and volunteer work, offering loving acceptance and support to so many others as she always had to us.

After the riots, I had wanted to go to Harrisburg. I wanted to see the suffering and make sense of it. But the people around me made it clear that Harrisburg was no place for someone like me. Nothing in my existence to that point seemed to prepare me for the tremendous weight of knowing the truth about the world's anguish, but I felt I couldn't live honestly without trying to understand.

The only way I knew to enter the world's pain was through my own. When I turned fourteen that fall, I was old enough to volunteer at a nearby Hospital for Crippled Children. Something in me made me feel I needed to face the crippled child still inside of me, to conquer the hurt that still hovered there, perhaps to offer some of the strength I had found to children struggling with difficulties so much more immense than mine ever were.

It was not Harrisburg. It was not racial injustice or explosive poverty. But it was a start for me, an entrance on a journey at the point of my deepest vulnerability.

My second night at the hospital, I rocked a five-year-old boy on my lap as I told him stories. He had recently had his left leg amputated because of a bone-marrow disease. I had seen him struggle on his small crutches and felt pain for him in his frustration to understand what had happened to him. His parents were unable to cope with the loss, and he was alone most of each day.

He interrupted my stories and looked into my face with his

immense blue eyes, then slapped his hand down on my left thigh where his should have been, and said, "Why?"

I wanted to tell him he would be stronger for it, that somehow God loved him in a special way to give him this challenge, that it was going to be OK. But I had no answer for him. I could only cradle him and catch his tears and try to push back my own as I whispered, "I don't know."

Ten years later, as I watched my friends laughing and pelting one another with snowballs, thoughts of him came back to me. I wondered where he was now.

I still didn't have an answer to his question. I was beginning to believe I never would. But sometimes the best of journeys are made up only of questions.

3. Harlem

On a cold afternoon two weeks before Christmas, we received word that a fire had started in Clifton Terrace, the huge tenement on the end of our block. Several members of Sojourners Community went to see how we could help.

The blaze had been contained on one floor, but several individuals and families were left without home or possessions. We quickly collected food and clothing for those in need of it, and that first night after the fire an elderly woman who lost her apartment moved in with us.

We never found out for certain what had caused the fire. It could have been faulty wiring. Or it could have been caused by one of the various methods people in our part of Washington used to try to keep warm in winter when the heat didn't work. Some kept ovens turned on with oven doors open; others bought electrical space heaters that sent electric bills soaring and posed a serious fire hazard. More than one blaze had been started by a blanket or curtain catching fire from the exposed red coils of an electric heater.

Clifton Terrace was a symbol of all that was wrong in our part of Washington, D.C. For years it had been the victim of landlord neglect and an extortion scandal that involved the former wife of the mayor. Now its halls were home to drug pushers and others who preyed on its poor residents.

Clifton Terrace still stands in Washington, D.C. But, under other names, it stands in cities all around the country. Clifton Terrace, and all the places like it, house the poor who have no other options.

I learned this first in the city that had upset my world when I was still in high school. That's also where I learned that even the Clifton Terraces were disappearing for the poor, leaving them nothing.

It was inevitable that I would eventually go to Harrisburg. Nothing dramatic. While still a teenager, I went as a counselor for a church-run day camp.

The journey was, at least in part, self-discovery. I suppose that our earliest strivings, perhaps most of the impulses throughout our lives, are to understand ourselves—in relationship to what we discover, to the world around us, and, at heart, to God.

But I believe that this journey was also a search for the truth. To live honestly, I had to go to Harrisburg, to see the truth that was there and to allow it to help me put Hershey in perspective.

I was still a Hershey kid, and I wasn't prepared for what I saw in Harrisburg apartments—bare rooms with cardboard boxes for furniture, screenless windows and kitchen tables covered with flies, places with no room for children to play but the streets. Some of the children came to camp hungry because their mothers could not afford to give them breakfast.

For the first time, I felt that the Jesus I grew up with, the Jesus I was bringing those children, was inadequate. They needed to know the tender care of the shepherd, but it seemed to me they needed so much more.

At camp the children seemed to thrive. I saw flashes of life and creativity and joy that burst forth in play; but these seemed to be slowly dying in the older children, crushed by feelings of despair and emptiness.

Toward the end of the summer, several of the children no longer showed up for camp. The staff was sent out to do a survey in the neighborhood that was home to most of them.

The change in the neighborhood was shocking. Where two months before we had recruited children for camp, we found vacant buildings with yellow notices posted on front doors.

"No Trespassing" signs were plastered everywhere, and next-door neighbors shook their heads and talked about city officials and their plans for "urban redevelopment."

It happened quickly. The eviction notices seemed to be popping up everywhere. When we asked one neighbor where people were going, she said with resignation, "Some have kin somewhere. Some don't. I don't know. Everybody's crowded already. I guess we'll be next."

City officials and business associates were pooling their forces and running over Harrisburg's poor neighborhoods like the bulldozers to come, making way for bigger and better business. And the suffering that came in its wake was considered a natural and necessary by-product. I had always looked at life as a set of options and personal choices; but I was learning that behind personal tragedies were political forces that had no regard for the people they crushed.

Jim Miller, the camp director, decided we should try to fight it. We focused on one building and one family. We got the local TV cameras to come and film the razing of an apartment building while one of the residents, with a four-year-old by her side and a six-month-old in her arms, talked about her desperate plight and the disappearance of her neighborhood. The TV cameras followed us to city hall, where we confronted the city council.

We made the local news that night. I was ecstatic. One of the Harrisburg city officials had found out that some of us were from "out of town" and accused us of being "outside agitators." I had devoured Saul Alinsky's *Rules for Radicals* that summer and was enamored with his confrontational community-organizing tactics—and proud to be among the company of "outside agitators."

I thought it would all make a difference. It didn't. It was a lesson I would learn many times over in the years to come.

The world of the children I had met in Harrisburg was so different from mine. But part of me could understand their pain—the part that had known what it was like to feel marginal. I thought that if I could just make people in places like Hershey see what was true, things would change.

Surely, I reasoned, everyone had at some time felt lonely or hurt; if they could remember what that felt like, they could understand poverty. And if people understood just how terrible poverty is, they would surely work to do away with it. I had found the key to changing the world.

I had forgotten that in America being strong was what counted most.

With the exception of a few family members, Kay and my mother in particular, nobody seemed terribly interested in my plan for changing the world. Nothing changed the way I was sure it would when I came back from Harrisburg with my stories. Few people even listened.

One who did was John Lynch, a seminary student and a member of my church in Hershey, who placed in my hands a copy of William Stringfellow's *My People Is the Enemy*. Stringfellow was an Episcopal theologian and lawyer who had gone to Bates College in Maine, then Harvard Law School, and worked for many years as an advocate for the poor in East Harlem. His book was an autobiographical reflection on his work in East Harlem, and I was deeply touched by the suffering and hope the book contained.

Despite a commitment I had made at church camp in the fourth grade to be a veterinary missionary in Africa (some exotic combination of a missionary from our church whom I admired and the lion doctor from the TV show "Daktari") and my father's vague hopes that I might be the first female cadet at the U.S. Naval Academy, I decided to pursue a prelaw degree at Bates College.

One of the attractions of the college was a spring work-study program in East Harlem. The very name *Harlem* conjured up many frightening images for me, but somehow I felt that in this place where suffering and poverty were so concentrated, in this place so alien from all that I had known and been, I would find a piece of myself. And I needed that piece to continue on my journey.

I remember that one of the hardest things about my decision to go was telling family and friends. The risks seemed at the time to be very great, and they feared for my safety. Our conversations about it were difficult for all concerned. It was their love for me that made them afraid and made them want to hold on to me. And it was that same love that ultimately made them let me go.

I was put off at first by the fact that the six-week work-study program in East Harlem was a religion course. After my first couple of months in college, I didn't set foot inside a church for two years. The deepest questions that haunted me—about suffering and justice—seemed to have no place in the churches I tried.

I abandoned Jesus because I felt the Good Shepherd wasn't tough enough to understand the hard realities that I was beginning to discover about the world. He was too nice to understand the kind of black rage that set homes on fire and too pretty to be bothered with the ugliness of poverty. But I was about to rediscover Jesus in an entirely different guise.

I left Hershey on a train in April 1974. My mind was full of thoughts, and I felt a deep excitement about the opportunity to see Harlem. As I got closer to New York City, my mood became subdued. And by the time the train was passing over Harlem, I began to feel fear and uncertainty about the whole venture.

Harlem was a strange and puzzling place to me. The huge tenements which housed hundreds of people overwhelmed me. The streets were full of children and dogs and peddlers and old men playing dice. The noise was jarring and constant, and the smells were overpowering—fried foods and cheap wine, rotting trash, human waste. On my first walk through Harlem, it seemed to me that to look into the eyes of Harlem's people was to see hopes crumbling like so many Harlem tenements.

I worked at Church of the Resurrection on East 101st Street. The church was a small, simple brick building across from a vacant lot where hordes of children roamed and played. A large, plain wooden cross hung in its otherwise unadorned sanctuary.

Mrs. Blorneva Selby was my supervisor and the dominating presence in the church. The night I met her, she was busy overseeing preparations of the fried-chicken dinner that was an East Harlem welcome for the twenty-two other Bates students and me, who had just arrived in the city.

I offered to help, but she insisted that I sit down and relax. I made my way to the piano and began to play. Soon Mrs. Selby came running over with a hymnbook, asking me to play her favorite songs.

After dinner she welcomed us all and said how grateful she was that she had been sent someone who plays "such sweet music" to play the piano for Sunday school. I felt as if I had arrived. Any question as to whether I would be accepted in East Harlem suddenly dissolved.

But Mrs. Selby also introduced me to a new and uncomfortable feeling, one that would grow more intense as East Harlem gradually brought truth into focus for me. While we were eating lunch one day, soon after I had arrived, she asked me, "So, is your father a doctor or a lawyer?" He is an engineer, but that didn't keep me from feeling my first twinge of guilt.

"I just figured you are from a wealthy family," she continued. A picture of Hershey's manicured lawns and my quiet field back home flashed into my mind, and I felt overcome with the tragedy of children whose only playgrounds are glass-strewn vacant lots.

I didn't know what to say. Somehow I wanted to prove to her my integrity, to make sweeping promises about my commitment to ending poverty. But the words stuck in my throat. Poverty was starting to get to me, and I wasn't at all sure I wouldn't go gladly running back to all the comforts of home as soon as I had gotten all the education I could out of Harlem.

The poverty in East Harlem was harsher and more concentrated than what I had experienced in Harrisburg, and therefore harder for me to bear at first. I was at times overwhelmed by the chaos and the noise. But as I stayed, I began to get a more whole picture of the many sides of this world. I moved often between feelings of fear on one hand and a deep and peaceful sense of being at home on the other.

I grew to love the feel of the streets—children running after the peddler of Italian ice as he pushed his cart, ringing its loud bell; women hurrying home at sundown loaded down with groceries; old men sitting on dilapidated park benches.

The children were often the most welcoming. Though I was a miserable failure at "double-Dutch" jump rope (I had always had enough trouble jumping over one rope, and two at once about did me in), they never gave up trying to teach me. They also gave me endless lessons at "The Bump," the current dance their culture had spawned; and by the end of six weeks, seven-year-old Apryl pronounced over my gyrations to the song "Rock the Boat"—"Pretty good for a white girl."

It might have been easy to try to understand Harlem from the acceptance I received from the children and the church members. And indeed there was a joy within them that flowed out of their deep faith and the strength that came from daily surviving the onslaughts of poverty.

But Harlem had its bitter side as well, the side that raged from decades of neglect and oppression. As surely as friendship was lavished upon me by those who grew to trust me, the hurt and rage were directed toward me as well. To have experienced only one side of Harlem's existence would have been to have missed the truth.

Sometimes the hurts came in seemingly small ways. Early in my stay in East Harlem, Mrs. Selby asked me to rake the glass from the "churchyard," which was mostly dirt and rocks and broken glass. I had been raking for only a few minutes when three small children came over to show me some mud pies they had made. We talked and laughed for awhile. But soon their mother came by and snatched them away, glaring and making a racial slur against me just before she marched off with them.

The hurt and anger I felt stayed with me most of the day. I had immersed myself during those weeks in reading books such as *The Autobiography of Malcolm X, Invisible Man,* and *Black Like Me* and felt I was beginning to understand racism. But this little flash of being accused on account of my race made me realize that I hadn't yet begun to know—and might never know—the daily grief and anguish that racism had rained down on people like that mother.

A few weeks later I was with a few other Bates students on our way to a church concert in Central Harlem. The feel of the streets was more dangerous in this part of Harlem, and as we turned a corner, we faced a large group of young men standing across the street from us. They yelled at us, interspersed with obscenities, "Whitey, go home!" and "Walk faster, albinos!" Then, just about level with my head, a gun was pointed out an open window beside us. I remember the soul-shaking fear that gripped me, the panicked looks we exchanged among ourselves, and the throbbing in my head that echoed the pounding of my heart.

We stepped up our pace and made it quickly to the church. When I realized we were safe, I felt tears come to my eyes. Tears of relief, perhaps. But they were also tears of anger and hurt and grief.

I recalled the faces of the children who were also on the street that night and who had heard and seen the vicious encounter; and I grieved over the seeds of hatred being sown in their young hearts. I replayed in my mind the conversation I had had the night before with Nana, a Puerto Rican woman who was the secretary at Church of the Resurrection; "I live scared," she told me, "and I hate the night."

I thought of eight-year-old Patricia and our conversation the week before. She had come by the church, smiling proudly, to show me her colorful new pocketbook, then grabbed me by the arm and begged me to take her for a walk. As we walked around the block, she told me how happy she was that she and her mother and her five sisters and brothers had moved down to the first floor of their large tenement building. "I was scared to walk up all those steps to the sixth floor. Women and men were always out there with almost no clothes on, and sometimes men touched me funny. I was scared to walk up all those steps every day."

Then I asked Patricia what she wanted to be when she grew up. "I want to be a gang leader," she told me, her eyes growing wide beneath a head full of cornrows, "so I can keep those *men* away."

The tears kept coming as I remembered Patricia's words. I felt powerless and didn't know what to do with the feeling. I wanted to curse God, to curse the system that perpetuated the suffering, to curse the men on the streets. I felt as angry at the victims as the victimizers, and somehow, for the first time, I saw how entangled I was in what I knew I couldn't change.

East Harlem was the birthplace of my political understanding of America. When I was in high school, at the same time that I had been trying to understand poverty in Harrisburg, I was writing term papers with titles like "Stopping Communist Aggression in Vietnam" (well researched and documented from a wide array of volumes of the *Reader's Digest*).

Like most children in America, I had been carefully taught that America was the world's greatest nation. We received the message in everything from our recitation of the Pledge of Allegiance to our gathering around TV sets to watch space launches and landings. Classes were suspended from elementary school to high school as we watched every Mercury, Gemini, and Apollo escapade in outer space and were proudly told, "We did it before the Russians."

I had learned well the lessons from a ten-week television series we were shown in junior high school. At the appropriate hour each week, our teachers again gathered us around a TV set, and we watched a show designed to help us "understand the Communist threat." I took careful notes.

Many years later the Berrigan brothers, Daniel and Philip, would become an important part of my theological training. But I was oblivious to the trial of the Harrisburg Seven, accused of conspiracy because of their activities against the Vietnam War, taking place next door the year I graduated from high school.

I had arrived at college just after the last gasps of antiwar activism. I remember my parents asking, at all the colleges we visited before I chose Bates, about "campus unrest." I shared their desire for me to be at a school unplagued by such extracurricular activity.

I turned eighteen three weeks after I arrived at college and just under the wire for the 1972 presidential election, the first in which eighteen-year-olds could vote. Kay and I had taken our civic responsibility seriously and registered to vote before leaving Hershey that summer, she making her first trip out of the house after a long bout with mononucleosis. The seriousness with which we approached the matter was a bit undermined by Kay's conversation with the registrar.

All was fine when he asked her name and address, but Kay faltered when it came to her age. She explained that she had just turned twenty the week before and was getting used to being twenty. Then he said, "Party?" and she answered, "No, I didn't have one this year; I was sick." He glared at her.

When she described it to me in the car later, I laughed and said, "I wonder if they're having second thoughts about giving us the vote."

The 1972 election was the baptism into electoral politics for most of the friends I associate with now, who poured their lives into the McGovern campaign. I have heard them say it was one election that really could have made a difference, the one that could have stopped the war. But fully trusting the path that my country was on, I never even bothered that November to claim the right my peers had fought so hard to win; my absentee ballot stayed in my drawer at college.

I had always felt proud to be an American, and proud of

what America stood for. I was thankful to be an inhabitant of the land of the free and the home of the brave. When I first encountered the poverty of Harrisburg, I viewed it as an aberration in an essentially contented world, kept peaceful and free by the righteous power of the United States. These beliefs were dashed to pieces by my education in Harlem.

I began to see that there was no coincidence in the fact that the complaints of the poor people in Harrisburg and East Harlem were the same. Both faced eviction at the whim of slumlords, suffered with substandard education and medical care, and had to make their homes in places infested with rats, roaches, and violence.

I was beginning to understand—slowly—that the conspiracy of greed that consigned tenants in Harrisburg and East Harlem to misery had tentacles that reached into every corner of the nation, and indeed across the globe. The affluence of the world's minority depended on an underclass that subsisted on a fraction of the world's goods.

One of the many people who came to speak to our group during our time in East Harlem made a simple statement and followed it with an illustration. He said that the American middle class, which composes 6 percent of the world's population, consumes 40 percent of the world's resources. He called this robbery from the poor and invited us to imagine ourselves shipwrecked on an island with fourteen other people, with enough water to last us several weeks, as long as it was rationed to three cups per person per day. Would any of us, he asked, drink eighteen cups a day, taking it away from the others because we felt somehow we deserved it more than they? Would we continue to consume at this rate as we watched the others die? This, he said, is the situation we live in on the island called Earth.

I was told that two-thirds of the world's population is hungry. Half of these people are literally starving to death. I found the statistics staggering.

It was clear to the people who spoke with us, most of them

pastors, lawyers, or social workers who had lived many years serving East Harlem, that the heart of the American economic system—free enterprise with an emphasis on profit and competition—was also the heart of destruction for masses of people who are made marginal by it. Essential to the bloated affluence and power of a few is hunger and unemployment for many.

In the middle of my stay in East Harlem, in May 1974, I was invited to a "Benefit Concert for Chile" at Madison Square Garden. The evening galvanized in me the feelings of shame that I was starting to feel toward my country.

Until that night I had never heard the name *Salvador Allende*. I did not know that he was a leader, popularly elected by his country, who was sympathetic to the plight of the Chilean workers. He had begun reforms in Chile, had raised the standard of living for the impoverished masses. And under his government the losers were U.S.-based multinational corporations such as IT&T who were no longer able to siphon off huge profits at the expense of the workers.

The U.S. government had engineered a coup, just months before, and Allende was overthrown. The workers were returned to desperate poverty, and rule by terror became a way of life in Chile. Assassination and torture, carried out by Chilean secret police trained by the United States, were instruments of state.

As I sat in the darkened Madison Square Garden watching graphic portrayals of the poverty and terror that now were daily life in Chile, I felt betrayed. Nothing I was learning fit with the image of America I had been raised on. My trust in America, righteous defender of freedom around the globe, evaporated that night.

As folk singer Pete Seeger got up on stage and began to sing, the people in the packed auditorium rose and clasped arms. I felt swept into the tide of emotion, into the tears and the unity and the resolve. I felt one with all those people and yet utterly alone. And I remember a young and angry voice inside of me saying that I would tear down the system—alone, with my bare hands, if I had to—until nobody suffered anymore.

Chile became a window for me into the behavior of my country around the globe. During my time in East Harlem I learned that what we had just done to Chile we did to Guatemala twenty years earlier. A sweep around the globe—South Korea, the Philippines, Iran, Argentina, Chile, Guatemala, El Salvador, Nicaragua, the Dominican Republic—showed a long list of countries ruled at that time by brutal dictatorships, supported by the United States, trained in terror by the United States, dominated by large corporations based in the United States. I learned names such as Somoza, Marcos, Shah Pahlavi—some of the most brutal men in history and all friends of the United States.

"Maximization of profit" was behind the wholesale evictions in East Harlem and the ghettos of Harrisburg. And that same sweeping tide was evicting peasants all over the globe from their homes and their lands. A vast majority of arable land around the globe was being grabbed by U.S.-based multinational corporations and used for growing items consumed in the United States—coffee, pineapples, sugar, bananas. The result was a comfortable middle class in America and masses of people landless, hungry, and exploited for cheap labor elsewhere. And wherever they were beginning to organize for their own survival, sophisticated methods of terror conceived in the United States were used against them.

In Vietnam patriotic rhetoric about stopping Communism was being used to mask the reality that the United States was just one more foreign power in a long line that tried to control the future of the tiny country. Our "war against Communism" was a war in support of a compliant South Vietnamese government, in support of the corruption that plagued it, in support of keeping the tiny nation powerless to determine its own destiny.

Unable to win the hearts and minds of the Vietnamese people—who saw our nation for what it was—we bombed the countryside, destroyed crops and villages, and took the lives of 1.5 million Vietnamese. In that war 55,000 American lives were also sacrificed. And of the Americans who came home alive, many were maimed, and many more suffered from depression, drug abuse, and the traumatic shock effects of the war.

I wrestled with what I was learning, finding no place to put this information that was so foreign to all that I had believed for twenty years. The triumphal emotionalism of my evening at Madison Square Garden gave way to a dread of what was changing in me. I felt that I had turned against America, and that choice seemed at the time to mean also turning against my past and my family and friends.

But in East Harlem I knew that I was not alone. Many faithful and courageous people, who had come from where I came from and made this journey before, spoke with us. They offered insights on the church that were new to me, seeing it as a base for engagement in the world, a countersign to the world's values of consumption and competitiveness that offered its life for the sake of justice. And each one of them offered the challenge that not to act on behalf of justice was to affirm the status quo, to accept injustice.

I will never forget meeting William Stringfellow, the lay theologian and East Harlem lawyer whose book had helped to bring me to Harlem. He offered searing political analysis of the Nixon administration and the Vietnam War and spoke at length about the selfishness and spiritual bankruptcy of American culture. He offered a passionate statement that came to the surface of my mind again and again in years to come: "Resistance is the only way to live humanly."

I was in awe of this man's brilliance and articulateness. But I managed to gather up my courage to approach him and share with him about the importance of his book to me, about my short-lived law career, and about my sense of losing roots and direction. He said to me, "It doesn't matter what field you go into. What is important is that you have integrity. And if you do, you will accomplish something. And if you believe in something, people will know it."

Stringfellow, along with all the others who spoke with us, shared the moral indignation that I was just starting to feel; but in them it was tempered by experience, maturity, and faith. And it was their faith that spoke most loudly to me. All of them had poured their lives into the struggle for justice and had watched conditions in East Harlem through the years grow worse and worse, despite their efforts. They all admitted that they could not have continued in their ministry without the hope that springs from their faith in Christ. Bill Webber, then president of New York Theological Seminary, captured this in a sentence: "Pessimism is a cop-out; optimism is impossible; all that's left is Christian hope."

In East Harlem I was also introduced to the writings of James Cone. His book *Black Theology and Black Power* had a particularly strong impact on me because it introduced me to a new Jesus. It had been impossible to ignore Jesus in East Harlem; he was at the center of the lives of the members of Church of the Resurrection and the people who came and talked with us. But I was often at a loss to understand this Jesus.

What I did understand was the angry, militant, black Jesus who came to liberate his people. I no longer believed in the Good Shepherd Jesus of Psalm 23; instead, I understood the liberator Jesus of Luke 4:

> The Spirit of the Lord is upon me,
> because God has anointed me to
>   preach good news to the poor.
> God has sent me to proclaim release to the captives
> and recovering of sight to the blind,
> to set at liberty those who are oppressed,
> to proclaim the acceptable year of the Lord.
> (vv. 18–19)

My understanding of Jesus was simply that—understanding rather than belief or faith. It was intellectual assent to a person who, in my arrogant assumptions of those days, agreed with me about suffering and justice. And once my understanding of Jesus as liberator was clear, the Scriptures opened up to me in a whole new way. I did not understand how for years I could have been so blind to the thrust of Scripture and the promise of justice that is so clear throughout.

With new vigor I started to read the Old Testament prophets, with their endless railings against the powerful and wealthy who oppressed the poor. Amos's cry, "Let justice roll down like waters," became a favorite image.

I began to understand Jesus as a fulfillment of the prophets' promises. Though I had read such familiar passages many times before, I started to see the radical social upheaval implicit in the Beatitudes: "Blessed are the poor . . . the hungry . . . those who mourn" (Matt. 5, Luke 6). And this upheaval was as plain as it could be in Mary's Magnificat, with its vision of the mighty being put down from their thrones while the poor were exalted, the rich being sent away empty while the hungry were filled (Luke 1:46–55).

I started to see that these were not isolated passages in a Bible otherwise intended to make us feel pious and holy and comfortable; the message of these passages was indeed the heart of Jesus' life and ministry and word to us. We were being called to let go of our privilege and affluence and follow this poor Jesus to the cross.

For the first time I understood the political significance of the cross. It was the political as well as the religious leaders of his day who put Jesus to death; and his death had everything to do with the threat that he was to their power and the status quo.

Jesus invited his followers into a radical sharing and caring that removed their allegiance from the power arrangements of the day. His followers were discovering a radical freedom in Jesus and the promised day of justice. And so this Jesus had to be put to death.

My mind was a bit boggled by this awareness. And I began

to feel that if only all the people who claimed to be Christians really *lived* like Christians, the suffering of the poor would disappear. I pictured the radical sharing that would happen if people would take Jesus' message to heart. I envisioned the dismantling of the multinationals, the crumbling of power concentrations in brutal governments, the birth of a new hope in the poor.

But in the midst of my dreaming, I also encountered another awareness—an awareness of my own weakness. In introducing me to a new Jesus, James Cone had introduced me to a new understanding of sin. Sin was not simply the personal and private immoralities about which I had been warned while growing up, but a much larger reality that pervaded systems and governments and institutions.

And sin was inaction; refusing responsibility. As Bill Webber put it, "Belief without action is only opinion." The church, he said, like Christ, must be in the midst of the conflict, must be a servant to the poor, must stand on the side of justice and hope. And he reflected on a different kind of poverty than what we were seeing in East Harlem—the spiritual poverty of most American churches, which had fled from the conflict and worshiped a pious Jesus and a privatized God and were no longer good news for the poor.

During my time in Harlem, someone had said to us that in order truly to live, it is necessary to believe in something so strongly as to be willing to die for that belief. As I remembered those words, two very strong, and opposing, feelings swept through me. I prayed that God would give me faith, would give me the kind of courage and conviction to be willing to die for a belief in justice and hope. But part of me hoped, not for faith or courage, but for the ability to forget. Take this knowledge from me, silence the cries of the children I've met, remove the desperate faces from my mind and their pleas from my heart.

I didn't know what to do with my anger and judgment, with all the feelings I had toward family and friends and all the good and sincere Christians back in Hershey, who seemed to me then to be missing so much of what it was all about. And most of all, I didn't know what to do with myself—with my sin and confusion and fear.

Art Brown, the Bates religion professor who had brought our group to Harlem, was a mentor and friend in those difficult days. Sitting on the tenth-floor balcony of the downtown YMCA, where our group lived those six weeks, with traffic and street noise way below us, the East River and the United Nations building in the distant view, Art offered a generous listening ear and all the wisdom of his years as I struggled to understand the changes going on in me.

As the time came close for leaving East Harlem, I took long hours thinking about my return home. I didn't want to hurt or alienate the people I loved, but I didn't want to swallow my feelings and be superficial about my experience either.

I walked one Sunday evening to St. Thomas's Cathedral, my favorite place those weeks for solitude and quiet. Each time I entered the cavernous sanctuary of the cathedral, the large double doors closed behind me and shut out the noise and chaos of the city. Only the occasional and faint rumblings of the subway beneath reminded me that I was in New York City.

I absentmindedly picked up a prayer book from the pew that night. As I paged through it, I discovered that it contained Scriptures and a meditation for each Sunday of the year.

I counted from Easter and figured that it was Ascension Sunday. Expecting to find some answer there, some word of help and reassurance, I anxiously read through the Scriptures. Christ's Ascension felt foreign and spooky to me. I was disappointed, closed the book, and started to leave the church.

As I got to the door, I stopped. I had forgotten to count the Sunday between final exams and my arrival here. I thought about it again, recounted twice, and confirmed that this was the Sunday *after* Ascension.

I ran back down the long aisle of the huge, empty cathedral to my pew and opened the prayer book again. The Gospel reading was from John 15: "Greater love has no one than this, that you lay down your life for your friends. You are my friends if you do what I command you. . . . You did not choose me, but I chose you and appointed you that you should go and bear fruit and that your fruit should abide."

I remember weeping as I read the words. In the midst of my confusion and doubt, I received those words as an embrace from God. I knew that my journey would be long, that I still lacked faith. But I felt invited on the journey by God, who received me as a friend. And I felt that some day, perhaps still years away, I would have the faith to be willing to die for my belief. I felt flooded with joy.

I moved on to the Epistle reading. It was a very familiar one to me from 1 Corinthians 13:

If I speak . . . but have not love, I am a noisy gong or a clanging cymbal. And if I have prophetic powers, and understand all mysteries and all knowledge, and if I have all faith, so as to remove mountains, but have not love, I am nothing. If I give away all I have, and if I deliver my body to be burned, but have not love, I gain nothing. Love is patient and kind; love is not jealous or boastful; it is not arrogant or rude. Love does not insist on its own way. . . . Love bears all things, believes all things, hopes all things, endures all things. . . . So faith, hope, love abide, these three; but the greatest of these is love.

These words also touched me deeply. I experienced them as beginning to soften the angry and arrogant edges, reaching the alienation that I was building up. They were a baptism, a cleansing, an invitation to be patient with myself and with the people I love. With these words implanted in my heart, I felt ready to face not only the long journey ahead but also the imminent return to Hershey.

I sat in the church a long time and let a flood of memories come to me in the stillness of that place. I laughed as I remembered my first day working at the food store that Church of the Resurrection had set up in the front foyer. Mrs. Selby had asked me to go downstairs and bring up the collard greens. I left, then returned and sheepishly asked her, "Mrs. Selby, what *are* collard greens?" She couldn't stop laughing at my introduction to what grew to be a staple in my East Harlem diet.

I remembered the day I was registering children at the church for the "Fresh Air" program—a two-week visit to suburbia for inner-city children—and police came and dragged a ten-year-old boy from the vacant lot across the street. As he was being handcuffed, the other children conjectured at his offense. Some said he was a drug pusher in their elementary school; others said he had stolen a bicycle. The scene brought to mind the words of an East Harlem schoolteacher who had said to us about her students, "In Harlem the status symbol is not achievement, but the ability to survive."

I remembered the day we found a rat in the church sanctuary. I thought of the Hispanic children who were helping me with my Spanish. And I smiled at the memory of the day it rained and we all ran into the streets to dance.

My mind wandered to other New York memories—to walks through Times Square and plays on Broadway, hot dogs at Coney Island and kite-flying in Central Park, double-dip cones in the ice-cream shop in Grand Central Station at midnight, and nickel trips on the Staten Island ferry at sunrise—the places and things to which friends and I escaped when Harlem got to be too much.

I thought about the fashion show coming up at the church and the colorful African-style dashiki that a church member had made for me for the occasion. I was always amazed at the range of activities the church had organized—from food store to Fresh Air program, prayer vigils to prison visits, rent strikes to fashion shows. I had never before experienced church at the center of people's lives in the way that it was here. The church was the spiritual, social, and political center, and all these aspects of life intersected in the members' Christian faith.

As the cathedral's custodian began to turn out the lights and close down the church, I wound up my thoughts with reflections on hope. I pictured Rose Gardella, who had begun a drop-in center for children in East Harlem. Every day she faced overwhelming suffering—abused children, drug-addicted children, children without futures. But she had given them a corner of their own, a place to create and play and talk. And she had seen lives turned around. Rose's words stuck in my heart that night: "Where there is no hope, there is no life."

A week later I was at Sunday morning worship at Church of the Resurrection. The service was in both Spanish and English, as always, and the singing was emotional and strong. The last sentence in my East Harlem journal reflects our sharing bread and wine together around the Communion table that Sunday: "Six weeks ago I shook hands with strangers; today I embraced friends."

That statement seems almost trite now, but words do not exist to describe the emotions of that morning. We hugged hard and cried hard, and Mrs. Selby told me she loved me "like a daughter."

I was the last of the Bates group left in New York City almost a week later. I watched as the others left one by one on trains and planes, and then I settled in to wait for my parents and Kay. On my last day there I took a final look from the tenth-floor balcony. I felt as alone as I'd ever felt. A deep exhaustion finally overtook me, and when my family arrived at the Y in the late afternoon, I was asleep.

The next morning we all went together to Church of the Resurrection. I will always be grateful to my family for having the kind of open-mindedness and courage to take such a step with me. I know that it was not easy for them to go to the middle of East Harlem, but they sensed how important it was for me.

After church we headed for Hershey. As we drove through East Harlem's streets—my last look for a long time—I remembered Art Brown's words about the gracious people of East Harlem, people like Mrs. Selby and Rose Gardella. "They open up their lives to us and accept us into their community for six weeks because they think it will make a difference. They're making a gamble that this experience will change your life, that you'll commit yourself to change their suffering." I knew that I did not want to disappoint them.

I also knew my lack of courage, my impatience, my need for results. And I tried to hang on to the words from Bill Webber that I had tucked away for moments such as these: "Joy is being in the struggle, not winning it."

As we left the city, someone in the car said, "Well, Joyce, I guess it feels good to be going home." The word *home* triggered a flow of tears as I realized that I didn't know where home was anymore. Just minutes out of the city, I was already failing my first test of loving my family. I felt only deep sorrow at leaving East Harlem—and disappointment and frustration at the realization that they would never understand. And as the New York City skyline faded from my view, I cried like someone who felt like part of her was dying.

All the emotion of that day came back to me three and a half years later as we watched firefighters bring the blaze under control in Clifton Terrace. As we gathered up food and clothing and comforted our new temporary houseguest, I thought of Mrs. Selby. I wished I could tell her that her gamble was working.

4. Sojourner

The same week the fire struck Clifton Terrace, I walked to the public health clinic on Fourteenth Street to enroll for health care there. We lived just a block off the neighborhood's main street, in an area of the city often referred to as the "Fourteenth Street riot corridor." The street had gone up in flames after the assassination of Martin Luther King, Jr., nine years before, and the scars from the riots were still in evidence—abandoned apartment buildings, burned-out storefronts, and vacant lots.

A few small businesses—mostly mom-and-pop groceries, fast-food carryouts, and liquor stores—had made a comeback. "King Solomon's Mansion of Love" did a fair business selling incense, candles, and exotic foods. And a few storefront Pentecostal churches were alive and kicking. The relatively new neighborhood clinic was a gesture on the part of the city government to show concern for this badly neglected part of town.

The small waiting room was packed with people—elderly people, crying children, and mothers trying to pull off the crying ones' mittens and boots. The walls were decorated with tinsel and Christmas greetings spelled out in crayoned cardboard letters. Someone had painted black the face of the plastic Santa Claus on the file cabinet.

After a two-hour wait, I was ushered into a smaller room by a young Hispanic woman who handed me several forms to fill out. A woman in the next room moaned and cried about a piece of glass in her foot, pleading with the doctor, "Please just amputate it." Across the hall an infant wailed.

The Hispanic woman wearily explained the forms to me, an explanation I was sure she had given many times before. She gave the impression of a compassionate person who was terribly overworked, probably underpaid, and who barely had the energy during the Christmas rush at the clinic to keep pushing on. I asked her where she was from.

"El Salvador," she said, allowing a smile to come to her face. Then her expression changed as she told me how painful it was to be so far from her family, especially at Christmas.

"Every year I save up my money," she said. "If I save carefully, I can save thirty dollars to call home at Christmas. That's for three minutes. Every Christmas I call. Every Christmas my mother answers. Every Christmas we cry together for three minutes. Never any words." She began to weep softly as she related the story.

On the walk home, I thought about her and about the many people I had met in the month since I had come to Washington, D.C. The suffering seemed overwhelming. Christmas was meant to be a joyful time, but I could only think of all the people I had met without homes or families or the comforts that could make the season a joyful one for them.

I felt sorry for all of them. But mostly I felt sorry for myself. I had a choice. I didn't have to spend Christmas in such a forsaken place surrounded by so much despair. Christmas had never been like this before.

I questioned then, as I often had since arriving in Washington, why I had come. And I wondered if it would ever be home.

I often thought about East Harlem, about how emotional and expanding and exciting it had been to learn and experience what I had there. I sometimes wished I could go back and experience it again for the first time—I wanted the newness and the awe all over again. But these come only once, and those days seemed very far away now. I had traveled a lot of ground since East Harlem.

I had spent a brief time in Hershey and then went with Deb to a summer camp in Maine, where, through connections with my college volleyball coach, I had been hired as a counselor and water-ski instructor. I was very grateful for the close bond that grew between Deb and me during those weeks. The summer was in every way the opposite of the six weeks I had just experienced in East Harlem. My campers were the inhabitants of the other side of New York's Ninety-Sixth Street, the dividing line between Harlem and downtown Manhattan. They were the daughters of wealthy corporate magnates, whose surnames showed up in the society pages of New York publications.

My thoughts that summer were often a kaleidoscope of memories and faces as I recalled East Harlem events or talks with Mrs. Selby or Nana or Rose. But sometimes the whole experience collapsed into my one long conversation with Patricia. She had embodied it all—the vulnerability, the fear, and the hope.

I remembered the last thing she said to me before saying good-bye. She told me that she was looking forward to the summer so that she could go swimming. When I asked her where she swam, she said, "Oh, in the summer they let the water run out of the fire hydrants for us." As I experienced the joys of our Maine lake, I often thought of her running through a gushing fire hydrant on hard concrete and broken glass— "swimming."

Late at night, almost every night, when all my campers were safely tucked in for the evening, I crept off to the lake for a moonlight swim. The night was always quiet except for the movement of the water and the call of the loons, crazy ducklike birds that gave out a plaintive cry and then dived beneath the water and mysteriously surfaced minutes later in another part of the large lake. Pine trees, standing like towering dark sentinels, ringed the shore, and the stars were beyond counting on nights when the moon didn't outshine them.

I reveled in the beauty of the night and the luxury of long hours of solitude, in the exhilaration and freedom I felt in that environment, in the peacefulness of it. The summer felt like recovery from the intensity of the weeks that preceded it.

Those solitary swims are my clearest memory of my summer there—those, and the image of campers and counselors all gathered around a TV set in the dining hall one August night for the historic resignation of a U.S. president. I don't remember the content of what Richard Nixon said that night, but I remember thinking that William Stringfellow was right about him.

Shortly after that night, summer came to an abrupt end for Deb and me with an emergency phone call from home. Grandpa had had a stroke. We got home to Hershey as quickly as we could.

Grandpa had been in the middle of a battle with cancer, and his already-thin frame was getting thinner. There in the intensive-care ward I grasped his frail, blue-veined hand and told him I'd be waiting for him, that it was about time we took another walk together—when he got well.

When I got home, I got out a photograph of The Lot in Gettysburg and drew him a large picture of the rushing water and the Old Man of the Falls for his hospital room. On my last visit before leaving to go back to college, I gave him the picture and told him I loved him. Then we prayed and cried together.

In late October, the day before Grandpa would have turned eighty, I got the phone call that he had died. I got on a bus in my college town in Maine and headed for Boston, where I would take a plane the rest of the way home.

I remember the brightness of that day—the red and gold leaves on the trees and a hot, yellow sun. Though the bus had only three other passengers, it felt stuffy. I felt closed in, full of grief, faint. And totally alone.

About halfway through the three-hour trip, a large woman, wearing a red knit stocking cap over a shock of bright white hair, got on the bus. With thirty-eight empty seats from which to choose, she gathered up her bundles, tottered down the aisle, and fell in a heap in the seat beside mine, exclaiming, "Praise God, what a *beautiful* day!" I tried to smile at her, wondering to myself if it would be impolite to change my seat and trying to figure out how I could get around her.

After a moment's pause, she reached over, took my hand, and, her warm eyes gazing into mine, gently asked, "Why are you so sad?" I found myself telling this stranger all about my grandfather. She asked questions and listened. And finally she said, "You must have loved him very much. How good of God to give you such a gift!" And with her subtle persuasion, I found my grief changing to gratitude.

Sarah Libby was a devoted Christian and an equally devoted Red Sox fan, who lived in a small room in an old rooming house in the shadow of Boston's Fenway Park and never missed a home game of her favorite baseball team. As we pulled into Boston, she gathered up her belongings and headed toward the door. Taking each stair slowly, she descended to get off. At the last step, she looked back at me and called, "Read Psalm 90!" and then disappeared into the crowds. At that moment I began to believe in angels.

I had a Bible with me. I had it with me a lot of the time in those days. Somewhere between East Harlem and midnight swims in Maine, Jesus got hold of me again. I don't remember the moment or the setting; there were no clanging cymbals or angel choruses. But somehow I moved from the intellectual assent I felt in Harlem to a belief that settled in my heart. I had rediscovered faith. And somehow Sarah Libby seemed to seal that faith forever.

I opened my Bible to Psalm 90 and began to read. A section of the psalm reflects on the fragility and ephemeral nature of life: "We are like a dream. . . . Our years come to an end like a sigh. The years of our life are threescore and ten, or even by reason of strength, fourscore." I smiled and wondered if Sarah Libby had known that my grandfather, "by reason of strength," had come just a day short of fourscore.

But what affected me most powerfully was the psalm's opening affirmation of God's power and presence:

> Lord, you have been our dwelling place
> in all generations.
> Before the mountains were brought forth,
> or ever you had formed the earth and the world,
> from everlasting to everlasting you are God.

I found comfort in those words, trusting that my grandfather was in God's hands. But I also trusted that I was in God's hands; that this "dwelling place," this home, was for me as well. I felt a sureness in God's purposes, despite my own weakness and frailty. I sensed God's love reaching back through the generations and forward to the children yet to be, and at the same time it was all around me like a comforting embrace. That assurance carried me through the funeral and for a long time to come.

Being back at Bates that winter was both a joy and a difficulty, and I sometimes felt as if I were leading a double life. I possessed an unequivocal love for Maine, and I reveled in the advantages that being there provided. I took skiing and rock-climbing courses, went white-water canoeing, and made frequent jaunts to the coast. I made the acquaintance of an old lobsterman, whom I visited with a friend once in Rockport; he gave us big, yellow Maine rain slickers to put on as we walked along coastal rocks in a storm, whipped by wind and pounding surf, and afterward gave us hot chocolate and told us lobster tales as we sat around a crackling fire.

Being both inept and unsympathetic to cutting open baby sharks or mixing dangerous chemicals (my greatest accomplishment in high school chemistry was melting my black plastic lab apron all over the contents of my chemistry locker), I took astronomy to fulfill my science requirement. I spent long and fascinating hours on clear, zero-degree Maine nights at the college's telescope, gazing at the rings of Saturn and moons of Jupiter and witnessing occasional displays of the northern lights. Though they were not popular with my dorm mates, I particularly enjoyed the special projects, such as hanging a huge metal ball from the ceiling of my dormitory to measure the earth's rotation.

At Bates we reveled in the abundance of snow, which usually put in its first appearance by early November. We smuggled cafeteria trays to the top of the campus's small mountain and raced them like sleds to the bottom. We endlessly shoveled snow off the lake for ice-skating, and each year we created prize-winning snow sculptures for the annual Bates Winter Festival.

But spring was always welcome—and always delightful in Maine. Bates had a six-week "short term" tacked onto the end of the regular school year, which East Harlem had occupied my sophomore year, but which usually consisted of staying on campus with just one course to take.

My junior year a friend and I tried to create an independent study. We decided to get a job on the night shift at the downtown Bates textile mill (famous for its bedspreads), learn about the lives of the mill workers, and write poetry about it during the day. We called it "Biology 401: Cerebral Osmosis and Spontaneous Generation." The curriculum committee called it unacceptable. We studied women's literature instead, played a lot of volleyball, and had numerous clambakes at the ocean—the main attraction of which was cooking lobsters over a steamy bed of seaweed.

After my experience of East Harlem, I became a religion major. I renewed my search for a church and found a small, community-based, working-class Episcopal church several towns away. I also felt in need of more intense prayer, Bible study, and support for my fragile faith, so I joined the campus's Christian Fellowship, a mixed experience at best.

Piety and political conservatism—to the extent that there was any political awareness at all—seemed to be the watchwords of this evangelical group. I felt both frustration at often being marginalized as the "radical" and pride that I had a corner on the "truth" that they refused to see. In the aftermath of East Harlem, there was little grace or tolerance in me toward such expressions of Christianity.

I was full of pronouncements and judgments—college was too irrelevant, my friends too materialistic, the Christians too apathetic. It wasn't until many years later that I recognized my responses in those days for what they were. Having experienced a renewed faith, I had no excuse for not following that hard call to the cross; I dealt with my fears and frustrations at myself, my weaknesses and temptations, by transforming them into judgments of others.

I often felt alone and misunderstood in those days, despite the enjoyment of many good friends and relationships. Often the ache for East Harlem and a feeling of being utterly alone on a journey whose path I could not see overrode all other feelings.

The mixture of friendship and solitude, pride and uncertainty, stayed with me through college. I began to crave a clear path, a way to put my faith to work for the things I believed in.

With the encouragement in particular of Art Brown, I decided to think about the ordained ministry. Rev. Thomas Guinivan, whose daughter, Ann, had been my closest friend during my growing-up years, had had a strong influence on my spiritual formation, and I still felt like a Methodist at heart. So I decided that, over Christmas vacation my senior year, I would go back to the church in Hershey to talk about my future in the United Methodist church.

Rev. Guinivan, however, was no longer the pastor there, so I spoke with another minister. I will never forget our conversation. I explained to him my desire to be involved in urban ministry, describing the importance of my experiences in Harrisburg and East Harlem in my faith journey. He explained that under the Methodist system, I would have to return to central Pennsylvania after ordination, and chances for urban ministry there were bleak.

I asked him if there weren't other options. He said that I might be able to get a "special appointment."

"And how long would that take?" I wanted to know. The conversation suddenly became very vague and convoluted. Several minutes later the truth emerged: A male pastor could get a special appointment in about five years—I would have to wait ten, he said.

I couldn't imagine waiting ten years to do what I felt called to do, and I considered this the end of the conversation. But then his face brightened, and he said, "Wait. There is another option open to you. You could just pick whatever city you'd like to work in—anywhere in the country—spend some time there, find a man to marry, and we would automatically transfer you there." As I was leaving, he was saying something like, "Let's say, for example, you wanted to work in Wisconsin, though you probably don't. Just go find yourself some nice dairy farmer . . ."

I decided then that I was actually an Episcopalian.

When I got back to Maine, I talked with Rev. Ken Child, the pastor of my Episcopal church. Women were not yet being officially ordained in the Episcopal church (though William Stringfellow had legally defended a few who had been unofficially ordained), and the topic of women's ordination would be the leading controversy at the denomination's General Convention the following September. I would be the first woman candidate for Episcopal ordination from Maine, a state with an extremely conservative bishop vocally opposed to the ordination of women. It was a challenge I felt up to.

With my future lined up, I felt both ready to get on with it and sad at the prospect of leaving Maine.

Along about mid-March, late on a wintry night, when a yearning for spring had begun to invade Bates, the cry "Snowbear!" echoed through the campus, as it always had about that time each year. Snowbear was not an animal or a thing but a verb. At the cry, everyone on campus threw on parkas, mittens, and scarves and headed to the campus's central quadrangle. When a sufficient crowd had gathered, snowbearing would commence.

This winter sport consisted of tackling everyone in sight and rolling in the snow, the theory being that the more snow we got on ourselves, the quicker it would disappear from the ground. It never seemed to rush spring, but it lifted many a wintry spirit. Caked with snow and barely able to move when it was over, I figured I had snowbeared for the last time.

Spring of my senior year was mostly consumed by the writing of my undergraduate thesis. I called it "Church Involvement in Saul Alinsky's Community Organizations: An Actualization of Harvey Cox's Definition of the *Diakonic* Function of the Church within the Context of a Theology of Social Change." The thesis was simply an attempt to put together a theological understanding of social change with the type of practical organizing tactics I had learned in Harrisburg—and to articulate the role of the church as both a pioneering force against oppressive social and economic structures and a healer of societal rifts.

The writing helped me identify an age-old dichotomy in the church that I was just beginning to see and be disturbed by. I had run into "social action" churches, with a liberal approach to theology and little place for the Bible. And I had been to "evangelical" churches, with an emphasis on the Bible and prayer and a primary concern for saving souls. I was equally uncomfortable with the nonbiblical approach of the liberals and the essentially nonpolitical position at that time of the evangelicals, who, if pressed, would throw their weight on the side of the status quo. My conservative understanding of the Bible and theology was at the heart of my belief in the radical political nature of the gospel, and I felt that I didn't fit anywhere.

In the middle of my research, a member of the Christian Fellowship handed me a magazine and said, "Here—you might like this." It was a rather undramatic introduction to the *Post-American*. I devoured it, immediately sent off to Chicago for a subscription, and was informed that the magazine had just moved to Washington, D.C., and was now called *Sojourners*. The magazine seemed to articulate my deepest concerns and became a spiritual companion in those days—a reminder that I wasn't alone in what I felt.

I hadn't exactly kept to a disciplined schedule toward finishing my thesis, becoming less and less of an academic as graduation grew closer and closer. I knew that I would need help just to get the title page typed on time.

The feat of finishing the thesis required going three days without sleep and drafting all my friends into a typing marathon the last twenty-four hours. My closest college friend, Deborah Hamilton McQuade, was also a religion major, with a thesis due the same day. The typing went on in shifts around the clock in every available corner of our dorm, racing to meet a 9 A.M. deadline.

At 8:06 on that fateful morning, Deb and I began to feed nickels into the Bates library photocopy machine. Twenty-eight minutes and 242 nickels later, we had the required two copies each of our theses. We jumped into my old Ford station wagon, headed for Art Brown's house, parked the car, and ran inside. It was 8:58. I handed my thesis to Art and said, "Do you accept them in early?"

He in turn pointed at my car and said, "Have you gotten much sleep lately?" I had missed the driveway by two yards and parked on his front lawn.

It was all over. All except the commencement rhetoric about our "grand and glorious fortune to be graduating in America's bicentennial year" and the painful good-byes. With diploma in hand, I was ready to sell waffles at Hersheypark.

I had felt I needed a break that summer, and being a wafflewoman at Hersheypark was a piece of cake. I was working mostly with high school–age kids five and six years my junior. "School spirit" was big among them, and talk often drifted to comparing football teams and cheerleading squads. It was always a real conversation-stopper when one of them asked me where I was going to school and I answered, "Yale Divinity School." As far as I knew, YDS didn't have a football team.

This was confirmed when I arrived there in September, just days before the General Convention of the Episcopal church approved a resolution to ordain women. The celebration rocked the seminary campus. My joy, however, was tempered—the Methodists had been ordaining women for two decades, and it seemed to me at the time to have made little difference.

I enjoyed seminary. I made good friends, got some solid

theological education, and learned that I could never make a living as a Greek scholar. Before long I began to wonder if I could make a living as an Episcopal priest.

Episcopalianism at Yale wasn't what it had been in Lisbon Falls, Maine, and I had a hard time adjusting to incense, robes, and high liturgy. I received tremendous support from many places for my pursuit of ordination, but from the institutional church, mostly roadblocks, it seemed. I knew that the fight would require all my energy, and I wasn't sure that I believed in it enough.

I devoured liberation theology and Karl Barth and Dietrich Bonhoeffer's "costly discipleship." But I felt most alive when I was on the other side of the city of New Haven.

Much of my experience of poverty had been intertwined with the lives of children, and I was anxious for a glimpse of life at the other end of the spectrum. When a fieldwork position was offered as chaplain at a public-housing project for the elderly, I decided to take it.

Twice a week during my year in seminary I traveled to Ribicoff Senior Center and Cottages on the other side of town. My job as chaplain included everything from visiting the sick to doing apartment maintenance checks, leading Bible studies to overseeing a "swine flu" vaccination program. Most of the 110 residents bore the triple pain of poverty, sickness, and loneliness. Many days all I could do was hold a hand and listen, and it never seemed like enough.

During the year that I worked at Ribicoff, city funds for the Visiting Nurse Association, Meals on Wheels, and maintenance services were drastically reduced. I was put in the position of having to tell a disabled woman that her nurse would not be coming back to care for her; a man who could not leave his apartment that he could no longer receive meals at home; and tenants who already struggled to pay their rent that they would now also have to pay for all repairs.

The brokenness and despair swelled, and it was my job to pick up the pieces. I could not reinstate the services, but I was mandated to "bring hope" to the place. The sense of power-lessness was profound. I was pushed to find a strength beyond my own, and my dependence on God and God's grace increased a hundredfold during that year. So did my anger at a city and a nation with skewed priorities.

There was not energy in me for building the kind of grass-roots organization that was needed to tackle the problem at its roots. I was a transient in New Haven, as I had been in Harrisburg and East Harlem. The only hope for my tenants seemed to rest in whatever caring community they could build up among themselves.

I devoted a great deal of my energy the second half of the year toward trying to foster such a community. One of the themes I emphasized in my preaching at the senior center was the one that had spoken to me so deeply as a child. I read Psalm 23 and retold the parable of the lost sheep, conveying God's care for us as a shepherd, tenderly loving each of us in our loneliness. But I also emphasized that there were so many sheep to watch over that God had given us one another to help with the task.

There were small inroads—a resident checking in on a sick neighbor, a retired electrician's helper offering to do small repairs for others. But there were also tough facades and long-standing suspicions born out of years of feeling neglected and unwanted.

Mr. Walters didn't like his neighbor because she kept too many plants, and Mr. Miller claimed that the woman next door was "stealing his electricity." Many people were unreached. The day I walked into Hilda's apartment and found her lying on the floor from an overdose of sleeping pills, I felt overcome by a sense of futility about it all.

What kept me going were the unexpected joys, the faith and gracious care of some of the residents, and the education I gleaned from a host of colorful characters representing a wide spectrum of aged humanity.

Mrs. Parus had been a concert pianist in Poland; newspaper

clippings, concert programs, and photographs plastered all over her walls attested to the truth of her claim. I often wondered what had brought her to this place—a flight from Communism perhaps, or a personal scandal or family tragedy. A large piano took up most of the space in her small living room. "It won't be long now until you'll be ready for a concert—we'll do one together!" she proclaimed as I sat behind the keys and awkwardly pounded out "Turkey in the Straw," the only song I seemed to remember from my years of piano lessons. She thumped on my back with her arm like a metronome, shouting, "But you'll never be famous unless you get your time down!"

She would not talk to me unless we went through this ritual every week, and she never gave up believing that I was a pupil arriving for my piano lesson. When I was through, she often would sit down at the piano, and her nimble eighty-two-year-old fingers would glide over the keys, moving from delicate sonata to beautiful rhapsody.

Jean Abbot and Miss García were two who had found in their friendship the kind of ministering community I had hoped to see take root among the others. Jean was from Scotland and had a delightful accent, as well as an infectious smile, with or without her teeth. She always welcomed me with cakelike Scottish scones and butter cookies and a special blend of Scottish tea, which she kept warm in her silver teapot covered with a colorful tea cozy bearing her family's coat of arms.

Miss García was paralyzed below her neck, and she spent her days making beautiful watercolor landscapes, painted with a brush held between her teeth. Her gift to me of one of these was a rare treasure. These two women were devoted to one another, and I often stopped by to see them when I needed to have my spirits lifted.

Perhaps my favorite was Mrs. Valearia Latham. She was a rotund black woman with pepper-and-salt hair and came from North Carolina—a mother of 13 children and grandmother of

104. She kept a closet full of sweet potatoes and collard greens and gave me my first dinner of pigs' feet, tails, and ears.

Mrs. Latham spent many hours reading her family Bible, and we often prayed together when I visited her. Despite her severe rheumatism, backaches, and hearing problems, she never engaged in self-pity and always was in a spirit to talk about her love of God.

Sitting beside Mrs. Latham was like being transported down south to her North Carolina home. She told me tales about the freedom riders who came through, her welcome mat always out for those who were fighting for the rights of her people.

At Christmas, when a group of seminary friends and I went around for a week spreading holiday cheer at one another's parishes and other fieldwork placements, she invited the Yale Divinity carolers into her home for a huge dinner. The menu was fried chicken, she explained as she winked in my direction, "because they probably eat pigs' feet with the same lack of relish that you do."

Mrs. Latham made perhaps the most unusual request I've ever received. She asked me if I would be willing one Saturday morning to help her walk five chickens back from the market, chop their heads off, and pluck and dress them. She planned to save the feathers in a pillowcase and make them into a pillow some day. It wasn't exactly in my job description, but she clearly needed the help, and I thought it would be an interesting education.

On the morning of the big venture, however, she called to tell me it was off. Word had gotten out to the neighbors, and I think it was Mr. Miller who said, "We have enough problems around here without having a bunch of birds running around like chickens with their heads cut off." (I think it's the only funny thing he ever said—and he was dead serious.)

My residents often kept me laughing. Spring brought the annual "garden contest." Resident judges walked around the cottages and awarded a prize for the prettiest garden out front.

When I stopped to congratulate the winner, she leaned over and whispered to me, "I've won it three years in a row now. The flowers are plastic. I bring 'em in every fall and stick 'em in the ground every spring—and the judges are too blind to notice."

On my last day at Ribicoff, Jean Abbot asked me to accompany her to the center to pick something up. I walked in on a surprise party. The residents were singing a song they had written about me—"Joyce to the World"—to the tune of the Christmas carol. I laughed so hard I cried. And I walked away from Ribicoff with that marvelous vision of all of them together, a community singing and celebrating.

In October of the year I spent in seminary, Jim Wallis, the editor of *Sojourners*, came to speak at Yale University. The most important thing I learned that evening was that an intentional community existed behind the magazine that had been such a constant companion since I was handed a copy six months before. Jim's inspired call that night was not simply to resist the forces that oppress and do violence but to form communities based on Christ's love—places of radical gospel hope offering an alternative to society's patterns of domination and militarism.

I recall that he quoted 1 Peter 3:15: "But in your hearts reverence Christ as Lord. Always be prepared to make a defense to any one who calls you to account for the hope that is in you." Jim preached that this passage implied that Christians lived their lives in such a distinct way that others were prompted to ask them what hope inspired them to do so.

His words were unsettling to me and made me raise with more intensity the question about whether I belonged in ordained ministry in the church. The image of Sojourners Community in inner-city Washington, D.C., with a ministry to the needs of its neighborhood's people and a Christian magazine that stood for justice, was very tempting. I got hold of a copy of his book *Agenda for Biblical People* and found there a vision of all that I hoped to give my life to. And yet I felt unsure.

I was plagued in those days with contrasts and disparities. It was often difficult to be at Ribicoff. But many times it was even more difficult to leave the suffering there and return to the comfort of Yale—to the imposing chapel and colonial-style buildings that made up what students in Yale's other graduate schools called "Holy Hill"—where I shared with another woman a spacious suite complete with bay windows, balcony, and fireplace.

Discussions of theology around crackling fires on wintry nights with friends, each of us smoking a very Yalish pipe, were a ritual. Sometimes I played the game, and sometimes I resented the pretentiousness. We were serious in our hopes to change the world, but it was hard for me to believe that anything that would upset the state of things would come from a suite at Yale. It had to play at Ribicoff Cottages if it were ever going to matter—and none of us *really* knew yet what mattered there.

But our friendships were important—forged in good times, late-night conversations, theological wrestlings, and dreams of the future. We helped run a coffeehouse dubbed "The Fatted Cafe" and joined in the annual "Seminary Olympics," the high point of which was the "Reformation Game": Everybody started together in the campus quad and then all split off and went their own way. Friends and I made an excursion to Boston one winter weekend, where, according to one, we would "do what every seminarian can do." He led us out onto the frozen Charles River, and with a brilliant orange sun setting behind us and the wind whipping our faces, he yelled triumphantly, "This is it! We're walking on water!"

We were young and slightly arrogant and wanted to change the world, as long as it didn't upset our plans too much. I started to feel that I didn't have any plans.

The church seemed as wealthy and status quo to me as any other institution. There were some in the church, and some at the seminary, who felt it should be otherwise, but the message hadn't yet reached the mainstream, it seemed.

The seminary was heady with feminism and new possibilities for women, but forces were also at work against that spirit. My second week at Yale, while I was standing in a line waiting to donate blood to a bloodmobile that had come to the campus, a professor standing next to me—an expert on C. S. Lewis— said under his breath, "Academic standards sure have gone down around here since they started admitting women." Documented studies said otherwise.

The Episcopal General Convention had passed an ordinance allowing the ordination of women. But the ordinance stated only that women *could* be ordained, not that they *had* to be. It was still up to me to convince an entrenched bishop of my merits and the merits of women in general for the priesthood. I no longer felt clear enough to be up to the challenge.

About halfway through my year at seminary, I suffered a flare-up of an old water-skiing injury. The Yale infirmary put my neck into a cervical collar to immobilize it. I remember laughing about it one night and telling my good friend Elizabeth Zarelli Turner, "You know, I think this is the closest I'm going to come to getting a collar out of this place."

I discovered the contemplative-political monk Thomas Merton during that time when what I had most of all was time to read. Elizabeth had come across a prayer in his book *Thoughts in Solitude*, which she typed out for me to hang on my wall:

I have no idea where I am going. I do not see the road ahead of me. I cannot know for certain where it will end. Nor do I really know myself, and the fact that I think I am following your will does not mean that I am actually doing so. But I believe that the desire to please you does in fact please you. And I hope I have that desire in all that I am doing. I hope that I will never do anything apart from that desire. And I know that if I do this you will lead me by the right road though I may know nothing about it. Therefore will I trust you always though I may seem to be lost and in the shadow of death. I will not fear, for you are ever with me, and you will never leave me to face my perils alone.

I knew that I was going somewhere, but I wasn't sure where. I didn't recognize at the time that losing my way was the path to finding it.

A word that seemed to be constantly floating around in my head those days was *community*. I read Dietrich Bonhoeffer's *Life Together*. It was a strong witness to me that this man so well known for his resistance to Nazism advocated Christian community—which took shape in his underground seminary—as the building block for a transformed society. The writings of Dorothy Day and the compassionate witness of the Catholic Worker movement—composed of communities that both ministered to the homeless poor and confronted the forces that created their poverty—also had a deep impact on me.

Some of us at seminary began to talk about creating a community together. A huge, old, abandoned building next to the campus, which had the perfect look for a haunted-house movie, began to be the object of our dreams. The building, formerly the Culinary Institute of America, offered not only spacious possibilities for us and the many others we hoped to recruit for the venture but also the chance to tell people we were living in the "CIA Building."

A few of us were taking a course with Fr. Henri Nouwen, whose book *Out of Solitude* had touched me deeply when I was still in college. The course had an emphasis on community as well as prayer, and each of us was required to spend some time in an intentional community of some type. While others made plans to visit contemplative abbeys and monasteries, Elizabeth, friend Dean Hammer, and I decided to journey to Sojourners Community over our spring break.

As I had read the magazine each month, I felt a growing kinship with the people who produced it. In my mind I had begun to feel that maybe Sojourners was the only place in the world where I might fit.

Spring in Washington reminded me of spring in East Harlem, and I felt immediately at home. We stayed in a community household whose living room was a child-care center during the day, with walls covered with artwork and toys stacked in the corner.

The first evening we shared a dinner of cheese chowder and homemade bread with the eight adults and two children who made their home there. Through the week we typed letters in preparation for a Holy Week antitorture campaign, took some of the neighborhood children up the Washington Monument, helped with cooking, and joined a sing-along that took place in our living room. The support and care the community members offered one another was always evident.

The week felt like a celebration to me. A deep joy pervaded the life of the community, even as it poured itself into a campaign against torture in many places around the world, helped an evicted family find a home, and dealt with a violent outbreak at the overnight shelter for homeless men it helped to staff. The joy seemed most evident in worship, when prayer and song flowed with ease.

I felt absolutely drawn to the life of the community, and yet scared of it. I was plagued with questions. Was it too easy to live here—or too difficult? Was it an escape from a responsibility to try to change the church? Or was this indeed the church, living together as the body of Christ in the way that Jesus had commanded?

The vision of the early church recorded in Acts 2 and 4 came to my mind often during that week. The first Christians lived as a caring community, sharing their goods, taking in the poor, breaking bread together, and being glad and generous and grateful and "of one heart and soul." I longed to live in a way similar to those early Christians—the ones closest to Jesus.

The community members at Sojourners were far from perfect in their attempt, and that was a comfort to me; I had a long way to go in my feeble efforts to be faithful. But they were trying with more integrity than I had seen anywhere else.

They were honest about the fact that they usually had more questions than answers. I knew it would probably be a very long time before I had many answers. But I discovered that week that I needed to live with people who were asking the same questions.

Faces from Harrisburg and East Harlem and New Haven came to mind. All the faces. What had I ever contributed? I had never stayed anywhere long enough to dig in deep, to work for change. Too many learning experiences, and not enough given in return. It felt like time to change that.

What was always overwhelming was a sense of solitude. Of being misunderstood. As if my anger and efforts were mine alone. It felt different here. I felt again that everything was turning upside down for me.

On our last day in Washington, Jim Wallis, just back from community meetings in Europe, met with us. I shared all the hopes and doubts that had flooded me during my week with Sojourners, the tug I felt to be with the community, but the difficulty of letting go of other things and the trouble I had trying to discern what was right.

Jim listened and responded with his characteristic sensitivity and wisdom—two qualities among many that made me decide several years later to marry him. At the end of our conversation, he said simply, "Often the right decision is to go to the place that feels like home." I thought of his words often in the following weeks.

Easter had a special significance for me that year. Christ's Passion had never seemed so real. I struggled to grasp the loneliness and despair of Gethsemane—and realized how many times in so many ways I, like Jesus' disciples, had fallen asleep at the crucial moment, or betrayed or denied Christ. It was part of my long path to understand the meaning of the Scriptures that say we must share in the sufferings of Christ if we want to know the joy of Christ. I was beginning to understand that unless I was willing to embrace the cross, I would never know the power of the Resurrection.

The faces of many people were with me again through the days of the Passion—Mrs. Selby, Patricia, Mrs. Latham. I saw

Christ crucified in the suffering that each bore, as I kept a solitary prayer vigil by candlelight throughout Maundy Thursday night and then a three-day fast. I felt weakness and weariness as I tried in the still darkness to understand what it all meant.

I read and reread Jesus' last prayer for his disciples, recorded in John 17.

Holy Father, keep them in your name, which you have given me, that they may be one, even as we are one. . . . Now I am coming to you; and these things I speak in the world, that they may have my joy fulfilled in themselves. I have given them your word; and the world has hated them because they are not of the world, even as I am not of the world. . . . Sanctify them in the truth; your word is truth. As you sent me into the world, so I have sent them into the world. . . . I do not pray for these only, but also for those who believe in me through their word, that they may all be one. The glory which you have given me I have given to them, that they may be one even as we are one, I in them and you in me, that they may become perfectly one, so that the world may know that you have sent me and have loved them even as you have loved me.

Jesus' final prayer for his disciples—and those of us who would come after—was a prayer for unity. His greatest hope was that they would be one. This was the blessing he left them with, the plea he went to God with.

I thought of all the things that keep us divided from one another—the rifts made by our affluence, our pride, our distrust; the things that keep rich from poor, white from black, Hershey from Harlem. It was not meant to be this way. I felt the truth of that more strongly than ever.

But the unity that Jesus offered was a threat—and still is— to a world divided. It incurs the hatred of those who benefit from the divisions.

Mrs. Selby and Patricia and Mrs. Latham had instilled in me a hunger for the unity Jesus spoke of in his prayer. To make the journey was now up to me. I prayed that I would have the strength to pay the price.

Easter morning dawned with a brilliance that bathed the

walls and pews of the Yale chapel, where lilies adorned the altar. In the bright light of day, the faces were still with me. For as surely as they had spoken to me of suffering, they had also spoken of hope. They embodied the truth that the deepest sorrow is the ground out of which can blossom the deepest joy.

I felt transformed that year by Easter and called to new hope—a hope born from a deeper understanding of Jesus that had come to me by way of people I had known and places I had been. It was a hope powerfully expressed in Jesus' prayer for unity, a hope I wanted to give my life to.

The decision to join Sojourners felt like a radical break and at the same time totally in keeping with the journey I had begun the day I stepped into Harrisburg. I felt a sense of deep and abiding peace for the first time in many months.

Two days after Easter, Jim came back to Yale to speak at the seminary chapel. I told him that I had decided to come and join the community. He was not surprised, and he reflected, "You never seemed like a guest." I had already made a commitment to a summer ministry job at the Grand Canyon but promised to arrive at Sojourners in the fall.

The next week William Stringfellow came and spoke at the seminary. Seeing him again, remembering his words to me in East Harlem three years before, seemed to be further confirmation of the step I was taking.

Just before the semester ended, I went with friends to see *Brother Sun, Sister Moon* at the local theater. The film was a bit ethereal and overly romantic, but nonetheless it offered me an introduction to St. Francis of Assisi that had a deep impact on me.

In the scene that left the deepest impression, the young Francis sits in a huge cathedral between his wealthy parents, all dressed in fine robes and worshiping a crucifix, on which hangs a kingly Christ adorned in a robe and crowned with gold and jewels. The poor people of Assisi are dressed in rags and huddle together at the back of the church. Francis is overcome with the injustice and inconsistency of the scene, and in a burst of rage, he jumps up and shouts, "No! No! . . . No!" He runs out of the cathedral, across a field of poppies, to the ruins of an abandoned church, where he kneels before its crucifix: Christ broken, despised, naked. This is the Christ he worships.

I was drawn in by the "eccentric little community" he built up in the old church, the life of the brothers, the commitment to poverty and ministry to the lepers who had been cast off from society. I wanted it to be this simple. I felt the same hunger to serve and give all to Christ. And yet I felt so terribly inadequate.

In that dark theater I wept a flood of tears. They were tears of fear and inadequacy. But they were also tears of deep joy. I felt that I was finally—at last—taking a step that would free me to abandon all else and follow Christ. I felt so sure then.

Now, two weeks before Christmas, as I walked against the wind down Fourteenth Street in Washington, D.C., past piles of gray snow, I tried to remember that certainty and joy. But it would not come. All I felt was the coldness of the streets, and all I could see was the Hispanic woman crying and a broken plastic Santa with its face painted black.

5. A Season of Hope

On Christmas Eve I was back at the overnight shelter where I had met María the month before. The frigid wind that visited the city that night had settled in and created an upsurge in the number of people needing shelter; this church was now open for women, and a much larger one had opened its doors for men.

After dinner the soup bowls were washed and neatly stacked away. Shopping carts and paper bags loaded with years' worth of collected string, cans, broken umbrellas, and other street items had been dragged in out of the snow and were parked in the church's foyer.

In a corner of the fellowship hall, a small circle of women sang "Joy to the World" and "Silent Night," slightly off-key, while others pulled sleeping mats onto the floor. When the singing ended and the mats were in place, the women selected their spots for the night.

It had been a fairly quiet evening. Dinner had progressed smoothly. Dozens of sugar cookies had been donated by the church for a Christmas Eve treat—a full turkey dinner would be served the next day. The singing had awakened the memories of the women, some of whom had not sung carols for years; some had cried. There was a warm spirit at the shelter, and I hoped for a quiet night.

When the lights were finally turned out, I took a chair in a corner next to Doris, whose head slumped forward as she nodded off. She suffered from an asthmatic condition that forced her to sleep sitting up.

Among these women without a home I thought of all the homes I had had. I had journeyed to New England before arriving at Sojourners Community. College friends were settling into careers or starting families. Seminary friends shared their enthusiasm for their plans at the start of a new academic year—hospital chaplaincies, pastoral counseling work, parish ministry internships. And as I considered my own choices, there was a twinge of sadness for all the dreams that must be left to die when a new one is begun.

Around another crackling Yale fire one night, pipes in hand, friends launched into a discussion about Ugaritic mythology. I tried to be relieved that I didn't have to worry about Ugaritic mythology—or class schedules or term papers or exams. Instead I panicked at the thought that I was going to die someday without ever really knowing what Ugaritic mythology was.

On an early-morning train headed back to Pennsylvania, I passed over Harlem. On this dreary, foggy, lonely day, the flood of memories came once more, and I felt again the ache to be experiencing Harlem for the first time. But it was three and a half years too late.

My journey north had felt like a pilgrimage of saying goodbye to many good homes. They were places that held many warm memories, but they would never be home again. And my lifelong home in Hershey had been put up for sale.

During my first weeks in Washington, my thoughts often escaped to the Grand Canyon, where I had spent the summer. That night at the shelter, memories came back in vivid detail.

I laughed as I thought of my difficult first adjustments to such a strange environment. At an altitude of 7,000 feet on the canyon's rim, the air was thin, making breathing difficult and getting sunburn easy. When I reflected on my difficulties in adjusting to the altitude to a wizened, old Grand Canyon resident, she suggested that I "stay inside and try not to breathe."

But before long the canyon felt like home, too. One of my first evenings there, I watched a storm move across it. Finger-like stabs of lightning danced high in the dark sky on the other side of the canyon, eighteen miles away, as sheets of rain began moving across it. Then, suddenly, the dark blue clouds parted and rays of sunlight shone through—casting a panoramic pattern of shadow and light across the canyon walls. And then the rainbow appeared—a soft arc, double in places where the clouds didn't intrude, spanning the canyon's edge and reaching down into its depths. The awesome sight was a perfect welcome.

I had a job on the summer ministry staff—an ideal place to launch a ministry career. The view behind me as I preached each evening was the sunset over the canyon, and no one ever fell asleep during a sermon.

I also worked as a transportation clerk to support myself. My job was selling mule rides into the canyon, raft trips through it, and helicopter flights over it. The most difficult part of the job was calling toll-free numbers in New York City to get credit-card authorizations under the category "transportation" and having to deal with the reaction when the voice on the other end asked, "By plane?" and I had to say, "No—by mule."

The most rewarding part was taking each of the rides I sold, at my employer's expense, so that I could describe them to the customers. I learned quickly that the breathtaking view from the rim of the canyon was only part of the picture. The descent into it offered another perspective on its vastness and changing beauty.

With a party of a dozen others on muleback, I left the rim of the canyon on the Bright Angel Trail one day just after dawn. I was convinced—because I had been told so many times— that mules are much more surefooted than horses on the steep canyon trails. My mule, however, seemed not to be aware of this.

Old Rosette, a big-eared, awkward beast of a beautiful chestnut color, stumbled often and walked very slowly, soon falling way behind the others. At our first break, the mule wrangler leading our party asked me why Rosette was so slow. Drawing on every ounce of expertise and experience I had had with mules, I replied confidently, "I have no idea."

We traveled the dizzying switchbacks of the Corkscrew, journeyed through the Furnace, an appropriately named narrow passageway between two large, sheer rock faces which trap the desert heat near the base of the canyon, and arrived at Phantom Ranch on the banks of the rushing Colorado River before dark.

After a brief sleep, we were on the trail again by dawn. We passed a group of wild burros, rode across a wide plain filled with tall, flowering yucca plants, made the last climb over Cedar Ridge, and surfaced by late afternoon.

Walking slowly and painfully and slightly bowleggedly, wearing my mule-munched cowboy hat and smelling like essence-of-mule perfume, I made my way to the general store and bought two pounds of fresh cherries. I ate these out on the curb in front of the store as I watched Grand Canyon humanity flow by—park rangers, European tourists, transient teenagers, mule wranglers, Navajo weavers, summer ministers—tipping my hat to tourists and spitting the pits. At that moment the Grand Canyon became home.

The raft trip was tame, providing beautiful scenery and the opportunity to spot eagles and soak up the cloud cover. But the most beautiful corner of the canyon could be reached only by foot, horseback, or helicopter.

Our helicopter touched down in a field of prickly-pear cactus, just a short walk to Havasu Falls, located on the Havasupai Indian Reservation at the base of the canyon. The falls cascade down a wall of the canyon into a blue-green pool and then over continuous shallow ledges. Bright trees hang over the pool, and the sun dancing on the water made it appear luminescent and of such brilliant hue that I supposed the Garden of Eden must have looked something like it.

The Havasupais had a history similar to that of other Native Americans. The federal government had stolen most of their land and pushed them to a small corner by the falls, where they carved out a living at the bottom of the canyon. Irrigating from the stream that feeds the falls, the Havasupais have been able to grow enough crops to survive.

Several Native Americans worked up on the rim of the canyon at the lodges and restaurants. They were usually given the worst jobs and treated poorly by the other employees. The Hopis had once been dominant in the area, but all that seemed to be left of their culture were a Hopi museum and an annual dance performed there for tourists by Hopis in colorful garb. The Navajos kept stands along the highway leading into the canyon, where they sold jewelry and blankets, and tried to raise herds and crops on the barren desert land. When I returned to visit the canyon in winter, the desert was dusted with snow, and the flimsy wooden stands were abandoned and battered by blasts of wind. The eerie desolation of the place made me wonder what kept the Navajos alive during the cold months.

I got to know well a young woman whose Havasupai husband worked in the bottom of the canyon during the summer; they got to see each other only once a week. I remember evenings in their tiny trailer, where she and I sat and watched the sun set behind the Ponderosa pines while I cradled their beautiful, dark-haired baby daughter. She spoke about the exploitation and hardship of her baby's people; about the young people torn between their culture and a "better life"; about the alcoholism that many gave in to in their despair.

As I got to know more of its people, I grew to respect the canyon's dangers. I was having dinner with the chief ranger's family when a fire broke out on the north rim. All the ranger families stayed glued to their radios during a disaster, waiting for word about the safety of their husbands and sons. While we ate dessert, we heard planes overhead flying rescue teams to the area, and old World War II bombers headed there with chemicals to drop on the fire, which ravaged 17,000 acres of forest before it was finally brought under control.

Rattlesnakes, scorpions, heat exposure, and dehydration were always dangers on the trails. And flash floods were often a problem, as storms came up suddenly and sent water cascading down the walls and through the gorges of the canyon. From the transportation desk we dispatched "drag-outs." In the case of fatigued hikers, we sent out mules. But in severe situations such as heart attacks on the trail, we sent out helicopters to make the rescue. And despite all our advice and warnings to hikers, there were several deaths on the trails that summer.

But hiking was still the best way to see the canyon. I liked to hike alone, especially at sunset. The canyon was at its most colorful then, and occasionally there were surprises, such as the rattlesnake that greeted me one evening—fortunately from a safe distance.

Friends and I took several long hikes, but always before us was "the ultimate challenge"—the twenty-one-mile hike across the canyon to the north rim. Finally, at the end of the summer, two friends and I decided to take the plunge.

We started down one night after work, with lots of Band-Aids, raisins, and water and with a small jar of homemade blackberry jam, a gift from a friend on the south rim to friends on the north. My memory of our descent is of millions of stars overhead and singing "Swing Low, Sweet Chariot" as we stepped into the darkness and slowly made our way down.

After about three hours of walking, we heard, faintly at first, the rushing of the Colorado River. The welcome sound got louder as we walked, and by two o'clock in the morning we were spreading our sheets on its bank to get some sleep.

My short night at the bottom of the canyon on the river bank was one of my best in twenty-three years of nights. A peaceful exhaustion overtook me, and I felt cradled in the hollows of the canyon and rocked to sleep by the sound of the Colorado.

As I was on the verge of sleep, I took one last drowsy peek at the stars overhead. And I allowed my senses to be enveloped by it all—the sound of the river and a chorus of crickets, the beauty of the stars, the warmth of the sand and cool of the night, the peaceful weariness.

As I began to shut my eyes, I saw a falling star streak across the patch of sky high above the canyon walls. Seeing no more for several minutes, I thought that perhaps the star was a trick of a tired imagination. But then there was another. And another. The stars kept falling in a magnificent display; I lost count at twenty-three.

Three hours later we were on the trail again, having been warned to leave before dawn if we hoped to make it to Roaring Springs before the worst heat of the day. We made our way across the canyon floor, a desert scattered with yucca plants, with jagged green leaves and tall shafts of white flowers that towered over our heads.

By eight o'clock in the morning, the temperature was already climbing over 100 degrees. By noon we were barely moving. But at the sight of Roaring Springs, we charged into the cool water and tumbled in its pools, taking a four-hour rest there while the sun blazed a hot trail across the top of the sky.

The time went by too quickly, and we grudgingly pulled ourselves away from the cool spring water and marched out onto the trail again. The moon, a large crescent, was visible in the bright blue sky above the red cliffs of the canyon. Large turkey vultures circled overhead, and lizards occasionally scampered across our path.

We had 3,000 feet to ascend in the last four miles of our trek. At sunset we found ourselves on a ledge high above a spacious canyon valley. We decided to have vespers.

I was elected to choose the Scripture and settled on Philippians 3:7–16. Having seen and stepped around so much evidence of mules on the trail, we could well understand how highly the apostle Paul valued Jesus Christ when he wrote, "I count [all other things] as dung." The Scripture exhorted us to "press on . . . straining forward to what lies ahead," toward the "upward call of God in Jesus Christ." We felt renewed and inspired.

It was a precious Communion that we shared together on that ledge. We prayed in gratitude for the wonders and safety of our journey. And as night closed in around us and stars began to appear overhead, we felt strengthened for our last three miles on the trail. With eighteen miles behind us, three miles seemed like so little.

It just about did us in. The trail got steeper. Pine trees signaled that we were nearing the top, but with the change in altitude came a drop in temperature and a wind that blew through our clothes, tailored for the desert and damp with perspiration. We wrapped ourselves in our sheets to try to keep warm (mine was covered with blackberry jam).

We slowly conquered grueling uphill grades, only to plunge down the other side back to the heat of the desert. We stopped at one point and allowed ourselves half an hour to sleep, but thoughts of rattlesnakes got us moving again. When we finally attained the rim, we all collapsed.

When friends arrived twenty minutes later at midnight (they were going to *drive* us the 180 miles around the canyon back to the south rim in the morning), we rallied to tell the story of the Great Crossing. We relived every emotion—exhaustion as we dragged ourselves from one shady ledge to another in the early morning, ecstasy as we fell into the refreshing water of Roaring Springs, serenity as we stopped for a sunset vesper service, desperation as it seemed the end would never come— and finally the rushes of relief and pride as we collapsed in triumphant exhaustion on the top.

Twenty-four hours after viewing the great meteor shower from the bottom of the canyon, I was soundly asleep on the north rim. I slept until noon the next day. Two days later I was finally able to wear shoes again.

Our hike was a memory I would always treasure. There were other moments as well that captured the beauty and unique life of the canyon that I would always carry with me.

I recalled the flame-red sun that hovered for a few moments on the western edge of the canyon and then dropped out of sight, just as a pale pink moon with light blue shadows—a huge, perfect sphere—appeared on the canyon's opposite rim. That night I walked home to my cabin along the tracks of the old Santa Fe Railroad, bathed in moonlight, guitar in one hand and Bible in the other. I walked by the dormitory of the mule wranglers, who were whistling and shouting in the dark; on past a small cabin, where round-faced Navajo children played and laughed on a porch. A coyote ambled across my path and then ran off through a patch of cactus and into a grove of towering Ponderosa pines, whose butterscotch-scented bark and thick boughs tinged the air with fragrant sweetness. It was a perfect Arizona scene.

On our last morning together, the ministry staff shared a sunrise Communion on the canyon's edge. We walked out to a point on the rim as the stars began to fade and the sky gradually turned from black to purple. We had balcony seats for the grand unfolding of a new day.

On the eastern horizon, a pinpoint of light appeared. Moments later the orange light flooded the canyon, creating brilliant color and dark shadow across its walls and chasms. We broke bread and shared wine in the radiant warmth of the morning sun.

Later that day, I took a last look at the canyon. I thought that I had seen it in all its moods and beauty. But a new sight was before me. A faint mist was rising from the Colorado River, and below me in the canyon were soft, billowy clouds. I thought of a banner, made by children from the Grand Canyon and hanging in the community church the day I arrived. The banner proclaimed, "Dear God—Today I Saw the Grand Canyon . . . Good Work!" When I finally had to leave, I felt as though I were leaving an old friend.

Two friends and I toured around the West before I flew back east, taking in the crimson buttes and low plateaus of Utah, a golden aspen–covered valley and wild geese in the shadow of Wyoming's Rockies, and a huge field of yellow wildflowers that carpeted the way to the majestic, snow-capped peaks of the Grand Tetons. We saw bison and elk at Yellowstone and caught the sun slipping behind the horizon through the pink vapor of a myriad of geysers. We watched clouds tumble down the face of a mountain in Glacier National Park, the swirling mist catching the morning sunlight and glowing on its journey down to the Logan River.

I was speechless at the beauty, and I began to wonder how I could face the concrete, chaos, and crowdedness of the city, which seemed at that moment so foreign and far away. When I got on a plane at dawn at the small airport in Kalispell, Montana, I felt utterly confused about the choices I was making with my life. I was headed to Pennsylvania by way of Louisville, where Kay and her family were, after several plane changes. It was early and I was tired, and I had to get from Kalispell to Missoula to Bozeman to Salt Lake City to Denver to St. Louis to Louisville to Harrisburg (as it turned out, my luggage went to Albuquerque).

I was exhausted, and the man in the seat next to mine was asking too many questions. I finally said to him, "I'm from Chocolatetown, Pennsylvania; I just finished a year at Yale Divinity School in Connecticut, where I was preparing to be the first female Episcopal priest from the state of Maine; I'm here in Montana returning from a summer of selling mule rides at Grand Canyon, Arizona, on my way to join a radical Christian community in Washington, D.C."

He stared at me oddly, laughed, and then said, "Who are you *really?*"

I looked back at him and said, "Look, if you don't believe me, you can read all about it in my forthcoming autobiography, *I Wanted to Be an Episcopal Priest but Spent the Summer Selling Mules.*" He had no more questions.

Several weeks later I arrived in Washington, D.C. For the first few weeks especially, it seemed like a very bad idea to have spent the months before coming there in a place of such profound beauty. I treasured the Grand Canyon memories, but they just seemed to make being in the city all the harder. I frequently longed for cactus and coyotes, for sweet-smelling Ponderosa pines and falling stars.

I recalled the nights when the moon was bright enough to

light my path into the canyon, and others when a moonless sky revealed millions of stars from my perch on the canyon's rim. I missed the feeling of being in touch with the cycles of creation, with storms and sunshine, with darkness and daybreak.

I missed the sunsets the most. Rides on the Fourteenth Street bus at the end of the day in Washington, D.C., revealed only momentary glimpses of hazy color between tenement walls. Days came and ended and nobody seemed to notice, except to be sure to be off the dangerous streets by dark.

Still, the welcome by Sojourners Community had been warm. I credit that in part to the ten-pound Hershey bar that helped to pave the way. I had visited my parents in Hershey just before Easter and bought the huge chocolate bar—available, along with fifty-pound bags of Hershey's kisses, only in my hometown.

I gave it to Jim Wallis to carry back to the community when he visited Yale just after Easter. Had he gotten on a plane at an airport near Hershey, there might not have been a problem. But a ten-pound chocolate bar in New Haven, Connecticut, is another thing. As he approached the airport security check with the huge, thin, rectangular package in a plain brown wrapper, the woman at the checkpoint said, "What's in the box?"

She was not amused when Jim answered, "A ten-pound candy bar." After a vigorous debate, she finally made him open the box and break off a piece of chocolate before she was convinced. It was reported to me that when the candy bar was opened again at the community in Washington, D.C., a look of joy spread over five-year-old Matthew's face, and he believed he had just seen a glimpse of heaven.

In those early days of the community, when we were all a bit younger and somewhat more idealistic and energetic, we shared a style of life that required some major adjustments. I am a "morning person" only to the extent that I do some of my best work after midnight. Every morning at 6:30, Jim

Tamialis walked through the dark house warning everybody that breakfast was in half an hour. I wanted to make a good first impression, a feat I accomplished with relative ease on my first morning at Sojourners. But by the end of the first week, I was rolling out of bed at 6:57 and groping toward breakfast minus my contact lenses and a cheery disposition; it was only the animated singing and Joe Roos's prayers that kept me going.

We lived and ate simply. One of the first tasks I was given in the kitchen was to "make milk." In central Pennsylvania we got ours from cows, and I didn't know how to "make milk." But I went to the large bins by the refrigerator as directed, took out a cup of white powder, and mixed it with water. The children later used the results for glue, and I was quickly given instruction in how to tell the difference between milk powder and flour.

My first week I produced something the household lovingly labeled "Black Hole Soufflé," but with practice my cooking improved. Before long I was as proficient as anyone else in making the ever-popular dish one community member fondly called "Rice and a Thousand Weeds"—created by stir-frying all the vegetables left in the refrigerator at the end of the week. Although I became fully aware that community living required adjustment and sacrifice, adjusting to "Savory Soybean Loaf" was clearly asking a bit too much.

For health, economic, and political reasons, we ate little meat, substituting for it beans in all shapes and colors. We learned to live by the motto "With enough ketchup, anything can taste like hamburger."

And we learned above all else to laugh at ourselves. I remember going to a wedding with another member of Sojourners shortly after we had both arrived at the community. At the reception, miniature hot dogs and small pieces of beef on toothpicks were circulating on plates through the crowd as we stood and chatted. At the end of the afternoon, we looked at each other and laughed. We each held an embarrassingly large fistful of toothpicks. (I was just trying to get enough protein.) But we did know how to celebrate. Birthday dinners were lavish affairs. There was only one time I remember that things didn't work out quite as well as they could have. Two birthdays in the house fell on the same day, and one celebrant wanted chocolate cake with penuche frosting for dessert, and the other ordered lime sherbet. The combination was deadly.

Our commitment to "sharing our assets" usually meant sharing college debts and cars on their last wheels. We were saddled with whatever cars happened to be brought into the community, and there were always cars with stuck doors or stuck gears.

There was, for example, the green Plymouth Fury (the name had nothing to do with the power of the car, but rather what it produced in the driver). It was prone to stall, preferring intersections during rush hour with a long line of traffic behind and a fire truck approaching from the right. At least it had no stuck doors; in fact, on right turns the driver's door swung open into approaching traffic.

In most theological circles, sin is broken down into two categories—sins of commission and sins of omission. At Sojourners we added sins of transmission—anything in the transmissions of our cars that could go wrong did. One car started only in reverse, and another stopped only in first gear. Some cars had standard transmission, some automatic, and one had dropped its transmission at the corner of Fourteenth and Euclid streets.

Few people other than community members can appreciate the joys of having a variety of cars at their disposal. Reverse could be found in the upper left position of the gear shift, or the lower right position, or in some cases only in three strong bodies pushing from the front. Reach under the dashboard in one car if you wanted to remove the emergency brake; do the same in another car, and the hood would fly up.

It always amazed me that our commitment to "simple living" seemed to make life so complicated. Another person new to the community discovered this in a most uncomfortable way. A robbery had been committed in our neighborhood, and police, considering everyone in the area suspect, were stopping cars on the street. They were checking drivers' licenses and car registrations, asking questions to test the truth of individuals' claims that they lived in the area.

David's answers to their queries went something like this: "I realize that my license is from Massachusetts and the license plates on the car are from Texas, but that's because I just moved here to Washington, D.C., to join this community and so did the person who owns this car; but the car isn't registered in her name or mine because all our cars are, on paper, owned by someone else in the community to keep things easier, and I don't know why the registration isn't in the glove compartment because that's where it was in the last car I drove. I live here in the neighborhood, but I'm not sure who we pay rent to because I've just moved into a household and we share all our chores and I happen to take out the garbage and sweep the steps, but I don't pay the bills. . . ."

With Christmas approaching, we were busy with preparations—decorating our tree, baking cookies with the children, hanging thirteen stockings of thirteen different sizes and colors from the mantle above the fireplace, and figuring out how to fill them.

As our household's gift to each of the others, we baked a dozen apple pies and took them warm out into the cold. We delivered four at each of the other households, announcing our gift by singing Christmas carols outside their windows and then allowing ourselves to be invited inside at each house to share the treat. By household number three, we had had enough apple pie to last us until the following Thanksgiving.

There was a lot of joy in our lives, and I was thankful for the worship, the children, the kindred spirits. I was deeply appreciative of the support that was offered me: the prayers of many in my household as well as the patient listening ears of Millie Bender and Bob and Jackie Sabath. Millie and Jackie's roles as pastors and the community's clear affirmation of the gifts of women were a deep encouragement to me.

Those first weeks at the community, I offered my energy wherever it was needed. On weekday mornings I often walked the children to the day-care center, a small parade bundled up to keep the cold out as four lanes of traffic sped by us on their way downtown. The day-care ministry, under the direction of Barb Tamialis, had expanded from a small operation located in a Sojourners household to a large center in the basement of Clifton Terrace. It provided a solid, low-cost play and educational experience for young children and offered many mothers in Clifton Terrace and elsewhere in the neighborhood their first opportunity to work.

The early-morning walks provided a daily look at what was commonly considered among the neighbors the best view of Washington, D.C. From the corner on which Clifton Terrace sat, the Washington skyline spread out between the Capitol dome and the Washington Monument.

For a time we held our Sunday morning worship in the day-care center. Our joyous singing was often accompanied by the chirping praises of the day-care guinea pigs—and the rush of water through the basement pipes every time anyone in any of the 300-plus apartments flushed a toilet.

I helped another community member direct the community and neighborhood Christmas pageant. We knew we had a lot of work ahead of us when we asked if anyone knew who Mary and Joseph were. One of the children, an eight-year-old, piped up, "Aren't they the ones who ate that apple?"

On Fridays I helped out with the Euclid Food Club. Located in the basement of the community's Euclid Street household, the food cooperative was an effort to enable our low-income neighbors to benefit from the lower food prices we paid when buying food in bulk for the community.

We picked up 100-pound bags of flour and rolled oats, drums

of honey and cooking oil, and cases of peanuts and raisins from places all over the city. And always we had on hand huge jars of kosher dill pickles for the children who came to the food club after school.

At a salvage store in the northeast sector of the city, we joined the other salvage-seekers and cart-crashers who maneuvered carts through narrow aisles to pick up bargain-priced boxes and cans. We arrived one afternoon at the checkout counter with cases of lasagna noodles and laundry detergent, cans of tomato sauce and grapefruit juice, and eighty boxes of brown sugar. Upon spying the brown sugar, the clerk exclaimed, "What are you doing—making corn whiskey?" When we explained that we were feeding forty and then some, he said, "I'm feeding twelve myself," and wished us well as we pushed our overloaded carts out to the loading zone.

As we bounced along the city streets in the van toward home each week and I attempted to keep twenty-four jars of taco sauce from colliding, eighty loaves of bread from tipping out of their cartons, and several hundred pounds of bulk items from sliding out the door, I was thankful that eggs (ninety dozen) were delivered Friday mornings to the store from a farm outside the city.

I also worked from time to time on the Sojourners renovation crew. The community had recently purchased a shell of a house for another household on Euclid Street, and a number of us worked for several months to make it livable. Taking our cues from the *Reader's Digest Do-It-Yourself Home Repair Manual*, we spent many a day covered with plaster or up to our knees in Styrofoam insulation.

I enjoyed those early days at the community, and yet some days there was an emptiness I couldn't explain. Choices seemed so stark then. There was a hunger in me for the beauty of creation, for a more "settled" life; but I knew that without being part of the struggle for justice, a part of me would die, and I would never make peace with the feeling that I had betrayed the gospel. The desire for community was strong, for serving Christ in the city and living on hope in the struggle; but did I have to sacrifice beauty and peacefulness and quiet in order to be faithful?

I didn't know how to make all the pieces fit together. Some days I felt—in the joy and unity of our worship, our shared commitments, and deepening friendships—that Sojourners was much more than I had ever imagined; and I recognized what a precious gift is community. Other days it seemed to be much less than I had hoped for.

I had come to Sojourners at a bleak time in the city. We had trouble with the heat in our old house during that bitterly cold winter, and guessing which radiator would spring a leak during which household meeting began to be a game.

The community had been gracious in encouraging me to take time to settle in, but after a couple of weeks I started to get anxious for regular work. I knew, however, that a religion degree and a year of seminary wouldn't help me much in the tight job market in Washington, and I wasn't eager for the job search.

A hardy army of cockroaches had invaded the neighborhood that winter, and we spent one evening hauling all of the dishes and food out of our cupboards and spraying for the insects, which we discovered dead throughout the house for days afterward. The day after the great cockroach adventure, the heat was off again and the house reeked of cockroach spray and I was all alone and there wasn't any work to do, so I wrapped myself up in a blanket and sat in the living room shivering. In that bleak moment, I told myself, "I'll stick it out through Christmas."

We took turns in the evenings doing "shelter run," a swing through downtown Washington to gather up homeless people for the overnight shelters. I thought of those nights now as the women in the shelter slept, about riding up and down Washington's streets, wrapped in a blanket and around the bag of hot baked potatoes we carried with us, protecting myself from the blasts of cold air that came out of our van's broken heater.

We watched for people huddled around steam grates trying to keep warm. It was a supreme irony to me that a handful of men could always be found huddled around the grates at the Department of Justice. The heating ducts below the capital city's great halls of power provide scant warmth for the powerless poor. In this city, hands that rub themselves raw for warmth exist in stark contrast to hands that shape the nation and the world.

Many of the hundreds of homeless people in Washington, D.C., live on the grates. And some of them die there. The wet heat from the steam grates leaves those who sleep there extremely vulnerable to burns and pneumonia.

Most of the people we approached responded immediately to our invitation to a meal and a cot in a warm downtown church for the night. We tried to prod those who were reluctant, but fear or stubborn independence kept some away. With these we left a hot baked potato and warm wishes for a safe night. That winter five people froze to death on Washington's streets.

Despite the hardened independence required to live on the streets, some people carefully watch out for one another. The night before Thanksgiving that year was a particularly frigid night, and Robert, one of the men we picked up in the van, expressed concern for a friend. He directed us to the bottom level of a deserted parking garage. His friend, Joe, had made a home for himself out of a rickety card table draped with old army blankets.

Robert tried to coax Joe to come with us and get out of the cold. "I'm OK, man, I'm OK," insisted Joe, a short man with a leathery face and bright eyes that seemed to shine in that dark corner of the garage. Robert tried again, but Joe was insistent.

We turned and were on our way back to the van when Joe called after us. "Hold up, man, I've got a Thanksgiving present for the people." We followed him to another part of the garage.

There stacked in a corner were dozens of cartons stamped with BISCUITS and a date.

"Caught a man behind the FBI throwin' 'em out," Joe explained. "He said they expired and there wasn't a nuclear war." The biscuits had been designed to survive several months in civil defense fallout shelters.

"Told me I could just take 'em away," Joe continued. "There's too many here for me to eat." We carried several of the boxes to the van and thanked Joe for his Thanksgiving donation to the shelter.

The first time I saw Charlie, he was wearing a long, bright red-and-white-striped stocking cap and pushing a shopping cart full of shoe boxes stuffed with index cards up Pennsylvania Avenue. Charlie had been prematurely released from an overcrowded psychiatric institution. He had a strange obsession with numbers, claiming to have driven the length of every highway in the country, beginning with Route 1 and going in numerical order.

✓Charlie spent his evenings at the Roy Rogers restaurant near George Washington University and his days at the Library of Congress, where he was in the process of transferring all the information in the card catalog onto the index cards he carried with him. In a year's time, he had copied information on about 6,000 books. When I asked him one evening why he was doing this, he gave me a condescending look that said, "Why not?"

There was a man on the streets who believed that he was a Soviet agent, another that the fillings in his teeth transmitted secret messages, and still another that he carried in his brain the formula for the atomic bomb. Many are extremely broken people with severe psychotic disorders—victims of deinstitutionalization policies that eject them from crowded institutions with little capacity to fend for themselves. Some people wind up homeless due to a history of neglect or abuse that has spanned generations.

Some of the women who came to the shelter were frightened,

needing a place of safety for the night away from an abusing husband or boyfriend. Many of the older women seemed tough, having learned over the course of years on the streets how to survive in a street world inhabited mostly by men. But they were still vulnerable to the street's particular dangers for women.

I met Rachel in a downtown park. This fifty-seven-year-old woman who had lived many of her years on the street was raped in an alley a few nights before. She had been there in a dark, hidden corner because all the downtown public restrooms closed at midnight and she had need of one.

Rachel expressed concern about a homeless friend whom she hadn't seen in several days. Exactly a year before, he had tried to comfort an ailing woman in an alley, and she froze to death in his arms. Rachel was afraid maybe her friend was alone somewhere reliving the trauma.

Almost all of the people on the streets urgently need medical care. A lot battle alcoholism; alcoholic seizures were common, and we occasionally brought patrons of the shelter to the detoxification unit at D.C. General Hospital. Most have bruised and calloused feet—some severe foot ailments and infections— from spending their days walking on hard pavement, often in ill-fitting shoes secured from church grab bags. Frostbite attacks many feet and hands during the winter months.

The arms, legs, and feet of the homeless take a constant beating from the elements. But even stronger is the beating that comes from constant rejection and a life lived without home, family, or security.

Many who try hardest to change their situation are victims of deeply entrenched racism, a severe shortage of affordable housing, and a lack of well-paying jobs. In one shelter were 200 men who worked full-time but could not afford a place to live on their minimum-wage salaries. Most people on the streets get knocked down again and again when they try to get up, battered by poverty, lack of education, lack of support, lack of opportunities. Sometimes all that is left is despair.

Some people have lived through unspeakable trauma. One older man with a heavy accent told me his story. "You are a nice Christian," he said. "But I am a German Jew. My family was executed. I came here with nothing. I still have nothing."

Last year I met a group of homeless people who live together under the Francis Scott Key Bridge in the wealthy Georgetown section of Washington. Among them are some teenagers who had been thrown out by their families or run away from their homes. One of the group, who had a mattress and sleeping bag up under the girders of the bridge where he slept, explained that they "live like a family and watch out for each other." The healthiest ones walk to the back doors of Georgetown restaurants to beg for food to take back to the others, including an elderly, sick man.

Recently, Georgetown residents had begun complaining about their presence. A tall, chain-link fence went up around the park near the bridge, and police began arriving in the middle of the night, shining flashlights on them and running them out.

The community under the bridge stands as a sign of the moral failure of Georgetown and Washington, D.C., and the nation to make a place for their most broken citizens. Wherever such a sign stands as a barb in the wealthy conscience, forces are marshaled to push away, keep out, and make invisible the people whose destitution lays out the judgment. How ironic that a memorial to the creator of "the land of the free and the home of the brave" harbors those who brave society's abuse and are allowed no home.

All of the people who live on the streets, women and men alike, share a vulnerability to violence. One man was doused with gasoline and set on fire by some teenagers while he was sleeping on a park bench. Some people receive beatings on the street or in some of the larger shelters, where cots are jammed against one another in large rooms, along hallways, and up and down stairwells.

Outbreaks of violence at the shelters were often triggered by an argument over a bed or blanket. During one incident, a man challenged another to a fistfight over a disputed bed. As the two started to square off, some quick thinking by a member of Sojourners averted a disaster. He stood behind the man who had issued the challenge, thumping him on the shoulders and giving him advice as if he were the man's coach. Suddenly he shouted, "Wait a minute! Hold everything. You can't fight him—he's a welterweight, and you're a heavyweight." The fight immediately dissipated.

I was thinking about this on Christmas Eve when a disturbance erupted in the far corner of the women's shelter. The voices began quietly, but they escalated before long into a shouting match.

The argument was over a coat. Sheila accused Mary of stealing her coat while Sheila was asleep. Mary jumped to her own defense, accusing Sheila of being a liar and calling her names, amounting to a string of synonyms for "prostitute."

Sheila told Mary she was a "no-good good-for-nothing."

And Mary responded, "Oh yeah? I'm better than you'll ever be. I'm an aristocrat of the highest order—with the Rothschilds on my mother's side and the Three Wise Men on my father's!"

End of discussion. Sheila couldn't top that one.

Things quieted down quickly, and both women joined the others in sleep. I reflected on Mary's words—and those of another Mary, recorded in the first chapter of Luke's Gospel.

My soul magnifies the Lord,
and my spirit rejoices in God my savior,
for you have regarded the low estate of your handmaiden. . .
You have scattered the proud in the imagination of their hearts,
you have put down the mighty from their thrones,
and exalted those of low degree;
you have filled the hungry with good things,
and the rich you have sent empty away.

In some sense, the rich were put down from their thrones that night. A claim of royalty, of power, of "somebodyness," issued forth out of homelessness and brokenness and powerlessness.

Mary and her homeless friends had been discarded by a society that despises them. The programs that could minister to their emotional and physical needs were being dismantled one by one.

In some cities sharp wire cages were appearing over steam grates to keep the homeless poor from sleeping there; though there is plenty to go around, some city officials, like some city landlords, seemed to think that heat is a commodity only for the well-off. Before long a southern city would begin a campaign for a "vagrant-free zone" as a step toward a "clean and safe" environment for new business and downtown redevelopment. A western city would pass a law declaring all garbage city property, so that people found scavenging for food could be arrested; for the first time, people could go to jail for breaking and entering a city Dumpster—for a loaf of outdated bread or a piece of bruised fruit.

In biblical times, at least a few stalks of grain or ears of corn were left to be gleaned by the poor. But even the crumbs are being denied to the poorest of our citizens. If it is true, as some have said, that a society is to be judged by the way it treats its poor, our country would suffer a harsh judgment.

On a global scale, "refugeeism" has become an epidemic. Hordes of the homeless—uprooted by disasters natural and human, by war and famine and the pronouncements of those who decide who eats—roam from one dark corner to the next, asking, "Is there room?"

They are those for whom there is no room. The inns are all full. There is only the drafty, dirty stable out back—if they dare to knock.

I pictured the gentle faces of María and her twin brothers. "And wrapped them in a sleeping bag and laid them in a dishwasher, because there was no room for them." It was indeed no place for children as precious as those. Nor was a manger for a newborn. The cribs of the poor are many.

Those bleak days of winter were turned into a season of hope when I began to recognize Jesus in the faces of María and Doris and Joe. And I was more deeply touched than I ever had been before by God's awesome choice to come to us as an infant on a pile of straw.

Jesus, the homeless one—a refugee in Egypt before his first birthday. His good news to the poor was not only a message of liberation but the promise that he would be with them always, among them. Poor as they are poor. Despised as they are despised. Incarnation. The Word made flesh and bones. Good news indeed!

I had discarded the shepherd Jesus for a time when I embraced the liberator. But I was beginnning to see that Jesus is bigger—and much smaller—than both of these. He is the shepherd who knows how to love and protect because he is also the sheep. The vulnerable one. The victim. The lamb that was slain.

What a scandal—this Messiah so longed for by the Jews who suffered under brutal Roman occupation. He came on no thundering white horse bearing arms. He came naked on a heap of straw. The good news was that he came to set them free and break the yoke of oppression. The best news was that he was just like them. And us.

The liberation had already begun—before his eyes even saw the light of day. The message of the radical social upheaval on the horizon had been entrusted to a woman—a poor Jewish woman. A victim of poverty through the Romans' exploitation, of racism from the surrounding culture, and of sexism by a religious tradition that defined her as property, Mary bore in her own being the mark of God's liberation. She was chosen to bear the Christ. She was already a sign of the good news; it was finding a home in her receptive heart and body.

What a precious moment for womanhood when Mary, still trembling with the news of what was to be fulfilled in her, ran to the elderly Elizabeth, bearer of a miraculous pregnancy of her own. And at Mary's greeting, the baby John leaped for joy in Elizabeth's womb. Mary's song of praise and hope flowed forth in this setting, and two miraculously pregnant women basked in the secret of the quiet revolution that was to be accomplished through them.

I opened my Bible that night and received an invitation to be, like Jesus, a sheep. I read from Matthew 25.

When the Son of man comes in his glory, and all the angels with him, he will sit on his glorious throne. Before him will be gathered all the nations, and he will separate them one from another as a shepherd separates the sheep from the goats, and he will place the sheep at his right hand, but the goats at the left.

Then the King will say to those at his right hand, "Come, O blessed of God, inherit the kingdom prepared for you from the foundation of the world; for I was hungry and you gave me food, I was thirsty and you gave me drink, I was a stranger and you welcomed me, I was naked and you clothed me, I was sick and you visited me, I was in prison and you came to see me."

Then the righteous will answer him, "Lord, when did we see you hungry and feed you, or thirsty and give you a drink? And when did we see you a stranger and welcome you, or naked and clothe you? And when did we see you sick or in prison and visit you?"

And the King will answer them, "Truly, I say to you, as you did it to one of the least of these my brothers and sisters, you did it to me."

Then he will say to those at his left hand, "Depart from me, you cursed, into the eternal fire prepared for you by the devil and his angels; for I was hungry and you gave me no food, I was thirsty and you gave me no drink, I was a stranger and you did not welcome me, naked and you did not clothe me, sick and in prison and you did not visit me."

Then they also will answer, "Lord, when did we see you hungry or thirsty or a stranger or naked or sick or in prison, and did not minister to you?"

Then he will answer them, "Truly I say to you, as you did it not to one of the least of these, you did it not to me."

And they will go away into eternal punishment, but the righteous into eternal life.

Everywhere I looked I saw the "least of these." I knew that my very salvation was at stake in how I related to them. And knowing that they existed, I could not turn my back on them. There were no excuses.

Jesus made it very plain, as I heard him say to me: "I am they, and they are me. That's me who stands, hungry, in the soup line. That's me who has no place to put my head. Look for me among the broken, the tortured, the discarded."

And that was where Jesus lived his life—among the lepers, the outcasts, the prostitutes and adulterers, the sick and lame and blind. He spoke the language of compassion and liberation and love. And if we are to follow him, we must do the same.

Words from Thomas Merton came to me: "Into this world, this demented inn, in which there is absolutely no room for Him at all, Christ has come uninvited. But because He cannot be at home in it, because He is out of place in it, His place is with those others for whom there is no room."

Jesus came to us poor, but he came with a promise: they who mourn shall laugh, and they who hunger shall be filled. And what laughing and feasting there will be on the day when the banquet is set for a new clientele!

From all over the world will come the refugees, the exploited, the ragged, the weary. They will trade in their shackles for garlands, their tattered coats for robes of splendor. Those whose food has been nothing but stark perseverance will revel in God's abundance.

And outside the great banquet hall, kept out by bars and fences of their own making, will be the hard-hearted, the selfish, the complacent. For once, a long time ago, a baby crept onto straw, and they thought the event too small to notice.

That birth was transforming my life again. As I looked around me that Christmas Eve, I saw little evidence of the hope that Mary so boldly proclaimed in her song of praise. The poor were still homeless and hungry.

But the vision of the banquet was there in that dark room, too. And I began to understand that the reign of justice is in-

deed accomplished wherever people live as if it were true. It
had something to do with faith.

Jesus was still looking for hearts in which to make his home.
I prayed that Christmas Eve that mine might be acceptable.
And I found a home in the invitation and promise "Abide in
me, and I in you."

In that dark room, where Mary and Sheila snored lightly,
and Doris wheezed with asthma, and all were asleep except
me, I laughed to myself when the clock in the church's tower
quietly struck midnight. I had stuck it out through Christmas.

6. Triple Jeopardy

The phone call came during Holy Week. A timid, young voice on the other end of the line stated simply, "My mother said you could help me." When Nicole finally introduced herself, I knew that a five-month search was over.

I had met her mother at the Women's Federal Correctional Institution in Alderson, West Virginia, while I was on an assignment there for *Sojourners* magazine. In our first conversation, Celia talked mostly about her oldest daughter. "Promise me you'll find Nicole when you get back," she pleaded as I left the prison. For weeks I tried to keep my promise to her. Phone calls to social workers and foster parents back in Washington, D.C., only revealed that Nicole had disappeared without letting anyone know her whereabouts.

I received letters from Celia and returned to Alderson to visit her. Slowly, over time, she offered me the pieces of her story. Terrified to think of having to make it on her own with four children, Celia had stayed for thirteen years with a husband who beat her. In recent months he had begun to abuse the children, so she took them and fled to a friend's home.

Her husband became enraged and threatened to hurt each of the children, beginning with the oldest, unless Celia came back to talk things over. On a Sunday morning, while Nicole was walking to church, her father and two of his buddies waited for her on a street corner and then gang-raped her. Nicole was fourteen.

The husband threatened similar violence against the next daughter, so Celia went to the house to talk to him. One of the men who had participated in the rape was downstairs in the house while Celia and her husband talked upstairs. A cousin of Nicole's, having heard about the rape, arrived with a gun and shot the man. By the time the police arrived, the man was dead and Celia was in the room, having run downstairs with her husband when they heard the shot.

Celia was handcuffed along with the cousin and taken to jail. A public defender told her that the circumstantial evidence was so strong that any judge would rule against her, despite the cousin's testimony of her innocence. She was, after all, the mother of the rape victim and therefore had the strongest motivation for the killing. The lawyer convinced her to plead guilty to manslaughter in order to avoid a first-degree murder conviction, which carried a possible life sentence in prison. She got four years, to be served at the federal women's prison in Alderson, West Virginia, 300 miles away from her children.

Nicole spent several weeks alone in the hospital, recovering from the physical effects and emotional trauma of the rape. Hospital personnel feared that telling her that her mother was in prison would only add trauma to trauma. So for weeks she bore the devastation and isolation of knowing that her father had raped her and believing that her mother had rejected and abandoned her.

After her recovery, she had to testify against her father in his rape trial. The ordeal was particularly difficult for her, and when it was over she disappeared. Her father was acquitted of the rape charge.

Months later, when she finally called me, I had no idea how I could help. I suggested that we have lunch together on Friday. It was a Good Friday I will never forget. Tears streamed down her cheeks like the rain that poured outside as she told me, "I don't have any money for food, and I'm going to have a baby."

She explained immediately that the baby wasn't a result of "what my father did to me." It was fathered by Charlie, a twenty-eight-year-old man into whose arms she had run when she got out of the hospital looking for someone to love her. Charlie, a Vietnam veteran, was at least responsible enough toward her and the baby to invite Nicole to live with him and his extended family—his parents, two brothers, and a sister with three small children.

These ten people shared a two-bedroom house, and Charlie's parents were putting pressure on Nicole to pay her way. Some low-level housing inspector was, according to Nicole, being paid off to keep quiet about their overcrowded home, which violated D.C. housing codes. If he was expected to keep quiet about Nicole, the inspector said, then he needed a small increase in the sum.

I didn't know where to start. Injustice overlaid with corruption overlaid with trauma formed the foundation of Nicole's life. We started with the basics. I got some maternity clothes from my sister Kay, who no longer needed them, and helped Nicole get her name on the city's welfare rolls. That didn't begin to scratch the surface of her needs.

Over the months I visited her often at her home with Charlie's family. A mangy old dog that the children kept in the front yard alternately growled and snapped at me on my arrival or ignored me. He often reflected the mood of the household, which seemed always either steeped in a lethargic stupor or about to explode with angry tension.

The front room of the house contained only a rundown couch, where the parents slept, a cloudy fish tank, an old television set that was constantly on, and an empty set of shelves, beside which was nailed Charlie's certificate of discharge from the army. The kitchen was in constant use, as the household had to eat in shifts from four overturned dairy crates that served as chairs around a small kitchen table, which was missing a leg. Upstairs, Nicole and Charlie shared a room with Charlie's two brothers, and his sister and her three children occupied the other.

Charlie, like his father, was an alcoholic and could not keep a job. Junior, his youngest brother, was mentally retarded and also could not work. The mother, bent over from arthritis and years of backbreaking work, still brought in money by cleaning rooms at a nursing home. The sister tried to juggle part-time work with the demands of three small children, one of whom was also mildly retarded.

Despite the odds against them and the angry frustration that often enveloped them, the family honestly did their best to try to care for one another. The whole family was present and cheering when Junior took second place in a race at the Special Olympics. The children were deeply loved, and their warm affection toward me—sometimes exhibited by flying leaps into my arms from the front bannister—came as a sign of hope and life in the midst of so much tragedy.

In August, Nicole, Charlie, and I made the six-hour drive to Alderson to visit Celia. Nicole had wanted to surprise Celia by bringing Charlie along, since the two had never met. The surprise was on us.

The guards at the prison refused to allow Charlie in, since he possessed no form of identification and was not mentioned on Celia's list of potential visitors. For three hours I tried to cut through the bureaucratic red tape, explaining the situation to prison officials all along the way. I finally got a call put through to the prison warden, who offered the ultimate no to my request to allow Charlie to see Celia.

We had driven so far, and Nicole was devastated. But she and I had a couple of hours with Celia. Then all of Nicole's hopes for the day were finally crushed when Celia began to challenge her on why she stayed with Charlie and to express her anger and disappointment that Nicole was getting herself trapped in the very same sort of mess that she had been in when she got pregnant with Nicole. Nicole tried to fight back her tears and finally ran out of the prison visiting room sobbing.

Celia began to cry, too. "I wanted so much for her," she cried. "I'm so sorry. I'm so sorry. I didn't mean to hurt her."

When she calmed down, Celia began to tell me about a new pressure in her life. Her husband had initiated a lawsuit back home to take custody of the children. Celia explained that such lawsuits, usually initiated by child-welfare departments of state governments, are fairly common, and women in prison often lose their children in court hearings—by reason of "abandonment."

I could hardly believe what she was telling me. Her husband was obviously in no position to have the children, but he wanted to prevent her from having them when she got out of prison.

Celia was particularly worried about the youngest. Lisa was just eight years old when Celia was taken away to prison. Celia had heard that she was doing poorly in school and was not happy in her foster home. I told her that I would try to check on Lisa.

Celia also talked about the anger and bitterness that had consumed her during her first year and a half in jail. But in recent months she began to recognize that she needed to trust God and knew that only her faith could pull her through. She wanted to trust—for her children's sake as well as her own. A tear came to her eye as she said, "You know, when the five of us were together, we used to laugh so hard sometimes. We'll laugh together again some day."

As she said this, Nicole came back in. As the apologies flowed, they gave each other a hug.

In September I got a phone call from a lawyer telling me that Celia requested me as a witness at an upcoming parole hearing. Could I come to West Virginia?

I left D.C. on a late-night train, pulling out of cavernous Union Station and then past the Jefferson Memorial—well lit even at that hour—and on into the blackness of the night. I had never testified at a parole hearing before, and I knew that this hearing was important for Celia's future. I tried to remember the Bible verse that says not to worry about what to say in court because the Holy Spirit gives the words, and prayed that I would be coherent on just a few hours of sleep.

At 4 A.M. the train stopped at Alderson, an especially desolate corner of the world at that time of night. I walked to the

Alderson Hospitality House, staffed by friends who open their home to families of the women in prison. A note directing me to a bed was posted on the front door. The parole hearing was scheduled for 11 A.M.

At 8:20 a call came from the prison, informing me that the hearing had been moved up to 9:00. I got myself together and to the prison as quickly as I could.

Celia looked beautiful—tall, slender, poised, and ready for the day. She gave me a hug when she saw me come in and introduced me to the other women sitting along the bench, waiting their turn to go before the parole board. The camaraderie was strong, and they wished each other luck as one by one they disappeared behind the huge double doors as their names were called.

Two and a half hours after I arrived, Celia and I got our turn. She had everything going for her. She had exhibited an exemplary demeanor in prison, was faithful in her work detail, had taken every course the prison offered, had a recommendation from the prison social worker and the added plus of an outside witness to attest to her character. She answered clearly and concisely to the woman and two men who asked her questions.

I was allowed only a few minutes to speak, just long enough to talk about her integrity and commitment and the fact that she had a daughter about to deliver a baby who needed her. Celia hoped so much to be out in time for the birth.

Then they fired questions at me: Had she repented of her crime? Was she sorry? What evidence was there of reform? Similarly, they turned to her: Why did she shoot a man? Did she feel remorse? Had she changed? They tried to intimidate.

We were both at a loss to know how to play this game. They assumed guilt. I wanted to plead her innocence. But that wasn't the way to make points in this game. It was too late for that. Only evidence of reform counted now.

It did not go well. I had to suppress a desire to scream at the board. Over lunch I apologized to Celia for having failed her. She told me she was deeply grateful that I had made the trip and said that my testimony and faith in her had given her hope to carry on.

In the end it didn't matter anyway. No one got early parole that day. The board had a reputation for being one of the toughest. The members apparently had their minds made up before the charade even began.

I spent the afternoon with Celia. We prayed together before I left. At 2:30 in the morning I was back at the tiny Alderson train station, waiting for a train that was half an hour late. I was exhausted but didn't drift off to sleep on the train for several hours. I was awakened in the morning by a woman who shoved a religious tract at me and asked, "Are you going to heaven?"

"No—Washington," was my foggy reply. By 8:30 I was home.

As the time came close for Nicole to deliver her baby, I was plagued with the feeling that I needed to do more for her. Finding a doctor and baby clothes for her was important, but it didn't address the real issues of her life. I didn't want to become her financier, and yet the disparity between our resources always disturbed me.

I had, with some ease, embraced a "simple lifestyle" when I joined Sojourners Community and moved into the inner city. But my growing relationship with Nicole affirmed that I could never know what it meant to be poor. I had too much education and too many resources ever to understand utter powerlessness and desperation. I was too well loved ever to know utter desolation.

Nicole helped me lose a fair dose of idealism and gain a lot of awareness about my limitations. Yet those realizations didn't make me want to turn my back on my hope of deeper transformation, but only to push harder to try to shed myself of privilege and make the struggles of the poor my own. Through Nicole, I was learning that my identification with their struggles came not from a commitment to a set of principles but from a deepening commitment to particular people.

From time to time I gave Nicole money when she asked for it. I always struggled to stay on the correct side of the fine line between compassionate generosity and a dangerous charity that would foster in her an unhealthy dependence on me. This was never easy. I had so much, and she had so little. And it seemed to me that, at the age of fifteen, she had every right to be dependent on somebody. Nobody else in her life was dependable.

I reasoned that I would do her a far better service if I taught her about budgeting money and eating nutritionally and inexpensively than if I kept handing her money. But her living situation mitigated against any independent use of her money, and the lessons never took hold.

One time when she asked for money for food, she came back the next day asking for more. When I asked her what happened to what I had already given her, she confessed, "Charlie and I used it to go dancing." When I opened my mouth to chastise her, she pleaded, "Isn't it OK to dance when you're hungry?"

I felt torn then as I often did. I wanted to take her head in my hands and say, "I'm glad you had a good time." Teenagers are meant to have a good time. And I wanted to shake my finger and beg her to be responsible to herself and the baby she carried. Expectant mothers need to eat well. I handed her some money and told her I was glad she had a good time.

Charlie's family possessed the gift of celebration. For all their troubles, they knew how to party on appropriate occasions. They always set aside money from their meager resources for sumptuous feasts on holidays and the children's birthdays.

I will never forget a cold winter night when Nicole called to tell me that the heat had been cut off at the house because of an unpaid bill. I drove over to the house, expecting to find the family huddled together around the open oven for warmth.

Instead, as I approached the house, I heard music blaring from the top floor. Inside, the family was dancing. The youngest child was giggling as she tried to show her bent-over grandmother how to pirouette and boogie at the same time. Pillows were flying and everyone was laughing, and Nicole shouted to me over the din, "We're trying to keep warm!"

During the months before Nicole gave birth, I struggled with the idea of inviting her to move in with me. At various times the family was threatened with eviction, and I considered the option more seriously. I wanted so badly to fix her life and make everything smooth. But those were my dreams for her life and not her own. The best I could do was simply be her friend.

Beginning the second week of November, I slept with the car keys by my bed, in case I would be needed to make a middle-of-the-night run to the hospital. On Thanksgiving Day my goddaughter was born. Nicole named her Celia.

The hospital felt deserted that Thanksgiving Day. I was alone in the maternity waiting room for several hours before little Celia made her appearance. I prayed like crazy for Nicole and the baby.

The silence was interrupted only once, by three teenagers who came through, smiling and giggling at the arrival of a baby boy to their teenage friend. I prayed for him, too. Then Charlie burst into the room, smiling. "It's a girl," he said proudly. We both wept.

At two hours old, Celia was as precious and beautiful as Nicole and I always knew she would be. I whispered to her through the glass that separated us that everything was going to be OK. Her peaceful sleep made me feel that the words were true.

I had a godmother's privilege to call her grandmother with the news. The prison officials in Alderson were quite cooperative on this special occasion and gave Celia the message to call me right away. She was thrilled at the news of a baby girl, asking me for all the details. "How big is she?" "What time did she arrive?" "Is she pretty?" she wanted to know.

"She's beautiful," I told her.

I was about to hang up, when I remembered a detail I had forgotten to mention. "Oh, and her name is Celia."

Celia was quiet for a few moments and then whispered through her tears, "Thank you. This is quite a Thanksgiving."

For the next month Nicole and I looked forward to talking with her mother on Christmas morning. I had arranged with the foster parents of her sisters Sharon and Felicia to bring them to my house for the call. Lisa's foster mother refused to let her come.

It was a continuing sadness to me that no persuasion on my part ever moved Lisa's foster mother to allow her to spend time with her family or me. Remembering my promise to her mother, it had occurred to me to try to challenge her foster placement through the appropriate channels. But this battle was one too many in a war that I already felt I was losing. I tried to accept the fact that I could do nothing for Lisa.

Charlie, little Celia, Nicole, her two sisters, and I spent the morning opening gifts, eating, and waiting for the phone to ring. At midmorning the call came. Nicole answered it and yelled, "It's her!" Sharon and Felicia begged for turns and then spoke to their mother. There were more tears than words exchanged that morning. By the time I got my turn, Celia was too emotional to say any more than "Merry Christmas" and "Thank you."

When spring rolled around, it became possible to make a trip to Alderson without fear of getting trapped in a blizzard in the mountains. Nicole and I decided that Palm Sunday weekend was a good time for Celia to meet her grandmother.

I tried again to reach Lisa's foster mother. This time she was more direct with me: "It is my duty to protect that child from the bad influence of her mother." I wished she could understand how tormented Celia was with fears for Lisa.

On Friday afternoon—just about rush hour—Charlie, little Celia, Nicole, Sharon, Felicia, and I packed into a Volkswagen station wagon, along with supper, a tape recorder, and a pile of rock-and-roll cassettes (Felicia's contribution). Charlie had made fried chicken for the occasion. To my relief, the batteries in the tape recorder gave out after about twenty minutes—just as we were finally getting out of Washington.

There was lots of talk until the dark enveloped us and brought with it a blanket of quiet. Rain fell gently most of the night, with a few pelting interjections. My godchild murmured softly from time to time, and Sharon and Felicia sighed as they changed positions in their semisleep, trying to get comfortable in the cramped quarters of the back seat. At one point I heard some faint singing and turned around to find Sharon quietly singing Celia back to sleep.

It had been a year since Nicole walked out of the rain into my life. It was a year of great turmoil for me. But in that peaceful moment, late at night on the road to Alderson, I knew that it had been worthwhile. I thanked God for the privilege.

The visit was a surprise for Celia. This time we made sure that everyone was on the visiting list and had appropriate identification. Part of our trip from Washington had been consumed with plotting the all-important details of the surprise strategy.

Nicole and I met Celia as she came into the visiting room. Moments later Charlie, Sharon, and Felicia with the baby came pouring out of the rest rooms where they had hidden. Shouts of "Surprise!" echoed all through the visiting room, and other prison residents and their visitors laughed and clapped at the sight.

Celia hugged each of her daughters and then focused her attention on her granddaughter. A big grin spread over her face, and she said, "I think I'm going to cry," as she scooped little Celia up in her arms. She had waited for four long months for this moment. She circulated the visiting room, exclaiming, "This is my grandbaby!" and found a photographer to take a family picture of all of us together.

A week later Celia called me with surprising news—her parole board decided to release her in December. The release date was much earlier than I had allowed myself to hope for after my experience with the parole board seven months before. The early release carried the additional good news of a week's furlough for Celia the very next week—a week that contained Nicole's birthday. The phone at Charlie's house had been disconnected for the third time in as many months, so I jumped in the car to go tell Nicole the news.

I was grateful that Lisa's foster mother allowed her to be present at the big celebration the next week. I went to pick up Lisa before getting the others. Dressed in her best Sunday dress and black patent leather shoes, with a smile as broad and sweet as I had ever seen on a child, Lisa walked shyly toward me and extended her hand. Then she let a tear escape and gave me a big hug. "My mama told me about you," she said. Of all the children, she most resembled her mother.

That moment of our meeting felt almost magical to me. Throughout the party celebrating Celia's early release and Nicole's birthday, I felt very focused on Lisa. Often during that day, our eyes would meet, and she would give me a big grin. I savored the day, knowing that it would be a long time before I would see Lisa again.

When all the calculations of Celia's time in jail were finally over, the prison officials determined that she could be released to a halfway house in Washington the first week of November. I went to visit her at the halfway house that week, expecting to find her full of hope at her chance for a new beginning. She was instead very tired and subdued—chain-smoking nervously, a habit she had never had before. She was not anxious to see her children.

It was Election Night, 1980. I will never forget it. The residents of the halfway house were gathered around the house's television set. As soon as it became absolutely clear that Ronald Reagan had won the election, the women began to cry. One sobbed hysterically, and another said in despair, "Things are gonna change." They seemed more aware than I was of just how dramatically things were going to change. As I left Celia, who had said little to me all evening, she said, "There's no hope anymore."

All of the children, with the exception of Lisa, and I were together at Charlie's house on Christmas Day. They had presents for Celia and anxiously awaited her arrival. The day dragged on, and still there was no sign of her. I finally called the halfway house.

"I don't have bus fare," Celia said weakly. "Tell the children." It was a flimsy excuse, but I did my best to sound convincing. The children's hearts sank as they realized their hopes for their first Christmas together in three years had just been dashed. All the presents remained unopened.

I couldn't figure out why Celia, so full of faith and committed to making it for the sake of her children, was now slowly destroying herself. Over the months, the forces eating at her became clearer to me.

She was released from the halfway house in January. After three years of confinement, she was finding freedom hard to deal with. So battered was her self-esteem, so wounded her spirit, that she could not find the confidence to carry on.

Despite the skills she had learned in prison, no one wanted to hire a woman with a criminal record. She went to job interview after job interview, only to find rejection at every turn.

Her children had suffered and now needed her, but she had little to give them. She didn't know where to start to reestablish their life together as a family. And now she lived, without protection, in the same city as her violent husband.

In addition, she suffered from a series of illnesses, including a serious infection that went untreated in prison. She had no money for the care she needed.

I wanted to encourage her, to take her by the shoulders and tell her she had to get herself together for the sake of the children. They needed her. She had a responsibility. But I knew I had no right. She was facing more than anybody should have to in ten lifetimes. And anything I could offer seemed only pious and shallow to me.

I didn't know what to do to help Celia make it, but I was determined not to let the tragedy repeat itself in Nicole. When little Celia turned two, Nicole started talking about wanting to go back to school. She had only finished eighth grade. I had seen her compassion and her sense of responsibility toward her sisters take over when she realized that Celia wasn't going to get them back together. And when she started talking about wanting to be a nurse's aide, I wanted to do everything I could to encourage her.

We found a nurse's aide program especially designed for young women like herself who had been unable to finish high school. She did well in her entrance interview, and Sojourners Community lent her money for the tuition. Together we tackled a multitude of obstacles—day care for Celia, money for books and a uniform, a quiet place for her to study, the need to convince Charlie that it was important.

In August, Nicole, little Celia, Charlie's six-year-old niece Latasha, and I made a trip up to Pennsylvania to spend a weekend with my parents. Nicole and Latasha reveled in the spaciousness of the house and the land, though Latasha, used to sharing a bed with three others, found it frightening to think of sleeping by herself. Neither could she adjust to sleeping lengthwise rather than crosswise on the bed, so she and I slept in my bed perpendicular to each other—at least she got some sleep.

Nicole shared excitedly about her plans for school, and my parents contributed to her school fund, as they had helped with needs around Celia's birth. Nicole returned to Washington determined to make everyone proud.

The trip home provided time to talk. For the first time, Nicole shared with me about the rape and the war within her between love and hatred toward her father. "I just can't understand why he did it," she said over and over. She asked me if I would help her find him. She wanted him to have the chance to meet his granddaughter. And she wanted to talk to him and tell him she was trying to love him in her heart.

I wasn't sure if it would be good for her to find him, but I couldn't refuse her persistent and courageous desire to forgive him. I decided to leave the reconciliation up to God.

The next week we drove to the gas station where her father was last employed. Nicole was nervous. When we got close enough to see that the gas station had been closed down, Nicole's face showed both disappointment and relief. We had no other leads on where to find him.

Nicole looked forward to the fall and the start of her classes with great anticipation. But one disaster after another threatened to derail her hopes. Her September welfare check got stolen from her mailbox, and with it the funds she was planning to spend on day care for Celia. She scrambled to find friends and relatives to keep her.

In October a fire started in the mattress in the children's room and swept through the top of the house. All of Nicole's new school clothes were burned in the flames. She was devastated by the loss but determined to go on.

During those two months Charlie got and lost three jobs. With each job lost, he intensified his dependence on alcohol and became more abusive. Nicole called me one night in November to ask if she and Celia could spend the night with me, fearing that Charlie might get physically violent. She called back a short time later to say that everything was OK.

For two years Charlie's promise to Nicole of an apartment of their own was dangled in front of her and then dashed every time he lost out on or got fired from a job. Nicole began both to long for and to fear a space of their own.

Through all of this Nicole kept going to classes, realizing that her only ticket out of despair was a good job. She excitedly shared with me all that she was learning, and she drafted all of Charlie's family into service as she practiced and gained proficiency in taking temperatures and pulses.

Graduation for her six-month course was scheduled for late February. She invited me to attend the ceremony, since, as she put it, I was her "second mother." I was all ready to be a proud parent with a camera on her big day. But that day never came for Nicole.

Early one January evening, she called and said there was a "family crisis" that she couldn't explain over the phone. I had long before stopped trying to guess what sort of crisis might strike next. I put my head in my hands for a moment and then piled on layers of clothing to face the cold.

The *Washington Post* was calling it the worst cold spell to hit the city in almost a century. At night, the wind chill factor dipped the temperature to forty below zero. It was so cold that night that the old dog that lived in the yard at Charlie's house had been brought into the front hall. He got up from where he was lying when I came in, and I instinctively reached out to pat his head. He snapped viciously at my hand, grabbing hold of two fingers and then letting go with a growl.

The house had been without heat and hot water for two months; two days later the city government finally forced the landlord to turn the heat back on for the duration of the bitter cold spell. Meals for ten were being cooked on an old hot plate. Celia had contracted bronchitis. Everyone in the house was bundled up in all the clothes they owned.

But it wasn't the cold or Celia's bronchitis that was the overriding crisis. It was Lisa.

Lisa was the one daughter Celia had taken back with her. But Nicole explained, as we sat on the old crates in the kitchen, that her mother had dropped Lisa off with her a week ago and never came back for her. "I can't keep her anymore," Nicole cried. "The housing inspectors are already after us. And besides, she won't listen to me. It's not good for her here." That was obvious to me.

Nicole was convinced that Lisa wouldn't listen to me either. But Lisa came and joined me in the kitchen when Nicole walked out. I would not have recognized her in any other setting. In the time since I had last seen her, she had grown into a beautiful young woman.

I asked Lisa if she would like me to take her back to her mother. She burst into tears. Through her sobs she explained that there had been some men drinking at her mother's apartment and one of them had tried to touch her. Lisa was fourteen now.

The pattern was beginning all over again. The innocence and magic were dead in Lisa. Sitting there on broken-down crates, wearing layers of clothing to keep out the cold, she wept and I shuddered in anger at the combination of bad luck and abuse that had set the course of Nicole's and Lisa's young lives. And I cursed myself for my own failure to make a difference.

I finally took her hand and said, "Let's go get some supper."

The incident with Lisa turned out to be Nicole's undoing. As with her mother, the pressure had built and built until one day something snapped, and it just didn't seem worth trying anymore to keep everything together.

Despite all my pleas to her to finish school, Nicole dropped out three weeks before she was to graduate. She decided that she needed to put more attention into her sisters' needs than her own. I tried to convince her that the best thing she could do for them was to get her own life together and get a good, stable job. But she was unconvinced, and I had no more pep talks left in me.

If someone had written Nicole's story as fiction, I would have said to the author, "Change it. Make it more believable. No one can have this much bad luck." But her story is true. She is a picture of what it means to bear the triple jeopardy of being poor, black, and female in America.

Nicole walked into my life on Good Friday, and it seems we never really got past it. If there is any resurrection at all in her life, perhaps it is this: that she has learned to dance when she is cold and hungry. Perhaps that is a legacy she will pass on to my goddaughter.

As for Lisa, we had supper together that night. I knew from experience with her sister that the fare I had to offer at home would be less than appealing to her, so we went out after some hamburgers. On the way to supper, she talked and I listened. She didn't understand why her mother's friend had tried to molest her. Nor did she understand why, when she was staying with Nicole, Charlie's older brother had paid Junior, the retarded brother, to try to force Lisa to go to bed with him— it was only a joke, the older brother explained later when Lisa ran crying into Nicole's arms.

She tried to sort through her feelings of fear, confusion, and shame. She was full of questions, and I tried to answer her as best I could while keeping my anger about it all under control. Why is it that the most vulnerable always suffer so much? I wished that she had had a mother the last few years to answer her questions and help her come to grips with her womanhood.

As we got out of the car, she said, "You're the only person I can trust." We barely knew each other. And then she added, "We're sort of kin, aren't we?" We decided over hamburgers that if there can be great-grandmothers, there certainly could be great-godmothers. We're sort of kin.

I took her home with me. We played a card game for a while, and then she talked some more. "I guess my mother doesn't want me," she stated. She talked about how painful it had felt to have her mother go away to prison and now to have been left at Nicole's.

It grew late, and we made a bed on my floor for her out of sofa cushions and a sleeping bag. She told me that she stayed awake all night at her mother's because of being afraid and she wouldn't sleep at my place either. Moments after she crawled into the sleeping bag, she was soundly asleep. I knelt down next to her, took her hand, and prayed for protection for her.

I lay awake a long time listening to her quiet, regular breathing. I knew that I had done the right thing that night—but I hadn't thought past the moment and knew that I would wake up in the morning realizing that for a while I had become the mother of a fourteen-year-old. I only knew that I was committed not to send her back to a place where she might be hurt again.

The next morning was filled with meetings for me, and Lisa went along to the magazine office and helped Sojourners Peace Ministry get a mailing out to our magazine subscribers. In the afternoon I tried unsuccessfully to reach Celia by phone. Lisa and I went home and made some cookies. While they were in the oven baking, Lisa asked if I would be her mother.

There were a thousand reasons why I couldn't take her in, but I thought about it anyway. In the twenty hours we had been together, she had clearly won a place in my heart.

I finally reached Celia the next morning. She had found a job, and we agreed to meet over her lunch break. I found my way to the federal building downtown where she had a cleaning job. We met in a dingy basement locker room. She had just twenty minutes for lunch.

Celia looked thin and tired and sick. Dressed in a faded blue cleaning uniform, she coughed and chain-smoked as we talked. To look at her was to see a pile of broken dreams and crushed hopes.

She had joined the underside of life in the capital city. Her work was dirty and degrading. With a small space heater as the only source of warmth, she cleaned the dark and cavelike cement-block basement of a building where upstairs power was brokered every day.

She had started drinking and began to stay close to men who she thought could protect her from her husband. They not only drank heavily but also dealt on a small scale in illegal drugs. They preyed on her failure and despair. At various times she had made a decision to get them out of her life and tried to do so, unsuccessfully. After several failed attempts, she resigned herself to their presence in her life and her dependence on their attention and protection.

Celia shivered in the thin uniform as she talked. The cold environs aggravated a problem she had with her back and her joints, so she worked in constant pain. And the unattended-to infection had worsened and spread, so that her doctor said she needed a hysterectomy—but she didn't know when there would be enough money for it.

I tried to remember the Celia I had known at her parole-board hearing—strong, confident, full of hope. And I recalled the words she had said to me about her children a month before the hearing: "You know, when the five of us were together, we used to laugh so hard sometimes. We'll laugh together again some day."

It was clear to me that day that those words would never come true. It wasn't because she didn't want to have the children back. She just didn't have the resources or strength to care for them all. "I'm trying so hard," she cried. "I just can't do it all."

She had begun to try with Lisa, about whom she felt the most guilt. Lisa had grown from a child to a woman in the years that Celia was apart from her, and Celia was unable to forgive herself for missing those years of Lisa's life.

Celia had put a great deal of time and energy into getting Lisa out of her foster home and back with her. But then she realized that this daughter who was no longer a little girl was becoming a victim of the men who used Celia. "I wasn't going to just leave her with Nicole," Celia said. "I knew my place wasn't good for her. I just wanted her to stay there until I could get a better place."

Celia had to get back to work. "I can't keep her," I said. "She can't go back to her foster home, and Nicole doesn't have space and needs the freedom to live her own life. Lisa needs to be with you. She needs her mother right now."

"All right. We'll try to work it out," Celia said as I left.

Lisa didn't want to go back with her mother. "She doesn't want me!" she protested when I talked with her later. "Can't I just stay here?"

I pleaded with her to give it a second chance to work with Celia. "You need each other," I said, "and she'll protect you."

I knew I was asking a fourteen-year-old to go back and face more than anybody should have to.

For two hours she refused to go back. A war went on inside of her between a child wanting to be a grown-up and a grown-up wanting to be a child. Deep wells of rejection and hurt bubbled to the surface as she talked about her mother.

She agreed to call Celia on the phone. They talked for a few minutes, and then Lisa reported what her mother had said: "I love you, Lisa, and I want you with me." Lisa cried. "I just don't know," she wailed. "I'm afraid."

I put an arm around Lisa's shoulder and said, "It's your decision. You think about it." I left the room.

Twenty minutes later Lisa came to me, tears streaming down her face, and said, "I'm ready to go back." Then she added, "Could I just stay here tonight?"

Before going to sleep that night, Lisa gave me a kiss on the cheek and handed me a large piece of paper. "This is for you," she said. Written in big letters were the words, "You are the Best of the West. Love, Lisa." "I'll never forget you," she said as she crawled into the sleeping bag.

As I was about to drift off to sleep, she suddenly said, "Once I wanted somebody to love me, so I tried to have a baby. It died. I didn't kill it. I would never have killed it."

There was silence for a moment, and then she asked, "Did you say your prayers?" There was another pause, and then she whispered, "Bless Nicole and my mother and you and my baby."

I didn't fall asleep. And it didn't surprise me when about an hour later, Lisa sat up suddenly and started crying, "I can't sleep. I'm thinking about my baby. I think I killed it. The doctor said so." She blurted out the story through her tears: "I was staying with Nicole and I was at the phone booth, and I had to run home quick to go to the bathroom. I think I ran too hard. I started to bleed."

The story continued to spill out. It had taken an hour for an ambulance to come as Lisa lay frightened and bleeding. As she finished telling me the story, she lay back down again and then smiled softly. "But it was OK. Nicole took real good care of me. She held my hand. And she just kept taking my temperature and my pulse to make sure I was going to be OK."

7. No Safe Place

I walked into the *Sojourners* office after a morning appointment and was immediately surrounded by concerned friends. "Hershey was on the radio," somebody said. "They're evacuating pregnant women and preschool children to the Hershey Sports Arena." I tried to picture the place where, as a child, I had watched hockey games and Ice Capades, now as an evacuation center.

Through the day, as friends and I packed up boxes of supplies and magazines for an impending office move, we kept the radio on, getting the latest updates from my hometown. At home later that evening, the television news showed the scene: the arena lined with cots, children crying, and their mothers trying to keep order under difficult circumstances. It was March 30, 1979.

The drama had begun two days earlier. I was cooking dinner for my household when a community member came in and told me there had been a nuclear power-plant accident near Harrisburg, Pennsylvania.

My parents' new home, just beyond Hershey in Elizabethtown, Pennsylvania, sat seven miles from the Three Mile Island reactor. My mother was the first to hear the news and the suggestion that people in the area might want to stay inside for a while. She watched as a neighbor plowed a field on his tractor and debated with herself whether to go tell him what she had just heard.

No one knew exactly how serious things were. And no one wanted to overreact. She finally went out to tell him. He listened and then kept plowing.

My attempts to call Mom and Dad that day were unsuccessful. Phone lines were jammed, as everyone had the same idea to try to reach relatives and friends in the area.

By eight o'clock, after repeated efforts, I still had not gotten through to them. I went with the others to our community's weekly Wednesday night meeting. We were in the middle of a Lenten series on the nuclear arms race.

That night we watched a movie filmed in Hiroshima the day after the atomic bomb was dropped. The devastation, scarred faces, screaming children, and lifeless flesh hanging off of living bodies hit hard. The immense suffering caused by blast and radiation generated many tears among us, and prayers for my family and the other people living in the nuclear shadow of Three Mile Island.

I finally reached my parents after the meeting. Brief news updates from government and nuclear-industry officials were telling them to stay put, assuring them that everything was under control and no one was in danger. Mom and Dad seemed calm—like others in the area, anxious to trust the reports coming from the "experts."

I felt the distance of the miles between us acutely that night. I wanted to keep in close contact with them and was frustrated by an unusual set of circumstances that complicated communication. The phone hadn't yet been connected in the new household into which I had just moved; the phone at the office would be disconnected soon in preparation for our move; and there was no telling when I might be able to get another call through the jammed lines. We promised to do our best to stay in touch regularly.

Little news seemed forthcoming the next day, confirming my mistrust of a nuclear industry with an image to protect. Two days later, the reports were frightening. The hydrogen bubble inside the reactor was growing, and the core wasn't cooling down. Radiation was being released into both the air and the Susquehanna River.

Reports from the Nuclear Regulatory Commission and Metropolitan Edison, the power company responsible for the plant, were conflicting. But by then even some of the experts—doing their best throughout the crisis not to provoke a panic and certainly not prone to overstatement about the danger—were beginning to talk about "meltdown" as a growing possibility. Three Mile Island's Unit 2 Reactor had become an immense, unstable, radioactive pressure cooker. Walter Cronkite's special report on the disaster that night was titled "The Nuclear Nightmare."

People were beginning to evacuate the area, though many were reluctant, as a few looters had begun capitalizing on the crisis and entering some of the deserted homes. As we talked on the phone that night, Mom and Dad decided that it was time to get out.

The next day was brilliantly sunny in Pennsylvania's Susquehanna Valley, making it hard to believe that serious danger was lurking in the air. The peril was imperceptible; you couldn't see it, or taste it, or even smell it. It was visible only in the emotions of the people it threatened.

I sat on top of the only remaining desk in our office, the others being moved out around me, on the phone again with Mom and Dad. They had reconsidered their decision to leave. I tried to accept it.

There was nowhere to go to be alone that day. Others were carrying all the furniture to our new office location two blocks away, and people were swarming from one office to the other. I remember spying a couch at the corner of Fourteenth and L streets downtown, left there for a moment by its movers when an office-furniture bottleneck developed at the new office. As traffic rushed by up and down Fourteenth Street, I sat there alone and tried to think.

Something changed dramatically for me the day radiation leaked into my home. The place of warm memories and security was suddenly invaded by an invisible and insidious and out-of-control danger. I thought of the mothers and young children in the Hershey arena and wondered whether anyone thought that it would actually protect them if the worst oc-curred. If TMI's Unit 2 Reactor exploded, even Washington, D.C., was in the danger area.

I got back to our new office just in time to hear the noon news report. Friends were sitting on boxes and corners of the floor listening as the radio proclaimed, "Everything is stable."

"Stable?!" burst out our news editor. "You know what stable means? That the lousy thing is still sitting there boiling at 500 degrees!" He was only slightly wrong—the reactor tempera-ture, we learned later, reached just over 5,000 degrees.

Four days after the crisis began, the reactor still wasn't under control. Metropolitan Edison continued to say there was no cri-sis. Options for getting rid of the giant hydrogen bubble inside the reactor were outlined in the *Washington Post* that day. It could be collapsed—but that would require building up even more pressure inside the reactor. It could be dissolved into water—but that would call for adding oxygen and increasing the possibilities of explosion or fire.

What was clearest was that if there had been a good option, the nuclear experts would have tried it by now.

I was awakened very early the morning of April 1 with a message that my parents had called to our Thirteenth Street household. They were on their way to my grandmother's home in Hagerstown, Maryland, and could be reached there in the afternoon.

Our community worship that Sunday morning was rich and encouraging. We suspended our usual order of things and spent a lot of time talking about our fears and praying together. The community sent me off to Hagerstown with prayers and expressions of love to my parents.

After the service, I walked home with a nine-year-old friend, apologizing to her for having to cancel our planned afternoon of flying kites together by the Washington Monument. And for a fleeting moment, I allowed myself to wonder if we would fly kites together again. Before I left the city, Jim Wallis and I talked briefly about what an evacuation plan might look like for the community and the neighborhood, should the reactor in Pennsylvania choose meltdown.

In Hagerstown we talked little over dinner about Three Mile Island, trying to keep my grandmother's fears to a minimum. I was thankful to be with Mom and Dad, grateful to be at a place with such strong and warm memories of family. Grandmother's pot roast was as good as I had always remembered it.

The bathroom was the only truly private room in my grandmother's small apartment, so my mother and I went there for a conversation. She recounted all the thoughts that had gone through her mind as they left the house, her sadness and the fear that they might never return.

She had considered bringing photograph albums and old letters along but finally decided to leave them. I told her that at the last minute I had grabbed all my journals before leaving Washington, just in case I couldn't get back into the city. The fear that the future might not be the same made us both want to hang on to the joyful and poignant fragments of the past.

That night I slept on my grandmother's ancient four-seater couch, where I had slept dozens of times before through the years. Kay and Deb and I used to take turns on the couch and two cots that, when set up next to each other, covered all of the living room's floor space. African violets still flourished in all the room's windows.

As I drifted off to sleep, I remembered all the Friday nights we had sat on Grandmother's balcony, listening to band concerts from the park nearby, where earlier in the day we had gone to feed the swans and eat ice cream cones. Those days seemed so uncomplicated now. And so far away.

The next day the hydrogen bubble in the Three Mile Island reactor mysteriously started to shrink. We all returned home. And it was declared that the nuclear nightmare was over. For conservative Pennsylvanians, used to nothing more dangerous in their air than the sweet smell of chocolate, the tendency was strong to believe it.

But now, ten years later, I recall the predictions of the medical experts at the time of the crisis: more birth defects and radiation-related illnesses, and cancers beginning to show up ten years after the disaster.

Elizabethtown, where my parents built their home on several acres of farmland, is normally downwind of Three Mile Island. But an unusual wind was blowing during the first days of the crisis, carrying the most severe fallout in the other direction. During subsequent venting of radiation, Elizabethtown got quite a few strong doses. But the winds of fate seem literally to have saved my parents and their neighbors from the horrible nightmare that people on the other edge of TMI have already lived.

A rusting sign bearing a picture of a Holstein cow and the words "Holowka Farm" swings at the end of a long, dirt lane in the western shadow of TMI's cooling towers. At the other end of the lane, a farmhouse holds an array of grand-champion blue ribbons that the Holowkas won through the years for showing their cows. They have been on this farm since their father bought it fifty-two years ago.

Marie and her brother, Paul, begin milking their cows at a quarter to four every morning. Marie described what happened on March 28, 1979: "I think I milked about three cows, and all of a sudden the barn windows started to rattle, and the barn started to shake. And my brother said, 'Oh, my God, that's an earthquake.' And I said, 'Paul, do you hear it under the ground?' It was going brrrp, brrrp, brrrp, like boiling water in a pot. I said, 'Paul, that isn't an earthquake; that must be something happening at Three Mile Island.' " The nuclear accident at TMI began at 3:58 that morning.

When Marie went outside after finishing the milking, her eyes started to "pinch" her and she had a funny taste in her mouth. The sky, she said, was "real blue," and she couldn't see for more than ten feet. She felt so weak, she fell three times on the way back to the farmhouse.

After the accident the Holowkas and many of their neighbors broke out in a rash that wouldn't heal. In May 1979, Marie developed a sore throat that lasted until August, when she was diagnosed with an infected thyroid. A year later, during a routine checkup, her doctor told her that she had cancer. He asked her if she felt scared. "Why should I be scared?" she said. "Everybody in our neighborhood has cancer."

Fourteen of their neighbors died one summer, most of them from cancer. "This is practically a new neighborhood," said Marie.

Marie Holowka has had six cancer operations and thirty-nine radiation treatments. She has lost most of her hair, her mouth is blistered, and she still has a tumor in her chest. She believes she was hit by a radioactive plume from TMI.

Since TMI began operating, the Holowkas have lost more than two hundred cows; their herd is down to forty now. "You just try to raise them," said Marie, "and they go so long, and then they just lay down and die."

Levels of radioiodine 131 were discovered in milk around the nuclear plant after the accident, and local milk companies refused to accept milk from farmers near TMI. The Holowkas now milk only for themselves and raise a few calves to sell.

Paul spends much of his time taking Marie to and from the hospital. Their 163-acre farm, once thriving with livestock and fields of tomatoes, corn, and beans, has fallen into disrepair.

The Holowkas, along with many of their neighbors, are convinced that their troubles stem from the towers visible from the edge of their property. They can't prove that their conviction is true. And no one can disprove it. What seems clear is that disturbing things are happening in the Susquehanna Valley.

Jane Lee began to see an increase in spontaneous abortions and stillbirths on her farm near TMI. Her veterinarian, Dr. Robert Weber, told her that "in a five-mile radius of that plant . . . we've got serious problems on the farms all around."

He used to perform one or two Cesarean deliveries a year. After the TMI accident, he was doing one a week. And he recently said to Lee, "Now I'm going day and night."

Jane Lee has documented a range of problems among animals in the vicinity of the nuclear plant. Litters of kittens have been born stillborn and hairless; dogs have been born without eyes; other animals were born dwarfed or retarded. Some livestock developed raw sores and lesions, others muscle deficiencies. Pigs have had trouble breeding, as did the county coroner's five thoroughbred horses, according to Lee. "The animals are giving us clear signals as to what's wrong with our environment," she said.

In May of 1979, Mary Osborn's daughter carried a bouquet of daisies home to her after school. Among the bunch were two severely deformed flowers, and when her daughter led her to the field where she had picked them, Osborn found about twenty-five more.

In October, Osborn sent both of her young children out into the yard to collect leaves for crayon rubbings. The maple leaves they brought back were too large to fit under the paper. One of the leaves, she said, registered radioactivity when a Geiger counter was passed over it.

Mary Osborn has begun a collection of mutant flowers and plants she has gathered in the vicinity of TMI. Among them is a 31-inch dandelion leaf picked from a ridge near the plant. She has a signed affidavit from world-renowned botanist Dr. James E. Gunckel, which states that among her specimens he found "a number of anomalies entirely comparable to those induced by ionizing radiation."

Joyce Corradi's oldest son, Tony, who was nine at the time of the accident, got violently ill after the family evacuated. Two doctors from Japan, who had done studies on survivors of the Hiroshima and Nagasaki atomic bombings, pulled out paint tiles and asked her to point out the color of what his stomach had ejected. They confirmed that his sickness was a reaction to radiation, according to Corradi.

Corradi said recently, "He turned nineteen yesterday. He seems healthy, he's productive, he's happy and, please God, let it be that way. But who's to say that somewhere down the road it won't be? What happens when he has children, or when his children have children? Those are questions children should not have to live with."

Joyce Corradi, Mary Osborn, and Jane Lee joined several other citizens near TMI who were frustrated by the lack of official response to their concerns about health problems in a door-to-door health survey in the spring of 1984. In the three areas they surveyed, they discovered a sevenfold increase over the expected number of cancers. Their report was verified by several independent physicians and statistics experts.

The Pennsylvania Department of Health immediately moved to undermine the report, according to those involved, and released its own cancer study in the fall of 1985. It concluded that no adverse health effects had been found in people living near Three Mile Island. The Department of Health study was discredited by both statistics and epidemiology experts: The facts had been diluted by the inclusion of 150,000 people— more than 40 percent of those factored in the study—who lived beyond the designated study zones determined by distance from TMI.

Dr. Gordon MacLeod, a friend of then Pennsylvania governor Richard Thornburgh (later to become attorney general during Ronald Reagan's tenure as president), assumed his post as the state's secretary of health twelve days before the TMI accident. Throughout the crisis, he pushed—against the wishes of other officials—for more medical input and an immediate evacuation of pregnant women and young children. He also tried urgently to secure from the federal government a supply of potassium iodide, a liquid that can be taken to block the ingestion of radioiodine and thereby protect the thyroid from damage. The supply arrived five days after the accident—too late for it to do any good—and thousands of the vials were unlabeled or contaminated.

During the presidential commission inquiry into the TMI accident, MacLeod felt that a Pennsylvania official involved in the crisis made "misstatements" to the commission. He wrote the commission a letter expressing his concern. Soon after, Governor Thornburgh asked for his resignation, stating "a difference in operational style."

But Dr. MacLeod was in fact prophetic at the time of the accident. Simply by consulting the state's vital statistics for the months following the accident, he found a dramatic increase in infant mortality in the areas surrounding TMI. After leaving his position as secretary of health, MacLeod was alerted by someone still in the Department of Health about a high rise in hypothyroid cases in children. It was critical that the data be released so that the condition could be treated and cretinism avoided in the children. But, said MacLeod, the data were "sitting on someone's desk for three months," until MacLeod himself released the information to the press.

U.S. government and Pennsylvania state officials, as well as representatives of the power company, continue to insist that the people around TMI were exposed only to safe levels of radiation—about the equivalent of an X ray, one official has stated. But we will never know for sure just how much radiation was emitted during the disaster. Official studies have shown that radiation levels went off the scales of the monitors, monitors were spaced at such a distance that significant gaps existed, and some were missing or malfunctioning. The critical data from the days of the crisis are gone and irretrievable.

But many citizens are convinced that their health problems are a direct result of the TMI accident. More than 2,000 lawsuits have been filed against Metropolitan Edison and its parent company, General Public Utilities Corporation (GPU). They represent, as one reporter put it, "an enormous catalog of human suffering"—cancers of all types, miscarriages, birth defects, leukemia, kidney and thyroid problems. Most of the cases charge "fraudulent concealment," accusing the power company of witholding information that would have enabled citizens to protect themselves from the danger. The official U.S. House of Representatives committee report on the accident, issued in March 1981, agreed with this charge, accusing the plant managers of "misstatements . . . that conveyed the impression the accident was substantially less severe . . . than what the managers themselves believed."

It came to light later that the late, prominent naval nuclear expert Admiral Hyman G. Rickover, as attested in a sworn affidavit by his daughter-in-law, had told her he had used his personal influence with President Jimmy Carter to pressure him to "suppress the most alarming aspects" of the presidential commission report on the TMI accident and release it in "a highly diluted form." Admiral Rickover had told her, according to the affidavit, that "the report, if published in its entirety, would have destroyed the nuclear power industry, because the accident at Three Mile Island was infinitely more dangerous than was ever made public."

The record of Metropolitan Edison and GPU has hardly been what one would call clean. Documented records show that Unit 2, which had been in operation for only three months before the accident, had a history of maintenance-caused failures in its main water feed system, which was the source of the accident. GPU has been issued warnings and fines for violations including plant operators asleep on the job, use of drugs and alcohol by operators, incidents of radioactive contamination in the plant, improper safety procedures, and a cheating scandal among its operators in training.

In 1983 GPU was indicted on eleven criminal counts related to falsifying and destroying safety data before the accident. The corporation pleaded guilty and was convicted on two of the counts; it pleaded no contest to the other nine.

The nightmare is far from over for the people around TMI. Of grave concern are 2.3 million gallons of radioactive water, a by-product of the accident. The nuclear industry wants to evaporate the water and release the radioactive gas into the air.

Citizens have mobilized to try to stop it, but history has shown that the nuclear industry usually gets what it wants.

Ten years after the accident, the damaged reactor still has not been decontaminated. Recent moves by the nuclear industry have indicated plans to halt the cleanup, which would leave TMI, as one resident put it, "an unstable radioactive waste site" into the next century.

Powerlessness, feelings of betrayal and the demise of public trust, concern for the future and one's children's future, continuing stress on marriages and families—all of these are part of the fallout of Three Mile Island.

Last month another of my parents' friends died of cancer. He was a neighbor for several years, the father of my first childhood friend. And so we live with our grief and our fears.

As a child, I always believed that the Good Shepherd, whose picture I kept by my bed, would protect me from all fears. But ten years ago, a fear crept into our lives that none of us had anticipated.

Through the years, in times of crisis, I have often turned to the Twenty-third Psalm, to the vision of that shepherd who leads and protects and consoles. In all my readings and prayings of that psalm, the images of pastures and still waters were always vivid; but I lacked a clear picture of the "valley of the shadow of death." Today, that image is disturbingly concrete for me. It is home.

For too many others on the globe, home has been contaminated by the scourge of radioactivity. Since Three Mile Island, we have had Chernobyl to show us the impact of a more serious nuclear-power disaster. Mary Osborn was recently invited to West Germany to talk about Three Mile Island with people in the path of the Soviet reactor's radioactive cloud. Some of the people she met gave her specimens of the strange flowers that have come up in their yards and gardens. One man talked about finding some very unusual dandelions—with leaves more than thirty inches long.

Osborn had found her mutant specimens within twenty-five miles of TMI; the West Germans lived almost a thousand miles from Chernobyl.

In all, at least twenty countries were affected by the radioactivity released from the Soviet power plant, contaminating water and milk supplies, crops, herds, and fish. A recent report stated that agricultural restrictions in Britain may remain in force for the next thirty years. The tremendous explosion at Chernobyl could not be contained within the reactor, nor its effects within geographic or generational boundaries. There is no telling the extent of the damage—in agricultural impact, long-term medical effects, and loss of human life.

Given what we know about the danger, it boggles the mind that we continue to pursue nuclear power as a "safe" option. The stakes are high—too high.

Dr. John Gofman was part of the Manhattan Project, which developed the first atomic bomb in the 1940s, the initial rationale for which was stopping Nazi atrocities and experimentation on humans. Gofman has had a tremendous change of heart. He is quoted in *Killing Our Own* (Wasserman and Solomon) as saying that in the United States "we have already accepted the policy of experimentation on involuntary human subjects" through our acceptance of nuclear energy. He continued, "I feel that at least several hundred scientists trained in the biomedical aspect of atomic energy—myself definitely included—are candidates for Nuremberg-type trials for crimes against humanity. . . . Now that we know the hazard of low-dose radiation, the crime is not experimentation—it's murder."

In response to officials who have said that the Three Mile Island accident released acceptable levels of radiation, Gofman said, "Setting permitted levels of radiation exposure for people is the same as saying you think it's permissible to have a certain number of random murders."

Given the immense suffering of people who are victims of the "peaceful atom," it has to be asked—why would decent human beings choose to point it at anybody? Aren't there some potentialities so horrible that they ought to be simply unacceptable? Shouldn't that have been the lesson learned at Hiroshima, when we saw for the first time what unspeakable devastation and horror were released by the atomic bomb?

✓ Instantly 75,000 people dead; 60,000 buildings leveled; survivors—men and women and children—severely burned and blinded. A heavy, black rain that showered the earth with deadly poison that will not go away, bringing a toll of tragedy that will last for generations.

If the warmakers felt compelled to unleash this secret, might they not have invited Japanese leaders to witness a test of its awesome power and offered them a chance to surrender, before incinerating Hiroshima's children? And once they saw the horror over Hiroshima, wasn't the only humane option to refuse ever to drop the bomb again? Instead we have had Nagasaki— a "test" of a different type of bomb—and an unprecedented arms race for which the Hiroshima bomb was only the starting gun.

Glimpses of our future can be seen by looking at the past. We have testimonies not only from Japan but, closer to home, from those Americans in Utah and Nevada who were witnesses to above-ground atomic tests in the 1950s.

Elizabeth Wright recounts sitting on the tailgate of her family's station wagon as a child, shivering in the predawn chill as she ate her mother's homemade cinnamon rolls and drank hot chocolate, watching an atomic test. The sight was unforgettable: the brilliant light, the immense fireball, and the grand finale—a huge and colorful mushroom cloud. Through the years she was often awakened at dawn by the tremors and light of the tests.

Military and nuclear-industry representatives assured Wright and her family that the tests posed no risk. But today the family bears an astounding legacy of suffering—a father dead of leukemia; a sister dead of an enlarged thyroid; a niece with a birth defect that left her with "a ganglion that doubled the size of her tongue and wound around, like a weed, inside her neck and down into her shoulder." Wright herself suffered a pregnancy in which her body destroyed the fetus, "dissolving it cell by cell." When a Geiger counter is run over her body, it clicks, and she lives with the unspoken dread: "When will the bomb inside of me go off?"

On the other side of the world, the legacy begun at Hiroshima and Nagasaki continues. Spurred on by the "success" of the bombings, the U.S. government began to move quickly ahead on nuclear development. As early as three months after the bombings, the military began searching for an appropriate testing site in the Pacific for further nuclear experiments.

In January 1946, the people of Bikini Island in the Marshall Islands were forced off their land, and their home became a nuclear target range. Bikini was the sight of twenty-three atomic tests. One, the seventeen-megaton "Bravo" bomb, showered the neighboring island of Rongelap with a two-inch layer of radioactive ash, contaminating its food and water supplies.

By the end of the day of the blast, Rongelap residents began to exhibit symptoms of acute radiation exposure: burns, severe vomiting, diarrhea, and hair loss. They were not evacuated until two days later. Miscarriages, stillbirths, and radiation sickness have been their heritage. Sixty-nine percent of the children under ten years old at the time of the blast developed thyroid tumors.

Two islands of the Eniwetok Atoll were completely vaporized in atomic tests, and the main island is considered unsafe for human habitation until the year 2027. Kwajalein Atoll—the world's largest—is now a target range for missiles launched 4,300 miles away in California.

In its Pacific wake, the U.S. military has left diseased and displaced islanders, disrupted culture, and permanently damaged ecology. While other people around the globe speculate on the horrors of potential nuclear war, the people of the Pacific are daily its victims. Atomic testing and dumping of radioactive waste have poisoned their home and severely violated their rights to both self-determination and a safe future. And the attitude of their victimizers seems to be summed up in a U.S. laboratory's report on the horror at Rongelap: the "habitation of these people on the island will afford most valuable ecological radiation data on human beings."

In the three decades since the Bravo test, data have been more than ample. Now, one can go to almost any continent or corner of the globe and find victims of radiation. From Hershey to Hiroshima, there is no safe place.

Albert Einstein, who helped to develop the atomic bomb and later regretted it, said at the dawn of the nuclear age, "The unleashed power of the atom has changed everything except our way of thinking." Indeed, since the first human being picked up a rock to hurl at another, the quest for military solutions and superiority has marked history. And the unprecedented destructiveness of the atomic bomb, far from holding those instincts in check, has propelled the nations into an unparalleled race for arms.

We are caught in a situation of tragic absurdity. Politicians talk about the need to build up our arms so that we can move toward disarmament. The United States and the Soviet Union have already armed the globe with 50,000 nuclear warheads, with the total explosive power of nearly a million Hiroshima bombs and the capacity to annihilate each other in less than half an hour.

Still new bombs continue to roll off the production lines at the rate of about three a day in this country. We now have the dubious distinction of possessing enough explosive power to destroy every man, woman, and child on earth many times over—such is the absurd logic of the arms race. And our situation is called a "national security state." Was there ever a greater misnomer in history? Who of us feels secure?

Six years after I had walked home after church with my kite-flying friend, I was visiting her in the emergency room of a local hospital. At the age of fifteen, she had tried to take her life. In a conversation I had with her doctor, he said that suicide is now the highest cause of death among teenagers. He attributed it to the fact that this is the first potentially "futureless" generation; that young people have to live daily with the reality that nuclear war may destroy all that they have: all hopes, all dreams, everything.

I know a seven-year-old who once said to his parents, "I wish you never had children." When they probed him on what he was feeling, he talked about his fear that he wouldn't get to grow up, that there were too many missiles pointed at us. He ended by referring to the Russians and saying, "Don't they know that *I'm* here?"

It was an insightful question. Maybe it would help the Soviets if they remembered that their missiles are pointed at little boys who like ice cream and baseball. And maybe it would help us if we could picture Soviet children who enjoy similar delights. Our nation may talk of the enemy as Communism or atheism; but our missiles are not pointed at an ideology—they are pointed at children, and grandparents, and everyone in between.

I had an astounding conversation one afternoon on a plane to Atlanta with an eighteen-year-old young man eventually headed to Fort Benning in Georgia. He was returning to army basic training. I asked him what the army was teaching him about the Russians, and he described an exercise he and his friends did frequently. One would hold up pictures of Russians, and the others would make derogatory comments and chant, "Slash 'em, stomp 'em; kill 'em, tromp 'em!"

Then I asked him if he thought the Russians were people. He looked astonished, and said matter-of-factly, "Of course not—they're animals." Every war, real or imagined, needs an enemy, someone whose humanity is in question.

Despite some recent encouraging changes in the Soviet Union, the cruelty of the Soviet system continues, as has been well documented. Its persecution of Jews and Christians and dissidents, its failed invasion of Afghanistan and brutal occupation of Eastern bloc nations, are unjustifiable acts of repression. The cries of the people of Czechoslovakia and Poland and Afghanistan cannot go unheeded.

But similarly the cries from Chile and El Salvador and Nicaragua must be heard. We cannot overlook our own country's support of ruthless dictatorships and its efforts to control the destinies of smaller nations. The "balance of terror" that has its grip on the globe encompasses more than stockpiles of nuclear weapons; and it will require a new way of looking at ourselves and the rest of the world to get us free of the madness.

Policy analyst Richard Barnet offers this truth: "To be obsessed with the Soviet threat in a world in which more than one billion people starve, half the global work force is projected to be without a minimally paying job by the year 2000, and industrial civilization is close to collapse because political paralysis and greed have kept us from solving the energy crisis is, quite literally, to be blinded by hate."

We have to ask ourselves: Is the Russian threat more dangerous than the nuclear weapons designed to keep it at bay? Barnet poses the question at the heart of the matter: "Is there any value, including containment of an outlaw nation or just retribution for outrageous behavior, that justifies risking the death of everything?" Is there indeed anything that excuses robbing our children of hope for a future? That justifies threatening to destroy all of God's children, and all of God's creation?

The Gospel of Luke records that as Jesus made his final entry into Jerusalem, he wept over the city as it came into view, saying, "Would that even today you knew the things that make for peace!" (19:41–42) I often wonder how much more Jesus weeps now. For all of our sophistication, we seem even further from knowing what things offer true security and what could help us live in peace with one another. Surely this man whom we call the Prince of Peace and claim to follow must grieve at our blindness.

In the 1970s, in the face of an escalating nuclear arms race, many Christians began seeing resistance to nuclear weapons as part of faithfulness to the gospel. The words and witness of many people had a profound impact on me. Elizabeth Mc-Alister and Philip and Daniel Berrigan, continuing a legacy they had begun in the Vietnam era, courageously and steadfastly offered their witness on behalf of peace.

Fr. George Zabelka, who served as Catholic chaplain to the bombing crew at the time of the bombings of Hiroshima and Nagasaki, turned his life around and began to work for peace. He pointed out that Nagasaki's imposing Catholic cathedral was near the bomb's ground zero. That day 300 Christians worshiping in the great cathedral were killed instantly; three orders of Catholic sisters were destroyed.

Zabelka said of that time: "One would have thought that I, as a Catholic priest, would have spoken out against the atomic bombing of nuns. One would have thought that I would have suggested, as a minimal standard of Catholic morality, Catholics shouldn't bomb Catholic children." Or any children.

Others pointed out that some of our missiles today are pointed at the Soviet Union's millions of Christians, sisters and brothers in the body of Christ who worship the same God we do. And, as author and friend Dale Aukerman described it, our missiles are pointed at someone else as well.

He recorded this scene: "On a ruined wall in Hiroshima is dimly etched the figure of a human being who was standing next to it when the flash came. The body, though instantaneously vaporized, stopped enough of the awful light to leave that abiding epitaph. When German theologian Heinrich Vogel gazed at the dim silhouette, the thought gripped him: Jesus Christ was there in the inferno with that person; what was done to him was done to Christ; the horror he had no time to experience, Jesus felt."

Jesus had told us that whatever we do to his brothers and sisters, we do to him. And indeed that must include their murder by nuclear genocide.

Jim Wallis preached about what may well have been Jesus' most unpopular command to his disciples: "Love your enemies" (Matt. 5:44). It was terribly difficult for them to hear, in this time when they were so brutally oppressed by the Romans. Certainly Jesus wasn't naive about the Romans' cruelty or their power. But he did not say, "Love your enemies unless they are Romans who might take away your life." He put no qualifiers on his words but instead showed by supreme example the way of nonviolent and sacrificial love.

The command may seem even more unpopular—and terribly naive—today. But we cannot distort the words to suit us: "Love your enemies unless they are Russians who might take away your freedom." As Jim articulated it, there is no time in history when Jesus' words are more relevant. Today our global survival depends on following them.

A rich promise comes to us in Paul's letter to the Ephesians: "But now in Christ Jesus you who were far off have been brought near in the blood of Christ. For he is our peace, who has made us both one, and has broken down the dividing wall of hostility" (Eph. 2:13–14).

The "far off" ones who were divided at the time of Paul's writing were the Jews and the Gentiles. Today his words could be addressed to Russians and Americans. No one on the planet is unaffected by our division. But affected perhaps most of all are our own souls.

Jesus came to break down the divisions among people. But we have added to that "dividing wall of hostility" brick by brick, missile by missile. We have armed it with the most elaborate weapons ever devised, limited in destructiveness only by the imagination of the scientists. And the more the missiles multiply, the more we are divided.

Perhaps the greatest tragedy of all is that this wall that divides the globe also goes right through our hearts. Nuclear terror can exist only if we have closed our hearts to the victims, both real and potential.

Surely we can't trust the nuclear powers not to unleash the arsenals. Every weapon ever devised throughout human history until now has been used. And, again, the possibilities of human or mechanical error are enormous. The stakes are even higher—much too high.

We have already seen both sides make grievous errors of mistaken identity in the air—with the deaths of hundreds of civilians as the consequence. How much more pressure must someone behind the nuclear trigger be under than the commander of the *Vincennes* in the Persian Gulf? In one two-year period alone, 147 false alerts occurred on the U.S. side, four of these escalating strategic forces to readiness for attack—one the result of a wayward flock of Canadian geese.

We have no security in our weapons. Our only hope is to trust in the God who is the creator and preserver of life. But instead of trusting God, we have tried to *be* God. It is both the earliest and most recent sin: the desire to have knowledge and power over life and death.

But only God has this power. And for us to try to seize it is blasphemy of the highest order; and to transfer our trust to explosive pieces of metal is, as others have identified it, idolatry.

Exactly one week after the disaster at Three Mile Island, I was on my way with others from Sojourners to Groton, Connecticut, to protest the launching of the first Trident submarine. We had come to say that, in this race toward "national security"—destination oblivion—we would prefer to be left behind.

We joined 4,000 others. As we streamed down a hill toward the Electric Boat plant, maker of the submarine, I caught my first glimpse of its immense, burnt-red hull. A bitterly cold wind whipped up whitecaps on the river where the 559-foot submarine was docked, and flags lining the dock snapped furiously.

Measuring five feet longer than the Washington Monument is tall, and carrying a price tag of $1.5 billion, the Trident is the world's largest, costliest, and deadliest submarine. The enormity of the cost registered when someone told me that if a dollar had been spent every minute since the day Chirst was born, the amount would not equal the price tag on the Trident program. The submarine would one day be equipped with twenty-four Trident II missiles, each carrying up to twelve individually targeted warheads, giving it the capacity to destroy as many as 288 different cities, each with a blast thirty times that which devastated Hiroshima.

Thousands of other people had come to celebrate this technological achievement. We had come to mourn. One person in our crowd held a sign paraphrasing President John F. Kennedy: "Humankind must put an end to the arms race, or the arms race will put an end to humankind."

While politicians and dignitaries inside the plant praised the submarine, Richard Proescher, an Electric Boat worker who had been fired for speaking out against the Trident, spoke to our crowd. He said that defense workers must convince the American people that conversion of defense plants to peacetime production is necessary: "The alternative is global destruction in the name of peace and freedom."

As the wind buffeted the crowd, numbing toes and fingers, and snow flurries began to fall from dark blue skies on this unusual April day, I pondered the immensity of the task before us. That mammoth submarine was a symbol of how large and deadly is our foe.

Scriptures tell us that we are in a battle, not with flesh and blood, but with principalities and powers. And at that place, in the shadow of that immense, burnt-red catastrophe, the powers felt tangible. The image of Jesus weeping came to me, and I felt compelled to pray. Perhaps, after all, prayer is our strongest weapon in this battle, our proclamation that the powers of death do not have us in their grasp.

I remembered our worship on Sunday morning at the height of the crisis at Three Mile Island, when a community member expressed her lack of trust that God would preserve the world from complete nuclear destruction. I shared her despair then and recalled times when the suffering of a neighbor, or newspaper headlines of war or starvation, made me cry out to God,

"How can you allow such suffering?" Times when the thought of such tragedies as Hiroshima or Auschwitz caused me to point to God and say, "If you are Lord of the universe, why didn't you intervene?" The thought of total nuclear war made this indictment even stronger.

But another community member spoke up and said that the fact that life goes on is a continual sign of God's intervention. Only God's constant intervention has saved us from ourselves. This God sent us Jesus, who broke the grip of death on history and forgives us still when we live as if it were otherwise.

God gives us a choice, summed up in words spoken to the earliest people of God: "I have set before you life and death, blessing and curse; therefore choose life, that you and your descendants might live" (Deut. 30:19).

That choice is always before us. And floating in front of me in the river that day was an option for death in the extreme.

But I remembered, as I watched it, other words of reassurance offered that Sunday morning: "The nuclear arms race is a sign of how much evil we can do. But if God created us with this much potential for evil, there must be an equal potential for good."

I felt the battle inside of me, as I had before, between my own sin and my desire to be conformed to the way of Christ. I was still in much need of conversion. And I understood that the sin that propels the arms race is all of our individual sins of power and greed and violence multiplied into a national sin. Change must start with each of us, with confession and repentance.

I prayed that day that the Trident submarine, with its unprecedented capacity for destruction, might be a place for this nation to make a U-turn. I hoped that this awful sign of our sinfulness would help us see ourselves for what we had become, convict us to turn from death, and encourage us to tap the immense capacity for good that surely exists in us.

Our fear will never change things, I am convinced; it will ultimately only paralyze us. But by faith, we are assured, all things are possible—even an end to the nuclear terror. I prayed, with limbs aching from the cold, for the strength to face and turn from my own sin; for the faith to trust in the God of life; and for the courage, in my own small way, to put my weight on the side of blessing and life.

8. Crossing the Line

During the summer of 1974, my mother had taught English at Fort Indiantown Gap, an old army base a few miles from Hershey, one of three places in the United States where fleeing Vietnamese refugees were taken after the end of the Vietnam War. Feeling a desire to understand better the war that had so dominated U.S. foreign policy for more than a decade, I decided to accompany her to the base a few times.

One morning Lin, a young woman in my mother's class who was relatively fluent in English, was summoned by Red Cross personnel to act as an interpreter between a young boy who had been seriously hurt and his doctors. Lin asked if I would accompany her to the infirmary on the other side of the compound. Security was very heavy at the base, and as we walked past clusters of military police, she explained in a whisper that it was her fear of them that had prompted her to ask me to come along.

A rope was stretched across a line several yards in front of the infirmary door, and lacking the appropriate security clearance, I was made to wait outside. Several minutes later Lin exited through another door and found herself in a maze of ropes, confused about how to get back to me. In the effort she apparently crossed a forbidden line, and immediately two military police grabbed her, one on each arm, and began taking her away. The look of terror on her face made me react instantly.

I overtook them and asked where they were taking Lin. Soon three other guards surrounded me, shouting that I was in a high-security area, in violation of code number such and such, and that I had to leave immediately or face arrest.

Despite my protest that a simple mistake had been made and

the problem could be easily solved, a commander was summoned. In a stern voice he yelled at me, grabbing at the identification tag around my neck and demanding to know what I was doing on the base. "You don't have proper security!" he barked and then threatened to put me in jail for trespassing on federal property, unless I left the base immediately.

The absurdity of their response was astounding to me. I finally told the commander that if they would let Lin go and let me get a message to my mother, I would leave. He ordered the guards to release Lin and then said to her, "Can you understand English? Go tell her mother she's fine." Still looking terrified, Lin went off in search of my mother. Scowling at me and pointing a finger, the commander said, "You—leave the base."

I followed him as he marched back to his office, parked myself in his doorway, and told him that there was no need to treat the refugees or me that way, that we were all decent human beings, and that if he had just taken the time to hear what had happened, this all could have been avoided. He ignored me and started shuffling some papers.

After a few moments of silence, he took out an official-looking form, demanding to know my name. He made me spell "Hollyday" for him and then looked at me and said, "That's a stupid way to spell it." (I had been told this before but never with such authority.)

He thrust the paper at me, declaring that it was my security clearance—just in case I got stopped again—and ordered me back to my mother's classroom. I thanked him and started down the long rows of barracks.

Lin's English was pretty good, but she could have used a lesson in the difference between being fine and being fined. When I arrived at the classroom, one of my mother's pupils told me that I had been fined and was probably going to jail. My mother had left to try to bail me out.

When I finally intercepted Mom and Lin on their way to see the commander, everyone was relieved. Lin grabbed my hand, squeezed it, smiled, bowed slightly, and said, "Thank you." It was the beginning of a long friendship.

I visited Lin and her family several times over the following years in their crowded home in a town on the banks of the Susquehanna River, where they had been resettled. She worked ten hours a day in a glove factory to help support her extended family of fifteen, fighting exhaustion late at night as she tutored herself in English and held tight to a dream of someday resuming the college education she had begun in Saigon.

Slowly, over the months, the stories came out. She told me about the bombs, the terror, the flight from her home by helicopter as Saigon "fell." She found herself on a boat with a destination unknown to her and then became separated from her family on Guam, unable to find them again for several months. She did not know what had happened to family and college friends who had been left behind; communication with Saigon was impossible, and she feared capture or death of her relatives because of her family's decision to evacuate the city.

It would be years before I fully understood the severity of our violation of the Vietnamese people—our intervention against their determination to resist foreign domination, our defoliation of their land through chemical warfare, the forcing of their young women into prostitution for U.S. GIs, the use against them of antipersonnel weapons, such as mines camouflaged as leaves that could blow the legs off children. But my first experience with military authority reinforced what I had begun to understand a few months before in East Harlem: those invested with the power to "protect the law" in the United States could be callous and, on a global scale, brutal.

Breaking the law, however, was about the last thing I imagined for my life. From my earliest days, members of my family and church had instilled in me the importance of the virtues of integrity and honesty and compassion; they had taught me a clear sense of right and wrong. It was those deeply held values that kept me out of trouble the first half of my life—and got me into it the second.

Friends in East Harlem and Harrisburg and Washington, D.C., were living reminders that this country systematically betrayed its own ideals. It was impossible for me to look into their faces and not question the authority of a nation's laws when those laws served as the foundational scaffold of exploitation at home and terror abroad. Just as it was hard to imagine watching Lin's rights being violated without responding, it was impossible to watch my home being violated by radioactive poison—and the globe by the threat of nuclear war—without acting.

I was doing all I could think of to register my protest. I worked full-time for a magazine that took upon itself a responsibility to educate the public and the churches about the dangers of nuclear war. I had chosen to live simply as a step toward withdrawing my support from a system that claimed many of my friends among its victims. I had braved the cold at Groton and prayed and sang endless verses of "All We Are Saying Is Give Peace a Chance."

But these efforts didn't seem like enough, given the magnitude of the peril. Waging war had always required risks and sacrifice, and as Jim Wallis pointed out, waging peace would require the same.

It was Daniel Berrigan who had said a couple of years before, when I was still a seminary student, that loyalty to Jesus Christ must supersede all other loyalties. He made clear that this loyalty inevitably leads to direct confrontation with governments that demand obedience—if only by silent acquiescence—to unjust laws and systems.

I had rediscovered Jesus when I saw him in the faces of the victims, but still I hadn't discovered all of him. Dan's words about loyalty forced me back to the Scriptures again, this time to try to understand more fully the nature of Jesus' confrontations with the authorities of his day. I wanted to understand why they had refused to let him live.

I read the Gospels again with renewed vigor, tracing the political confrontation that began with Jesus' birth. No sooner had Herod received word of the birth than he tried to make the three kings from the Orient unwitting accomplices in the baby's death, so threatened was he by this child. But the powers were foiled, the wise ones took another route home, and Jesus and his parents fled into exile in Egypt.

But Herod did not give up. He ordered a massive slaughter that claimed the lives of all the baby boys two years old and under. The joyous birth of Jesus was accompanied by weeping and untold grief for the mothers and fathers of Judea.

I understood with new clarity the ministry of John the Baptist, a foreshadowing of Jesus' ministry to come. I pondered the third chapter of Luke's Gospel, which opens with a list of government and religious authorities, laying out the political geography of the day. But the Word passed by the governors and tetrarchs and high priests and appeared in the wilderness.

This Word is at home in strange environs—a stable, a wilderness, at the edge, on the margins. It came to a frightened, young Jewish woman and a baptizer who wore camel's hair and ate insects and honey. It came as good news to the marginalized ones—and bad news to those who waged oppressive power. So threatened were these authorities by the Word that several were later notorious for their collusion in Jesus' death.

John got right to the point when he said to the "brood of vipers" who had come to hear his words, "Who warned you to flee from the wrath to come? . . . Even now the axe is laid to the root of the trees" (Luke 3:7, 9). He made clear that there was only one way to salvation for them: to repent. To offer confession and change their ways, for the mountains of power were going to crumble, and the poor in valleys of sadness would be raised up.

Several verses later, in a passage I loved for its wonderful irony, John again laid things out clearly as he talked about the coming work of Jesus. " 'His winnowing fork is in his hand, to clear his threshing floor, and to gather the wheat into his granary, but the chaff he will burn with unquenchable fire.' So, with many other exhortations, John preached *good news* to the people" (Luke 3:17–18).

The juxtaposition of that unquenchable fire with the announcement of "good news" went right to the heart of the message of Jesus: It was good news to the poor and a threat to those who supported the arrangements that oppressed them. It was good news to those who mourned, who lived in poverty, who were persecuted and reviled, for the day was coming when they would laugh and be possessors of the land and celebrate in triumph.

Jesus himself inaugurated his ministry reading from the words of the prophet Isaiah, declaring his vocation to preach good news to the poor, free the oppressed, and heal the sick. He ended with a reference to the Jubilee year—the year of "institutionalized justice," when slaves were freed and land was redistributed, when debts were forgiven and the poor were given a new start.

Jesus minced no words when he proclaimed again and again the judgment that was to come on the "faithless and perverse generation." He reserved his sharpest condemnations for the political and religious leaders, calling Herod a "fox" and the Pharisees "hypocrites" and "white-washed tombs" who put on pious facades to hide their sin. He named their love of money an "abomination in the sight of God."

To advocate for the victims meant at times to break the law of the land. It meant, for Jesus, breaking the religious laws by healing on the Sabbath. It meant casting out from the temple those who used it as a den for robbing from the poor.

The authorities did not like this man who refused to play by their rules. They did not like his "kingdom," where the poor were exalted. They did not like his community movement, where compassion and inclusion flew in the face of greed and elitism.

The Gospels are filled with attempts by the Pharisees to entrap Jesus in his own words and plots to eliminate him. Finally, he was dragged before both Roman and Jewish authorities, condemned as a threat by both the government and the religious establishment.

He was a political criminal, victim of a state execution. But the powers could not contain him. The tomb's seal was broken open. The most airtight security the state had at its disposal was not enough. And with that ultimate victory over the power of death, that ultimate act of resistance to their authority, the powers were silenced.

The apostles, huddling fearfully behind closed doors during the trial and execution, found new boldness after the Resurrection. They were the continuing sign that death had been defeated. And their boldness led them into all sorts of trouble. They got dragged into courts and were imprisoned, stoned, and crucified.

As I searched the Scriptures, I went back again and again to the Letter to the Hebrews, which describes the experiences of the early followers of Christ.

Some were tortured. . . . Others suffered mocking and scourging, and even chains and imprisonment. They were stoned; they were sawn in two, they were killed with the sword; they went about in skins of sheep and goats, destitute, afflicted, ill-treated . . . wandering over deserts and mountains, and in dens and caves of the earth. (11:35–38)

As I read those words, I could not help thinking of Christians in El Salvador, in South Africa and the Philippines, in Poland and South Korea and the Soviet Union. The words describe the experience of Christians today around the globe who suffer torture, exile, prison, and ultimately death for their belief that Christ has empowered them to throw off the chains of oppression and poverty.

Following these words is an invitation.

Therefore, since we are surrounded by so great a cloud of witnesses, let us also lay aside every weight, and sin which clings so closely, and let us run with perseverance the race that is set before us, looking to Jesus, the pioneer and perfecter of our faith, who for the joy that was set before him endured the cross, despising the shame, and is seated at the right hand of the throne of God. Consider him who endured from sinners such hostility against himself, so that you may not grow weary or fainthearted. (Heb. 12:1-3)

This passage brought to mind Dietrich Bonhoeffer, Sojourner Truth, Martin Luther King, Jr., Dorothy Day, Fannie Lou Hamer . . . Despite so much evidence to the contrary, they lived their lives believing that the victory over death had already been won, that Resurrection had already come. All of these and so many others acted boldly in their faith to confront the forces of death, to challenge injustice in its many forms. And all paid the price for their choices, joining that "cloud of witnesses" who go before us offering courage and strength.

They understood Jesus' words when he said to his disciples, "If the world hates you, know that it has hated me before it hated you" (John 15:18). And each of them faced a test and had to claim boldly, as did the disciples, "We must obey God rather than men" (Acts 5:29).

I imagined that each had searched the Scriptures and wrestled, as I had, to find a faithful response in their particular historical situations. The gospel speaks anew in each historical moment, and in every situation Christians are called upon to show what they believe and what they refuse to believe, what they must do and what they refuse to do.

I could not dismiss the exhortation at the beginning of the thirteenth chapter of Romans: "Let every person be subject to the governing authorities. For there is no authority except from God, and those that exist have been instituted from God." But I soon learned from Jim Wallis and others that Romans 13 could not be read without Revelation 13, the image of the blasphemous beast that arises, exercising authority and demanding the worship of men and women.

John had received his revelation when the Roman empire was at the height of its oppressive power and moral decadence. The Scriptures indeed recognize the need for the state to protect human life from the power of chaos, and they ordain its authority to do so; but they also acknowledge the demonic possibilities inherent within any state.

Certainly Dietrich Bonhoeffer understood this as well as anyone as he struggled to find a Christian response to Adolf Hitler and the atrocities of the Third Reich. So many other Christians had become complicit with the evil by their silence or were co-opted by the power of a state that demanded their obedience for its own justification.

They have now been indicted by history, and by their own children and grandchildren. Not long ago, the documentary film *Holocaust* was shown to German youth. Their overriding reaction was to question their parents and grandparents: "What did you do about it when the ovens were being prepared for the Jews? How could you not speak out?"

Bonhoeffer once said, "The only thing that needs to happen for evil to triumph is for good people to do nothing." He and all the other faithful witnesses throughout history ultimately had to answer the question every Christian must face: Where does my loyalty lie? And they had to decide, when the will of God is being violated, do I obey God's law or human law?

Nuclear weapons—with their unprecedented threat to destroy all of God's creation, their power to divide up the world into hostile factions, and their robbery from the poor—were as clear a sign as I could imagine of a violation of God's will. Particularly in the wake of Three Mile Island, I felt that until I disobeyed the law of the land demanding loyalty to nuclear policy, my inaction was complicity. And until many of us registered strongly and visibly our refusal to fall in line behind the madness, there could be no hope of turning it around.

A decade later, I am still convinced of that truth. Now the alarm has been sounded; the peril has been recognized. Almost every major church denomination in the country, as well as groups of physicians and physicists and many others, have written statements condemning nuclear weapons.

But such statements, and years of government summits and

disarmament talks, have led to the destruction of only a hand-ful of missiles from our mighty arsenals. True freedom from the nuclear threat is nowhere in sight.

I once heard Rev. William Sloane Coffin, Jr., preach, "They are lovers of the law who uphold it when the government breaks it." He offered the words at the first Symposium on Sanctuary in Tucson, Arizona. They were given as an encour-agement to sixty Central American refugees who had been ar-rested for living "illegally" in the United States, and sixteen church workers—key leaders in the sanctuary movement—who had been indicted for aiding the refugees.

Among other offenses, the church workers were accused of conspiracy. But theirs was only a conspiracy of compassion. They had broken the law that says refugees fleeing for their lives from war and persecution deserve no shelter or protec-tion.

I was preparing to break another law that violates the stan-dards of human decency: the one that says preparations for mass murder and a total assault on the creation are acceptable. I wanted to be able to answer when my children and grand-children ask, "Where were you when preparations for destroy-ing the world were being made?"

In September of 1979, six months after Three Mile Island boiled over, the Air Force Association's weapons exhibition—"arms bazaar"—came to the Sheraton Washington Hotel. Weapons contractors displayed the latest weapons technology, while government agents, military chiefs, and Third World rep-resentatives wandered among the wares. Skimpily clad models talked about nuclear capabilities and handed out pens and tie clips in the shape of missiles.

We passed out leaflets, talked with the sponsors, met with the hotel owners to express our concerns. On the evening be-fore the last day of the arms exposition, we held a candlelight vigil outside the hotel. As we prayed, the air force officers in their dress whites, elegant women on their arms, passed by.

Kneeling there sheltering my small candle from the wind, I remembered the Scripture about the work of Christians being folly to the rest of the world.

As night fell and the wind picked up, I crouched closer around my candle. The image of Christ as the light of the world was strong. I felt enveloped in an awareness of how much light he had brought to this world's darkness—and my own—and how fragile that light was, snuffed out momentarily by the forces of hatred and oppression. And suddenly I felt as if the only thing that mattered was keeping that ridiculous candle lit.

The next day we returned to the hotel. I felt as though many people were with me that day. The burned victims of Hiroshima were there—the ones who had first shown me the suffering and made the pain real. Twenty-one of us carried large pictures of them and attempted to take them into the hotel, to make the pain real for the nuclear traders, too.

I felt as though I were carrying my family with me—my parents, at the edge of the crippled and still-leaking nuclear reactor; and Deb, living equally close to the plutonium deposits of Rocky Flats, Colorado. I thought especially of Kay and her new son, my one-year-old nephew, Travis. I felt that I was especially there for him—for his future. That he might have a future.

I felt gratitude for a host of friends who had shown the way—who offer prayers in dangerous places, hold candles in dark corners, and cross forbidden lines. The ones who, from Connecticut to Georgia to Washington State, protest the deadly Trident submarine; who sit on railroad tracks all across the country to block nuclear shipments; who are on trial or in jail for Plowshares disarmament actions. Those who persistently cross the line onto the Nevada nuclear weapons test site; who face imprisonment for their war tax resistance or for welcoming Central Americans labeled "illegal" and "alien"; those who dauntlessly advocate for the rights of women and unborn children and death-row prisoners and homeless people and people of color.

As we walked toward the hotel, I thought of that "cloud of witnesses" and of suffering Christians around the world. I remembered words from a South Korean Christian: "In my country courage is commonplace; in your country what should be commonplace is called courage."

Those words helped put things into perspective. This was such a small step—it was nothing compared to the suffering of him and so many others. But, for a Hershey kid, it felt like a fair leap.

As we neared the hotel entrance, I hoped that this one small step might give me the grace and strength to take more. I was praying for courage when the handcuffs tightened around my wrists. And then I felt oddly peaceful.

One of the rewards of our witness was the way it drew Sojourners Community closer. It affirmed for me the need to live closely connected to others, to feel their support and love, to gain courage from their boldness, wisdom from their experience, and strength from their faith. I understood more clearly how crucial it is that we live "disarmed lives" with one another—freely confessing our sins and wounds, giving and receiving forgiveness—offering an alternative to the world's ways.

It had a surprisingly bonding effect on my family as well. My choices had not always been easy for my parents, and through the years we had had our share of long and vigorous discussions about my decisions to go to Harrisburg and East Harlem, to leave seminary and move to inner-city Washington. They were not always pleased, feeling that I was often choosing against my own best interests, but in every case they ultimately extended me freedom to live my own life. I feared that my decision to face arrest might be particularly troubling and potentially divisive.

But two months after my arrest, my mother wrote me a letter that was as deep a confirmation of my life as I had ever received. It said much more to me about her care than it did about what I had chosen to do.

The testimony for Christ that you and the others gave as you knelt on the sidewalk with your candles was certainly tremendous—and may have had an effect on more of those people than you will ever realize. Your description of the whole scene brought tears to my eyes—and I was so proud that you are my daughter. . . .

I know this nuclear arms race is a terrible thing and must be stopped. If all Christians everywhere had the courage to speak out and demonstrate against it, surely something could be done. But we don't stand together enough to fight any of the forces of evil. (I do see why you gain strength from living in a Christian community.) And so these evils grow worse and worse until an individual or a small group has the courage to step out from the crowd and lay everything on the line for that cause.

We are studying Amos in the Bible class at church right now. Amos was a very ordinary man who didn't hesitate to speak out even against the king and religious leaders for their part in allowing and encouraging the sins existing in Israel—and he stressed that judgment and punishment would come for all. Don't back down or compromise on the things that you believe in, Joyce.

Through the years I have felt fortunate both to witness and to participate in many prayerful, nonviolent actions for justice and for peace. They have always held out a glimmer of hope for me in a world that seems so entrenched in its arrangements against the poor and vulnerable.

The first was in September 1978, a year before I walked up to the Sheraton Washington Hotel and refused to leave. Five friends, three of them from Sojourners Community, illegally moved into an apartment building that had been home to six low-income families. Like so many others in our neighborhood, the building had been purchased by real estate speculators who had plans to renovate it, transform it into a single-family dwelling, and sell it at a huge profit.

This trend of "gentrification"—which I had first witnessed in Harrisburg several years before—was becoming an epidemic that was sweeping unchecked through our neighborhood. Furniture and belongings piled on curbs in front of homes where the poor had been evicted seemed to be an almost daily occurrence.

Five families had been put out on the streets, and only one woman, a mother of two young sons, was willing to stay and fight for her home. On a Friday afternoon, she broke a bottle of sparkling grape juice on the outside wall of her home, while neighbors cheered. Young friends of her three-year-old son, all from the Sojourners day-care center, planted a tree in the yard and carried signs that said, "Let Donnell keep his home!" Together we celebrated "neighborhood ownership" of the building. Then the five moved in.

Very early the next morning the police arrested them, charging them with unlawful entry, and removed them from the building. All of Sojourners Community had come to watch, and a kind neighbor, seeing some of our young children in their pajamas and thinking he was witnessing an eviction of the usual sort, offered, "I can help if you need a place to stay."

At their court arraignment later that day, a public defender watching the proceedings suggested that our friends plead insanity—since "anyone who thinks they can fight real estate speculation in D.C. is crazy." They didn't, and they went off to jail.

We didn't save the building or stop real estate speculation in Washington. Perhaps the best that can be said is that the attention focused on the action made what seemed to be an invisible scourge a public issue, bringing to light the plight of the many victims of gentrification.

In May 1983, during Peace Pentecost, 3,000 of us filled the cavernous Washington Cathedral with song and prayer, feeling the Spirit moving powerfully there and the next day when 242 of us carried bread and flowers into the Capitol Rotunda and were arrested for praying for peace.

Two years later friends from all over the country came again to Washington, D.C., for Peace Pentecost 1985. A mighty stream of people flowed through the streets of Washington to six different sites. Some went to the White House to protest budget priorities that fuel the arms race and cut off services to the poor, while others offered opposition to U.S. policy in Central America at the State Department. One contingent went to the Supreme Court to oppose the death penalty, and another to the Department of Health and Human Services to offer a feminist protest against abortion. Two embassies were the sites of protest as well that day: the Soviet Embassy for its brutal occupation of Afghanistan and the South African Embassy for its racist policy of apartheid.

Those days brought moments of great exhilaration and hope. And, though we didn't end the arms race or apartheid, there was a feeling of being part of a long legacy of nonviolent protest that has included among its victories an end to legal segregation in this country.

There have been astounding victories as well as countless defeats in nonviolent campaigns throughout history. Many efforts have been met with utter brutality by their opposers, bringing numerous deaths and causing detractors of nonviolence to talk about its ineffectiveness. These same critics never seem to talk about the millions of lives that have been lost in history's wars. And each successive war seems to point only to the ineffectiveness of the previous one to settle humanity's disagreements.

With every effort we made, I became more deeply convinced that nonviolent resistance offers a promise of breaking through the spiraling cycle of violence that wracks the globe. But many times our efforts seemed very small, and hope was hard to muster. I remember our community and some friends shivering on the steps of the Capitol, holding signs pushing for a nuclear freeze, long before it was popular and when the whole world was riveted instead on the U.S. hostages in Iran.

On a sweltering day in June 1984, we reached an impasse with the authorities at the Department of Energy, the government agency that sends out the signal for the "nuclear train" to move with its cargo of nuclear warheads from the Pantex plant in Amarillo, Texas, to its various destinations (or "Armadillo, Texas," as one of our community children was heard saying to a local TV news reporter while he was explaining what our protest was about). By midafternoon all that was left of our children's wagon-and-bicycle "Peace Train" was a string of wilted streamers and popped balloons; "leaflet lethargy" had set in; and the police still made no move to remove the thirty-five people who had been praying at the front entrance of the DOE for seven hours. We had long before nixed "We Shall Not Be Moved" from the list of songs appropriate for the occasion.

At three o'clock we ended our vigil with a prayer. Our protest got little attention, but five of us did in fact make the local six o'clock news that night. In a blatant act of civil disobedience (hoping not to be discovered by Park Police), we plunged hot and exhausted into the waterfall at Rock Creek Park after our tiring ordeal. We were the major focus—along with a Salvadoran refugee family that eventually joined us—of the annual first-hot-day-of-the-year human interest story on Channel 4, called "Washingtonians Beat the Heat."

On those kinds of days it's easy to feel ineffective. I think often of the words of Ammon Hennacy, a lifelong resister who was once asked why he kept protesting, since it didn't seem to have much effect. His answer: "I don't know if I'll be able to change society, but I'm determined that society is not going to change me."

His words seem especially important now, as the powers try so hard to extract our loyalty. We are an obstacle to their schemes, and they are determined to undermine our efforts and our hope.

We have seen what they can do. Sophisticated new technologies make surveillance and data gathering on those who oppose U.S. policy ever easier. We have seen the sanctuary movement infiltrated by government agents wearing tape recorders to meetings and Bible studies. We have witnessed increased harassment against friends by the FBI, the Immigration and Naturalization Service, and even the Internal Revenue Service—including incidents against Sojourners.

Not long ago we received word that the Federal Emergency and Management Agency, usually known for its assistance during such natural disasters as tornadoes and floods, was granted power to contain "dissidents" during defined national emergencies. Ten sites thoughout the United States were being readied as camps for holding dissidents during "emergencies" such as a major U.S. military escalation in Central America. One of them, we were told, is Fort Indiantown Gap in Pennsylvania.

I often turn back to the Letter to the Hebrews when I start to doubt that anything we do makes any difference; when the powers seem so big and we seem so small; when, despite our efforts, things only seem to go from bad to worse. I often take comfort in the verses that end the eleventh chapter, following the long list of faithful men and women and the various sufferings that befell them: "And all these, though well attested to by their faith, did not receive what was promised, since God had foreseen something better for us, that apart from us they should not be made perfect" (Heb. 11:39–40).

These verses put an astounding responsibility on all of us. Although we may never see results, faith demands that we act. We act for the sake of the faithful ones who went before us and showed the way, trusting that we would follow—and for those who will come after us on this journey.

I remembered these verses especially as I was walking toward the edge of the Nevada Test Site, the place where our country's nuclear weapons are tested underground in the Nevada desert. The legacy of many sisters and brothers in the faith was strong there, as some had protested nuclear weapons at this site a generation before I had arrived.

The sun was a blaze of yellow near the eastern horizon, and even at the early hour, heat radiated in waves from the desert's gravelly floor. Ten hours before, we had traveled out to the canyons beyond Las Vegas to witness a dark, expansive sky decked out in millions of stars. Now, in morning light, the sky

was a blue haze, and the cactuses that had looked so frighten-
ingly grotesque in the dark appeared simply unusual in an
otherwise barren landscape.

A tumbleweed occasionally rolled across our path, and a
small lizard once skittered out of the way and under a pale
rock. Apart from these, we and the large buses lumbering
along the road were the only movement in this part of the
desert.

The buses conveyed workers to the gate of the test site, and
we had arisen for four mornings at 4:30 in order to drive from
Las Vegas to greet the early shift on its arrival. We were people
of faith from all over the country who had gathered at the test
site to commemorate the fortieth anniversary of the bombings
of Hiroshima and Nagasaki. We carried banners and water,
prayers and folded paper cranes, the delicate Japanese symbols
of peace.

Sixty-five miles to the south lay Las Vegas, a city of glaring
glitter and gold, where gigantic casinos like Caesar's Palace and
the MGM Grand line the Strip, and where even the local
McDonald's has a gaudy, fountainlike sign with moving lights.
One casino features live trapeze acts over the gambling tables.
Slot machines are more abundant than water and can be found
everywhere from the airport to the local K-Mart.

To the north is the Beatty jail, where people of conscience
who cross a forbidden white line are sent for a time, some to
clear the local cemetery of tumbleweeds. Farther north, a four-
hour drive from the test site, is the Tonopah County jail, where
time is served when Beatty's few cells become filled. The road
to Tonopah traverses endless desert, the only source of refresh-
ment being a few bars along the long stretch. Across the road
from one, a huge sign flashes "BROTHEL"; in Nye County, Nevada, prostitution is legal and thriving.

But these places seem distant, as if in another world, when
you're walking the edge of the Nevada Test Site. Larger in
area than the state of Rhode Island, this chunk of desert is

pockmarked with craters from nuclear explosions. The perimeter is marked miles from the actual site. You cannot see it; you can only feel it.

The feeling is eerie. As one person put it, beyond that mountain are preparations for the end of the world.

We walked—each of us alone—from the highway to Camp Desert Rock, an area a hundred yards from the test site's white perimeter, which during the 1950s was the base for young soldiers who were exposed to atomic blasts in order to measure their effects on human flesh. At 8:16 A.M. on August 6, 1985, precisely forty years after the bomb was dropped on Hiroshima, Japan, the first of our group crossed the white line onto the test site. The last group crossed at 11:02 on the morning of August 9, forty years after the bomb devastated Nagasaki. Arrests were made by the local sheriff and test-site authorities.

In this stark desert place, I understood why people of faith often head to the wilderness to seek God. In the barrenness—the emptiness—one is forced to abandon all else. As I walked, the image of the people of God wandering for forty years in the wilderness came to mind; and it was easy here to recognize the forty years of moral wilderness in which our nation had been lost since the day we accepted the use of nuclear weapons.

I tried to imagine back forty years to that day. The power intended to ensure our freedom only led us into a different kind of captivity. For once the awful secret was unlocked, we were caught in a race that had no end.

Jesus was crucified 75,000 times that day. Could 75,000 cries for mercy have included "Father, forgive them, for they know not what they do"? Or was this prayer absent, too difficult to utter on that dark day stabbed with light?

For many on that day the past exploded, dreams evaporated, the promise of a future melted away. We might have fallen on our knees, reached down into the ashes we had made of homes and lives, and spread them on our foreheads as a sign of contrition, begging for mercy for the terrible thing we had done.

But instead we have raced ahead, preparing each day for a million more crucifixions, equipping ourselves with the capacity to make our earth a lifeless cinder in space. And if we do, who will be left to say, "Father, forgive them"?

The unimaginable was imagined—and carefully plotted and prepared and carried out. Mothers and brothers and daughters remain only as sharp shadows on stone, as dull aches in heavy hearts, as laughter that exploded in the wind.

As we walked, we did so as an act of repentance for what our country had done and with an awareness of our own sin and complicity for not more clearly renouncing this monstrous evil. As I neared the test site's perimeter, I uttered a prayer into the desert wind: "Father, forgive us. For now we know. But still we do not stop."

9. Doing Time

The colorful banners proclaimed warm invitations: "Celebrate the New Year with us!" and "Ring in the New Year here!" Nothing particularly odd about these messages hanging from Capitol Hill cafes and pubs—except that this was the last weekend in September. As I made my way around the Hill on a magazine-related mission, the thought occurred to me that Capitol Hill was either way ahead of the rest of us or miserably behind the times (I will not confess my bias here).

The mystery of the banners didn't become clear until I spied one that read "Party here for the Fiscal New Year!" The banners were referring to the year determined by money, the one that begins on October 1.

A week later, when the new fiscal year descended upon us, I got a lesson on the importance of perspective. Whether or not the arrival of October 1 was something to celebrate depended on whether you were sitting in a Capitol Hill cafe or the D.C. jail.

It was October 1981. I was serving the first of five consecutive weekends for a second act of protest at the nuclear weapons exhibition in the Sheraton Washington Hotel. Weekend sentencing was one way the authorities had of dealing with "non-dangerous" lawbreakers in a severely overcrowded jail.

I remember the conversation that night in a holding cell as we waited—for what seemed like endless hours—to be processed into jail, wondering if we would get processed in before it was time to be released. The guards handed us trays with dinner: a recognizable slab of lime-green Jell-O and a glob of cold noodles with a congealed pile of bland yellow gravy a guard identified as "turkey tetrazzini."

"Appreciate it," she said. "It'll get worse from here." It was the second day of the first Reagan budget.

The guards and the women with whom I shared the cell launched into a conversation about the changes the new budget was going to bring. Jail is one of the best places to listen to understand the real impact of national policy.

Jail personnel had been warned about the upcoming changes: lower-grade food and dwindling supplies and services for inmates, loss of jobs for some guards and others as the labor force at the jail was cut back because of lack of funds. The women on my side of the bars spoke fearfully about an end to educational and job-training opportunities, to medical services and drug rehabilitation programs. They wondered how they would pay their rent and feed their children.

Most were already in desperate circumstances that had pushed them to pass bad checks or sell illegal drugs or peddle their bodies. And despite the fact that they thought anyone in jail who didn't have to be there was a bit crazy, they understood better than anyone how those nuclear weapons we were protesting—whether or not they were ever used—were already robbing them and their children of a future.

The conversation ended when one of the women, expressing frustration at the way circumstances were determining her life, put a pile of noodles on her spoon and shot it across the cell, where it stuck to the wall. One of the other women threatened to hurt her if she did the same with her Jell-O.

On that first night, as I waited for my turn to be fingerprinted, photographed, searched, showered, sprayed against lice, and handed a blue prison jumpsuit, I replayed in my mind our witness at the Sheraton Hotel two nights before, a year after we had attempted to take the Hiroshima pictures inside. As the politicians and arms dealers passed by us in evening attire on their way to an elegant banquet inside, fifty-one of us started up the hotel's driveway toward the entrance with loaves of bread. We wanted the people inside to remember that while they feasted at taxpayers' expense and lent their support to the nuclear arms race, many children in our city went without bread and other basic necessities.

We were arrested for blocking the driveway—an offense that was officially entered on our records as a charge of "incommoding." This was a source of great amusement to the women who joined us in the police wagon, picked up off the streets for sexual solicitation. As we all slid from side to side as the wagon negotiated turns on the way to the police precinct, hands cuffed behind us, they laughed heartily.

I spent that night stretched out with the others on the concrete floor of a holding cell under the D.C. court, a contact lens gripped in each fist. One of the bits of jail-survival trivia that had been passed on to me was that hard contact lenses, if placed over the gums just above the eye teeth, will adhere and not move; but try as I might to trust this advice, my fear of swallowing a lens prevailed.

Sometime in the middle of the night, I heard a racket outside the cell. In the dim light, I saw a woman with bright purple eye shadow caked on her eyelids and a large red heart tattooed on her left arm being let into the cell across from ours. She looked over at our cell, at the nineteen of us women who had been arrested at the hotel sprawled out on the floor, and said loudly, "What in the world did *they* do to get in here?!" Gloria, who had met us in the police wagon, said with a giggle, "They incommoded!" And then added, "At a *hotel!*"

Singing had been an important part of our protest, and very early the next morning it began again. A few voices started it, and as other women began to shake off a stiff drowsiness, they joined in. From the cell across from ours, Gloria shouted, "Hey, do you all know 'Amazing Grace'?" Soon the two sides of the cellblock were trying to outsing each other, and strains of the hymn thundered through the long corridor.

I groped blindly toward the chrome contraption that served as drinking fountain, sink, and toilet for our cell, searching for water for putting my lenses back in my eyes. I pushed what I thought was the tap for the sink, and the deafening roar of the jail toilet immediately silenced the singing. Gloria glared at me from across the corridor, pointed a finger, and hollered, "Now, *that's* incommoding!"

The entire cellblock erupted with laughter, with Gloria laughing the hardest. When the singing of "Amazing Grace" resumed, a brusque male guard came back to find out what all the commotion was and silence us. Gloria jumped up and said to him, "It's only the *gospel*."

Charlene, the one with the tattoo, rather bluntly told the guard what she thought of him. He began an argument with her, which finally ended when she fluttered her enormous fake eyelashes at him and said, "Don't you know you agreed to marry me last night, baby?" Flustered and embarrassed, the guard stomped off.

When Charlene found out we were demonstrating against nuclear weapons, she started shouting about the danger of the Russians. Then she said, "Now, if you'd demonstrate for a woman to be president of the U.S.A., I'd join you. Take Mrs. Maxwell [a guard], for instance. Mrs. Maxwell, you ever thought about running for president of the U.S.A.?" Mrs. Maxwell never had.

More than any other place I had been, jail was a political education, a spiritual pilgrimage, and a lesson in absurdity. As prisoners in the D.C. jail, we were denied hardback books— unless they were religious. Did the authorities think that a blow to the head or solar plexus delivered with a Bible would do less damage than, say, a hardback copy of Tolstoy's *War and Peace?* Or did they simply believe that no one would launch an attack with a Bible?

Reading material was hard to get hold of in jail, so we often took requests from other inmates and carried in copies of their favorite books the following weekend. This worked well, though it was a bit embarrassing to arrive each week with a Bible and a pile of cheap romance novels.

Toothpaste and deodorant were issued to us, but shampoo was prohibited. The inevitable question came to mind: Is shampoo more lethal than deodorant? By my third weekend I had figured out a way to smuggle shampoo into jail in a toothpaste tube.

Charlene may not have been appreciative of what we had done at the hotel, but so many others—inmates and guards alike—expressed support. Even my arresting officer expressed his gratitude.

The banquet had fallen on the same night as a big fight, and much of Washington, D.C., was out cheering for hometown hero Sugar Ray Leonard. While he was filling out my forms, the young, black officer confessed that he had had plans to watch the fight that night. When I apologized for ruining his evening, he smiled and said, "That's OK. What you're doing is important. *We're* the ones suffering for all this money being wasted on bombs and nothing for what we need, like schools."

His response was echoed by cabdrivers picking up people at the hotel, several other police officers, and later even the young clerk of the court, who took one of our "Bread Not Bombs" buttons and wore it in court throughout our arraignment.

The three of us women from Sojourners—who along with four Sojourners men were the only ones given jail time because of our prior convictions—passed those first three weekends in the jail processing area in what was built to be a temporary holding cell for one occupant. A cot and a bunk bed covered all the floor space in the tiny cell. A fluorescent light shone constantly, and Psalm 139:12—"The night is bright as day; for darkness is as light with you"—became a mainstay for comforting meditation together.

As constant as the light was the noise. Lionel Ritchie's "Endless Love" was indeed endless that fall, as the prison radio blared it at high volume round the clock. From time to time an urgent voice on the jail intercom interrupted to call a security squad to a particular cellblock to quell a disturbance. The pandemonium picked up at night following police drug sweeps on the streets and raids on houses of prostitution.

The only sure signs of the passage of time were the arrival

of meals shoved under the cell door and the announcements of prisoner counts. Every few hours all prisoner movement was "frozen" while the guards swept through and counted us. Until their combined numbers jibed with central security's number of prisoners in the jail, the count was repeated—sometimes three or four times.

The advantage of our position in jail those three weekends was that we met lots of women who passed through. We saw some several times. Shirley was unforgettable.

We had first met her in the police wagon on our jarring ride to the police precinct. Two red ponytails stuck out askew from under a bright red beret Shirley had cocked on her head. She laughed often and talked incessantly.

She had an endearing innocence about her. "When I was little," she related, "I took a tube of toothpaste and squeezed it into my baby brother's ear. I guess I've just always been bad." She let forth with another high-pitched laugh.

Shirley had tried and failed at several secretarial jobs and in between them went back to the streets. She made little money as a prostitute and got caught often by the police. She put in frequent appearances on Friday nights at the D.C. jail. As she talked, she said from time to time—as did so many others— "I just want to make something of myself" and vowed to get off the streets as soon as she could keep a job.

The three of us in our small cell were a curiosity to some of the women, who wanted details about both our protest and our life on the outside. One of us, doing her best to describe Sojourners, used the phrase "ecumenical community." When one woman asked what that meant, she explained that "people from all different backgrounds come to live together and share all that we have and do the same thing." The woman thought a moment and then said, "Oh . . . so it's an orgy."

On our fourth weekend we were rousted out of bed by a guard in the middle of the night on Friday. A raid on a local house of prostitution had caught a dozen women, and our cell was needed for some of them. Carrying our sheets and blankets with us, we followed the guard through a series of electric doors, up an escalator, through more electric doors, past the guard bubble, and into individual cells on a cellblock in the south wing of the jail.

I was thankful for small blessings. There was "lights out" on the cellblock about midnight. The beds were mattresses on slabs of metal, and while not entirely comfortable, they were a step up from the sagging springs downstairs. Although the tiny window in my cell had been blacked out with paint like all the others in the jail, a small corner had chipped away, and I could catch small glimpses of the outside world; I had a view of a cemetery. And the food upstairs, I soon learned, was hot (although I discovered that turkey tetrazzini at any temperature is cruel and unusual punishment).

On Saturday afternoon Sylvia, whose cell was a few doors down across the corridor, asked if I had a book I could send down to her. After I carefully slid a book her way, she began to talk about her life. With arms draped outside our cells and faces pressed against the bars, we shouted to one another for almost an hour.

Sylvia was three months pregnant. She was also addicted to heroin. She was supposed to be getting methadone treatments to wean her from the heroin, but she had been brought in late Friday night and was told that the infirmary was closed on weekends. Her hands alternately dangled limply and trembled as she spoke about her abusive father, her escape from home and into drugs, and how much she wanted this baby. Her hands were all that I could see of her.

That night—sometime in the middle of the night—I was awakened by screams and moans. Sylvia had thought the effects of her withdrawal from heroin wouldn't get unbearable until Sunday. She was wrong.

I could hear her pounding on the walls. Calling to her to try to calm her was futile, as her pain consumed all her attention. The entire cellblock was immediately awake, with all the women at their cell bars, shouting up and down the corridor and conjecturing on how soon the guards would arrive to help her. Minutes passed, and no one moved from the guard bubble.

Sylvia's moans grew more intense, and I could hear her body thudding over and over against the floor. I thought of the tiny life she carried.

"Rattle your bars!" the woman in the cell across from me yelled down the corridor, hoping we could together get the attention of the guards. The swelling roar of the shaking bars swept through the cellblock, but still the guards were unmoved.

"Try your lights," the woman on my right shouted. Up and down the tier of cells the lights switched rapidly on and off, and the bars thundered, and still there was no response from the bubble. I was stunned by the guards' blatant refusal to respond.

As the din and Sylvia's screams escalated, so did my sense of desperation to get her help. Someone should have been holding her, wiping the perspiration from her forehead and the terror from her eyes. Her agony and our utter powerlessness finally collided in my spirit, and I sat defeatedly on my bunk and started to pray. It was the only option left.

Sylvia was taken away early in the morning, and I did not see her again.

As I tried unsuccesfully to fall back to sleep that night, I thought about my feelings the night before, my first on the cellblock. I remembered most clearly the sound of my cell door clanging shut in the middle of the night. I had thought back then to the crowd of 600 people who had been at the vigil at the Sheraton Hotel, and then the 51 of us who walked up the driveway; I pictured the 19 of us women who were taken to the police precinct together, and then the 3 of us who were sentenced to jail time. But that night, in that cell, it was just me.

I stayed awake the night Sylvia was taken away until the first tiny stream of light came through the chipped paint on my window, thinking of the women all around me, the ones who had come in alone, frightened. The ones for whom the cell door clanged shut for months, even years. Those who weren't sure when they'd see a lawyer or if their families would ever come to visit them.

Jail for us was always an experience of support from many quarters. Visitors and letters flooded in, gifts of books and writing paper came, and promises of prayers while in and of longed-for delights such as fresh fruit and homemade bread upon release were always kept. We were especially touched that some of our neighbors active in the tenants union Sojourners had helped establish—who had not understood that we had freely chosen to go to jail rather than pay fines to the court—had pooled from their meager resources fifty-seven dollars to help us. But for many others, imprisonment meant estrangement from family support and friends.

On Sunday night of our last weekend in jail, getting out took almost as long as getting in our first Friday night. We had only one door to go, when the 7:30 count was called; it took forty-five minutes to clear. When the door finally opened, we expected to walk through it, past the electronic fence laced with razor wire and the guard tower, shouting out our prison numbers as we passed and leaving the District of Columbia Detention Center (the "D.C.D.C.") behind us for a while.

But instead an inmate flanked by two guards shuffled in. He was an old man, with a black, weathered face and hollow eyes. His large hands were cuffed together in front and secured to shackles that circled his waist, which were fastened by chains to leg irons. The left pant leg of his faded blue prison clothes had been torn to the knee, revealing beneath the leg iron a deep gash in his ankle that was bleeding onto the floor and appeared to be infected. The guards treated him harshly, and when he begged to sit down, one said, "You gotta stand, boy."

Another guard ordered us outside. The sweet taste of freedom was tainted by my silent questions about the man. I wondered which was more painful to him—the agony of cold metal against his raw flesh or the indignity of their raw white power against his black flesh.

The face of that man haunted me for months, as did my imagined picture of Sylvia's. I had witnessed little behind bars to counteract those pictures of human suffering. Even among those women who had been generous and kind to us, who had talked so often about their hopes for a new start in life, despair was hard to fight. Jail is an alien land for the human spirit. It calls for constant vigilance against indignity and defeat, and few seem to win the battle.

A glimmer of hope came to me one rainy night near Dupont Circle. I was stopped at a traffic light. When the light changed, the cab in front of me began to move—in reverse. I leaned on the horn, but it was too late to stop the cab from backing into the car.

The excited young cabdriver got out, waving her arms in frustration at herself, and saying over and over, "I'm sorry. I'm so sorry." The red ponytails beneath the cocked beret were unmistakable, even on a dark night in driving rain.

We briefly surveyed the situation—no visible damage to either vehicle. Shirley apologized once more and said she was new on the job. I hoped to myself that her driving skills would improve more rapidly than her typing.

Her agitated and impatient passenger was making his way toward us, and I just smiled at her and said, "Good luck. You deserve to make it." A puzzled look came over her face. Then she smiled back and took off into the rainy night.

Shirley had once made a joke about being a repeat offender in jail, saying something like, "I guess if I can't be a scientist or a journalist or a violinist, I'll just be a recidivist." I became one too, in May 1983.

Some 3,000 people from across the country had come to the Peace Pentecost event organized by Sojourners that May. During a congressional debate on funding for the MX missile, 242 of us were arrested for praying and singing in the Capitol Rotunda.

The changes in the jail were noticeable. The predictions of the guards a year and a half before had come true. Prison services were cut back in successive Reagan budgets that placed increasing priority on military defense.

This time we were each issued just one sheet. Several beds were lacking mattresses, and prison jumpsuits missing buttons. The prison diet went from bad to worse—high in sugar and starch and generally low in nutrition. "Extras" such as salad dressing were no longer available, and a sugary drink in half-pint cartons labeled "Jungle Juice" seemed to be the only regular dietary staple.

Supplies of all types were running low: One woman inmate was infected with an incurable and sexually transmittable disease when a jail doctor reused a disposable instrument during a routine jail-entry pelvic examination. The number of guards was cut back, and a suicide in the jail was attributed to lack of supervision.

As money on the outside for job training and educational programs dried up and basic support services for the poor diminished, desperation escalated, and with it the crime rate. Increased drug sweeps and a general crackdown on crime packed the jail to almost twice its official capacity. And so the jail, with fewer resources, had to deal with ever-increasing numbers of inmates.

The jail had become so crowded that the gym area in the women's wing was converted into sleeping space for sixteen, which is where the three of us women from Sojourners who received jail time served our sentences. In the men's wings, TV rooms and floor space in the corridors between cells were also jammed with metal bunks, and some of the wings had begun double celling. Tension in the jail escalated.

Two months later it exploded: The population of the jail, which was built to hold 1,350 residents, peaked at 2,400. People were packed in on top of one another so tightly, and basic medical, food, and social services were so inadequate, that a minor riot broke out the third week of July.

Inmates set mattresses on fire and refused to return to their cells. Officers armed with shotguns were sent outside to the walled recreation area to control residents who were destroying equipment. In early 1986 it came to light that the prison population had exceeded a federally imposed ceiling and that prison officials had falsified counts in order to avoid prosecution.

The jail also became a dumping ground for another type of resident. My first night back in, when I was still alone in an "intake cell," the woman in the cell below me was punctuating her moans of despair through the night with a regular banging of her cell bars. I pictured her with hands clenched around the bars, moving back and forth with all her might in a plea of desperation.

"She'll be handcuffed to her bed tonight," a guard told me after I expressed concern for the woman the next morning. "She really doesn't belong here, but the mental hospital is more overcrowded than we are—she's lucky she's not just wandering the streets like most of them."

I remembered Sylvia. One thing that had not changed in jail was the suffering.

Our first evening in the gym, a number of women drifted over to our bunks. One by one they shared their stories.

Cheryl had been forced out of her home and onto the streets as a teenager when her mother abandoned the family and her father told her he couldn't afford to keep her. Jackie had stolen checks from the office where she worked as a secretary, she explained, so that she could afford to keep her three young sons in a parochial school. "It's the first chance they've ever had for a decent education," she said as she began to weep, "and they're so smart."

Ruby spoke next and got even Jackie smiling as she explained that she had found a check written to a Sally Harvey. She described the scene when she tried to cash it at the bank: "The bank teller told me that Sally Harvey was a tall Caucasian with blond hair. I told myself, 'Uh-oh.' "

Wanda timidly moved over and joined our circle on the bunks. Looking down at the floor with her arms folded to try to hide cigarette burns on her face and hands, she talked about how her father had burned and sexually abused her as a child when he lost his job and stayed home all day angry.

Wanda's story gave Terese the courage to speak. She said she had recently suffered a miscarriage after being raped. She lost so much blood during the miscarriage that the doctors ordered a blood transfusion; but so ruined were her veins from her heroin addiction, the transfusion could not be performed.

That night we were rudely awakened at about 2:30 by shouting guards. While everyone mumbled about their interrupted sleep, a guard explained that since Monday was Memorial Day—a holiday—the prison laundry was washing sheets that night, and our turn had come. I had just had mine for a day, but the guards insisted on taking it away anyway.

I was aggravated by the stupidity of it—and the fact that in just two hours we would be awakened again for breakfast. Few things are worth getting up for at 4:30 in the morning—and a breakfast of cold, watery powdered eggs and warm, grape-flavored Jungle Juice is not one of them. Keeping inmates perpetually tired seemed to be a way of draining off energy that might turn disruptive.

But the others seemed to take this intrusion in stride. By the time I had deposited my sheet and was back on my bare mattress, Wanda was already asleep again. She was sucking her thumb.

I will leave it to the sociologists to argue heredity and environment, and the politicians to nitpick over who deserves what, and the pastors to decide where moral responsibility lies for the trap these women are in. Most are victims of sorely lacking financial and emotional resources, government priorities that exclude them, and politicians and bureaucrats who wish they would just go away (as some of their families wished since the day they were born). They carry abusive pasts, live desperate presents, and face seemingly hopeless futures. And with all of this to shoulder, some of them make bad choices. And they become victims of those as well.

With some glaring exceptions, these women are perpetrators of crimes in which they themselves are the primary victims—most notably prostitution and illegal drug use. They tend to be accomplices in thefts and robberies rather than the main players, who are often boyfriends or male relatives. And of those rare few who commit extremely violent crimes such as homicide, their victims are frequently abusing boyfriends or spouses.

In lives fraught with violence and tough talk and tougher choices, there remains in each a core of vulnerability—a point where the tears come, where the pain and the fear spill out. For most it's when they talk about their children.

Most claim that they did what they did to be able to feed their children. They fear the scars their young ones will bear because of their jail time and the separation. One woman talked lovingly about her four young children, who had waited for several hours to get a half-hour visit with her behind glass on the other end of a visiting-room phone that worked sporadically. Another proudly told how her fifteen-year-old son had gotten a summer job in order to make enough money to pay her bail.

No attempts have been made by the prison authorities to address adequately the great tragedy of mothers separated from their children. In January 1984 a pregnant woman inmate claimed that she was in labor but was not attended to by the infirmary staff. After a long delay, she was finally taken to D.C. General Hospital, located at the edge of the prison grounds. She gave birth before reaching the delivery room. Her premature baby died the next day. In relating this story to me later, another woman resident said sadly, "Maybe it's better. They would have taken her baby away anyway."

Making up less than 20 percent of the prison population, women are treated as an afterthought in the system. This is perhaps nowhere more evident than in the medical services.

The intake examination is notoriously insensitive and dreaded by every woman who talked about it.

One friend was told she had an infection and given medication for it. Refusing to use it, she took it after our release to our community doctor, who identified it as a dangerous drug that had been off the shelves for three years. Banned medications, it appears, get "dumped" in U.S. jails as well as Third World countries.

I will never forget a scene I witnessed as we were getting ready to leave the jail following our five-day sentence. Three other women came into the room where I had been told to wait. Two were guards who stood over a young inmate in a late stage of pregnancy.

The young woman was near tears as the guards put on and then took off of her one thin prison robe after another, trying to find one large enough to cover her. The guards began to get exasperated by the futility of the task, and the young woman hung her head in shame. Finally one of the guards looked up and down the woman's exposed body and said, "Isn't it just amazing how much the human skin can stretch?"

The young mother's eyes met mine, and we each shed a few tears. I wanted her to be some place where she would be honored and gently cared for. And I wanted her child, so soon to be given new life, to be welcomed with joy and received with tenderness. I had been told about a woman who had given birth unattended in a jail cell here, and I offered up a prayer of protection for this sister and her precious baby. I left the jail that day wondering what kind of future that child would have.

On June 12, 1985, while a vote was taking place in Congress over $27 million to fund a war of terror against the people of Nicaragua, a group of us knelt in drizzling rain in front of the U.S. State Department. We held crosses bearing names of Nicaraguans who had been killed by the U.S.-funded contras. Our action was just one of hundreds of actions happening all around the country as part of the Pledge of Resistance, a network launched by Sojourners and other organizations that had grown to include at that time 80,000 people committed to respond to U.S. military escalations in Central America.

The wheels of justice ground ever more slowly. It took an unbelievable seven and a half hours to process twelve of us from the State Department and six other women into the jail. The question-and-answer part of the process went fairly quickly with the others, as the answers were the same in every case: "Hair—black," "Eyes—brown," "Place of birth—Washington, D.C.," "Employer—none." For whom this jail was designed was made very clear when a few guards were caught trying to save themselves some time by filling this information in ahead of time.

The process bogged down considerably with the rest of us, and one of the other women, hungry and impatient, finally yelled, "Oh, man, they all have different colored eyes and stuff!" A sixty-year-old Catholic sister from Ohio in our group said very calmly to her, "We have as much right to be in jail as you do."

My arresting officer had thought that "Holly" was my middle name, and my numerous efforts all along the way to correct the error were futile. I finally got used to responding to "Day" when names were being called in court and holding cells and police wagons (feeling a warm connection to Dorothy Day who—two generations before me—worked against the occupation of Nicaragua by U.S. Marines and first went to jail here in Washington as a result of demonstrating at the White House for the vote for women). But when I tried to convince the jail that I wasn't actually "Joyce H. Day," chaos ensued. And all the confusion helped me understand why some of the women I met on the inside got disoriented when they forgot which of their aliases they were using.

At 1:30 in the morning, processing complete, we were finally offered the obligatory right to make a phone call. "Anybody you want to call at 1:30 A.M.?" I asked the woman beside me, another participant in the witness at the State Department. She grinned and said, "I think they've already figured out I won't be home for dinner."

At 1:35 we heard our first news report over the blaring prison radio. The lead story was about the vote. The House of Representatives had overwhelmingly passed the aid package to the contras. In this business you win some, you lose a lot.

The next day in the infirmary holding cell, I scanned the graffiti while waiting my turn for the dreaded jail physical. "Did you hear about the sixty-second sex maniac? Ya got a minute?" was scrawled across one wall.

In smaller but neater print, someone had written, "If I trust in God, why be scared?" I wondered who had put those words there. All who entered the jail had to make an initial visit to the infirmary and took their turn sitting in that cell. The words had probably reassured many, perhaps most of all the one who had penciled them there.

I remembered a story that Jim had told me about his brother, now my brother-in-law, Bill Weld-Wallis. When Bill was being released from jail in Michigan following a nuclear arms protest, Lauren, a three-year-old friend from the church day-care center where he worked, accompanied her mother to bring him home. Lauren gave Bill a big hug and then began looking around and behind him. When her mother asked why, she said, "Isn't Jesus coming too? We've been praying all week that Jesus would be with Bill in jail."

Jesus had made his home in that Michigan jail and the D.C. jail as surely as he had in all the other places where people suffer and are in need of him. And faith in him was rampant behind the bars.

My thoughts about the strength of faith I had seen in so many women in the jail were interrupted when a young woman sitting on the bench across from us in the cell began a conversation with Millie Bender, a close friend from Sojourners sitting next to me. "Doesn't this hurt your heart?" Tanya asked as she pointed to Millie's scar.

Two years before, Jim and I had rushed Millie to the hospital on Labor Day. Open-heart surgery and weeks in the hospital had followed. More than anything else in a long time, Millie's heart attack had drawn Sojourners Community closer and given us a new appreciation for both the preciousness and fragility of life.

In one day's stack of notes and cards that Jim and I had brought to Millie was an invitation to the dedication of Timmy McLaughlin, born in our community a few months before. The front of the card quoted Ephesians 3:14–19: "that Christ may dwell in your hearts through faith; that you, being rooted and grounded in love . . . may be filled with the fullness of God."

I remembered Millie's tears as she read those words in her hospital bed. She explained, "This was the Scripture that was with me last night. I couldn't sleep, and between midnight and two o'clock I just prayed. I prayed for the community, my family, and friends. And I wept to know how deeply I love and am loved. And how much this hurting world needs communities of faith, people who are taking the risk to love one another."

Many scenes from those weeks came into my mind—members of her Sojourners and Bender families, with our hands clasped over her bed, praying together the Twenty-third Psalm; five hours of waiting during her surgery; in the recovery room, Millie's tired and bruised body hooked up to a respirator, monitors, and IV tubes, which beeped and hissed and dripped and blinked. She looked so vulnerable then. She could communicate only with her eyes, which spoke of pain but also determination and love.

Now Millie was telling Tanya how grateful she was for the gift of life and the chance to advocate on behalf of life for others. A beautiful and gentle woman with scars of her own—needle marks running the length of her arms—Tanya wanted to know why we continued to protest when it didn't change anything.

As I watched Millie respond, I thought about a sermon by

Rev. Allan Boesak, an outspoken opponent of apartheid in South Africa, in which he paraphrased author Alan Paton: "We will go before God to be judged, and God will ask us, 'Where are your wounds?' And we will say, 'We have no wounds.' And God will ask, 'Was there nothing worth fighting for?' "

We were there because we had decided there were a great many things worth fighting for. That feeling became stronger with each jail visit.

Millie was explaining to Tanya that her belief in God demanded that she be faithful in resisting, even when it required taking risks and meant perhaps never seeing success. Tanya nodded and said, "Yes, God knows your heart."

Then Tanya continued, "God is giving me a second chance— just like he gave you a second chance. God always gives us second chances. I'm going to beat these drugs this time. Keep protesting—'Drug programs not war.' " As she finished these words, she was called in to see the doctor. She stood up, gave Millie a hug, and said, "Take good care of your heart—and pray for me."

When Tanya was taken out of the holding cell, another woman was brought in. She immediately sat on the floor in a corner, resting her head on her knees. I watched her awhile, then went over, crouched beside her, and asked if she was all right. She slowly raised her head. Her eyes were bloodshot, and she looked terribly tired.

"I'm OK," she said, and put her head back down. I touched her shoulder and asked, "Are you sure?" She started to cry and then pulled out a photograph of a beautiful child with dark hair in long, shiny plaits, dressed in a bright red dress. "Vanessa is going to be two tomorrow," she cried, "and I'm not going to be with her. It's the first time I've been away from her. I carried that baby in this place."

Slowly Yolanda's story unfolded. She had been working as a prostitute for several years, but she quickly added, "It's different for me—it's better. My husband is my pimp, and he treats me good." She looked imploringly at me as she said,

"He can't get a job, and we need the money—to give Vanessa the best."

She was addicted to heroin when she came to jail about two and a half years ago. "They kept me on 'meth' for a few months. It would have killed the baby if I went off." Vanessa was born addicted to methadone on June 14, 1983.

When I put all the pieces together, I knew why there was such a familiarity about Yolanda. She was the one trying on the prison robes two years before. And Vanessa, who was born about three weeks later, was the baby for whom I prayed.

Yolanda had been released from jail four days after Vanessa's birth. Gradually, over a period of weeks, Vanessa was taken off methadone. Her future was uncertain at best, but she had already proven before the age of two that she was a survivor.

Yolanda I wasn't so sure about. She buried her head again in her knees and wailed, "I tried so hard to be good." In this place where everything seemed impossible, I wasn't sure what to hope for—or to say.

The only wisdom that came to me was Tanya's. Her indomitable faith made anything seem possible. I put my arm around Yolanda's shoulders and said, "God always gives us second chances." And I prayed again for a child whom I had now had a glimpse of—a winsome child with dark hair and bright eyes and a captivating smile—that she might find enough miracles in life to pull her through.

10. Strong and Vulnerable

The book was called *I Never Told Anyone*. I don't even remember the editor's name, but she had compiled a collection of writings by women survivors of child sexual abuse. Page after page offered stories of violence forced on young girls—from infants to teenagers, from uncomfortable touches to acts of brutal sexual torture.

I could not put the book down until I finished it some time in the middle of that Saturday night several years ago. And then I could not sleep. I couldn't stop myself from feeling the pain and the anger, from taking time to grieve and weep and pray.

I have such vivid memories of that night. I began to experience waves of pain that matched the descriptions I had heard from mothers of the early stages of giving birth. In the few hours that were left of the night, I drifted in and out of sleep, feeling at times utterly alone and at other times in the presence of death.

But toward morning I felt a profound sense of the presence of Christ—beside me and within me. And with that assurance, I finally fell asleep. I was awakened soon afterward by a phone call from a close friend with the news that she had suffered a miscarriage through the night.

Three hours later, Sojourners Community was gathered in our Sunday morning worship. We grieved the loss of a child and prayed for the family into which it would have been welcomed. We were drawn very close together in our sorrow, and I consecrated our Communion that morning in memory of a child we had never met but who in its short life had taught us all a great deal about life and community.

I confess a proclivity in life toward the things that are concrete and tangible; I am not so comfortable in the realm of spiritual mysteries. But occasionally I have experienced one of those rare and extraordinary moments when a touch of God is so profound that I begin to glimpse the possibilities, to see myself healed and whole.

Through the experience of that night, I felt transformed, knowing that I had been loved and held by a God who is both far-off mystery and intimate companion. At the heart of the experience was a death. But beyond that death, something new was given birth in me.

I had always been uncomfortable with the weakness and marginality that mark women's history. At an early age I had become determined to distance myself from that powerlessness, to cultivate gifts for success in a male-defined world, to dash the stereotypes and prove myself on the world's terms.

I hadn't been exempt from discrimination. I remember wanting to be a drummer in elementary school, but only boys played drums at that time, so I took up the viola. In college, our women's varsity basketball team had practice at seven o'clock every morning—we ranked in priority for gym space just under men's one-on-one basketball and Ping-Pong intramurals. And I got an inescapable introduction to sexism in the church when I sought ordination.

But I always took the approach that I had options; other women might be limited by gender, but I could always find a way to pursue my hopes. I thought I was different.

My experiences with Nicole and her family and my time in jail had drawn me into sympathy—but not empathy—for the victims of an oppression that is both very subtle and often cruelly blatant. It was easy to touch their pain as long as it did not relate to my own. What died in me that long night was my alienation from other women, my pride, the distance and barriers I had built to insulate me from their suffering—and from my own oppression as a woman.

This leg of my journey has been perhaps the most difficult. It has involved walking not only into others' pain but also into my own. It has meant rage and tears not just over what is happening to people I identify as being in circumstances very different from my own but also over what is happening to my many sisters, my people, to me.

Several years ago the women of Sojourners Community began meeting together regularly. I remember the release that came as we shared our stories during our first gathering. No one had been untouched by discrimination, harassment, and violence directed toward us as women.

Sexual advances by college professors and sexual harassment in work settings were recounted, two experiences of rape and another of incest were painfully shared, and confessions of confusion about how best to deal with frequent verbal assaults on the street poured forth. The common thread in all the stories, as in those of all the women I had met in jail, was vulnerability. We were trying to come to grips with how to live with the knowledge that we can be physically overpowered at almost any time by almost any man.

Our experiences varied, but we acknowledged that the very threat of sexual violence affects all of us. For most women this threat is epitomized by the reality of rape, an act of unilateral violence done by men to women—considered by many criminal statistics experts to be the fastest-growing violent crime.

Rape is the first thing I feared late one spring afternoon when three men surrounded a friend and me on our way home from the *Sojourners* office. We got away with some bruises and a wrenched shoulder on my part; they got away with the three dollars we had between us. We were grateful for safety from greater harm, and the incident seemed relatively minor at the time; but for days after, we both found wells of anger at our powerlessness and vulnerability erupting.

We live in a world in which violence against women has reached epidemic proportions. The statistics are almost unbelievable. It is estimated that a rape occurs in this country every eight minutes, and that if current trends continue, one in four women will be raped in her lifetime.

Domestic violence is proliferating beyond all bounds. According to the FBI, one of every two married women is beaten by her husband at some point during her marriage. Most of these abuses go unpunished, as domestic assaults are more often viewed as situations requiring mediation than as criminal offenses. What men can't get away with on the streets they often get away with in their own homes.

In a recent study at D.C. General Hospital, it was found that 12 percent of rape victims were children under twelve years old. It is estimated by Parents United, a support group for people who have been affected by child molestation, that one in four girls, and about half as many boys, are being sexually abused, 75 percent of these by their own family members. In a recent survey 10 percent of women responded that they were victims of incest.

But the statistics don't tell the personal horror. I remember holding a friend for close to an hour, sobs wracking her body as she told the story of her pain, of hands wandering over her small body years before. She commented through her tears, "I know why there's so much broken glass on the streets of this neighborhood. I just want to destroy something, to release some of the anger." There was no way to hold the pain adequately.

She finally curled up tightly as her sobs turned to whimpers. She talked then about the shame and the fear, about feeling sometimes like a young child who just wants to scream for help.

The foundation of the epidemic is the subjugation of women. Rape is its threat, and pornography is its propaganda.

For four years the *Sojourners* office sat on the edge of the downtown pornography district. A walk to the subway required cutting through the heart of that area, enduring the barrage of blaring music, flashing lights, graphic life-size pictures, and the shouts of the barkers trying to rope in customers for the "world's best collections" of adult books, peep shows, and nude dancers. With every walk down Fourteenth Street, I felt personally assaulted—a feeling shared by most of the women I know.

Pornography has been used strategically throughout history to portray women as less than human. Jewish women were targeted in Nazi Germany to generate anti-Semitism, and Asian women were a primary focus of pornography in the United States during the Vietnam War. Such dehumanizing portrayals of women paved the way for rape, a widespread tactic of terror in almost every war since the first was fought.

Pornography exploded from a $5 million business fifteen years ago to a $5 billion business in 1984, grossing more than the conventional film and music industries combined. Of the ten most profitable magazines on the market, six are "men's entertainment" magazines, with *Playboy* and *Penthouse* outselling *Time* and *Newsweek*.

Escalating brutality toward women has accompanied escalating profits in the pornography business. From the Playboy "bunny" image to the macho acts of sadistic torture and bondage that are rampant in pornography, the message is the same: women must be made nonthreatening, either placated as pets or violently whipped into submission. As David S. Wells, editor and publisher of five men's magazines, put it: "Men don't want to be equal; it's as simple as that."

It is no coincidence that the pornography business exploded in the mid-1960s, after a revitalized women's movement offered new possibilities and empowerment for women. Like rape, pornography is about power, with sex as the weapon.

The roots of the current epidemic go deep. Some are found in our society's basic assumptions about women and men. In a recent study, researchers determined that 66 percent of the thousands of men interviewed had a "conquest mentality" toward women.

Such attitudes are developed early. Although some changes are occurring, our society is still plagued with stereotypes that encourage young boys to be aggressive, competitive, and physically superior, while most young girls are taught to be passive, submissive, and physically attractive. Such assumptions, and their evolution into the gender dichotomy of "protector" and "protected," lead to the imbalance of power that is the taproot of sexual violence.

A society's rituals reveal a great deal about its beliefs. Many women in the United States still participate in marriage ceremonies in which they are "given away" by their fathers to their husbands—a throwback to understandings of women as property—and in which they promise to "obey" while their husbands "love and cherish" them; the traditional pronouncement of "man and wife" makes clear whose identity is the derivative one. Typically the term *bachelor*, applied to single men, conjures up images of an independent and freewheeling lifestyle; whereas single women have been saddled throughout history with the labels *spinster* and *old maid*, viewed as hapless and hopeless women unable to snag a husband.

Another prime indicator of a society's view of women is its incidence of rape. University of Pennsylvania anthropologist Peggy Reeves Sanday conducted a comprehensive study on rape in ninety-five cultures. She concluded that several factors prevail in the societies with low incidences of rape: women are respected and influential in all sectors of life, sharing decision making with men; the societies' religions include female deities, and women are active in religious life and ritual; the societies are structured cooperatively, with little distinction between women's and men's work; and fertility and the nurturing of children are highly regarded.

In rape-prone cultures women have little or no part at the highest levels of decision making or in religious rituals; God is viewed as exclusively male; men tend to stay aloof from raising their children and to demean "women's work"; boys are taught to be aggressive and dominant, and masculine violence is glorified in patriotic militarism and war; and violence in general is accepted as a fact of life and prevails in the popular culture—in advertising, on television, and in movies.

It's not difficult to guess into which category our society falls.

Women in the United States are several hundred times more likely to be raped than women in some other cultures.

Sanday concludes that rape is not a biological drive within men but comes from a conditioned social response. Her research verifies that violence against women will remain an epidemic until we transform the roles, structures, and symbols of our society that perpetuate relationships of dominance and submission between men and women.

I would argue that the rate of abortion is another factor in evaluating women's status in a society—and another form of violence against women. It gives me great sadness that the secular feminist movement in this country has made support for abortion the litmus test of commitment to equality for women.

Only in a society where women feel unsupported and where raising children is less than highly regarded does abortion reach epidemic proportions. A million and a half children a year are lost to abortion in this country. Many women suffer tremendous guilt afterward, knowing that what was destroyed was not some unknown mass of tissue but a child, endowed with all the potential that life might have offered.

Many women also suffer physically from abortions—even the "safe" ones carried out in clinics and hospitals. Some women are rendered infertile. And the women highest at risk are the poorest ones, who already suffer from inadequate nutrition and poor health care.

It is no secret that many men have abandoned, or been minimally involved in caring for, the children they have fathered. The standard feminist argument states that since most men are free from the burden of raising children, equality for women demands that we also claim this freedom. Abortion is viewed as an issue of a woman's right to self-determination.

But this society's acceptance of abortion wrongly pits a woman's right to self-determination against a child's right to life. It negates any hope that women and men can share the sacred gift and responsibility of raising children. And, as feminist writer and friend Ginny Earnest has expressed it, it signals a lack of intention to build a world in which there is justice for women and the guarantee of a good life for children.

Ultimately, abortion threatens to deny the power of God, who is the creator and preserver of life. "You formed my inward parts, you knit me together in my mother's womb. . . . Your eyes beheld my unformed substance; in your book were written, every one of them, the days that were formed for me, when as yet there was none of them," writes the psalmist in Psalm 139, one of my favorites. Those words are a powerful affirmation of life and its promises. To protect life at its beginnings is a way of worshiping and trusting God.

Destroying our unborn children cannot be an answer to our dilemma, when there are so many other answers that affirm life. We must commit ourselves to a vision of justice and work for adequate sex education and health care for all; advocate for responsible sexuality and male responsibility for children; work to change public policy priorities on behalf of women and offer support for women with crisis pregnancies through the community of faith. Until we are committed to such an agenda, women will feel compelled to seek abortions.

But until we have arrived at a world in which the thought of abortion is obsolete, there can be no room for condemnation of those women who feel that abortion is the only answer for an unwanted pregnancy. Some women, facing an increasingly bleak economic future, feel pushed to abortion out of economic desperation.

Two out of every three poor adults in this country are women, and their impoverishment is rapidly growing. There is such a strong trend that social scientists and feminists have labeled it the "feminization of poverty."

Statistics help tell the story. Women earn, on the average, about sixty cents for every dollar a man earns. It takes a woman nine days of full-time labor to earn what a man makes in five days, and women with a college education earn less, on the average, than men with a high school diploma. If wives and female heads of households were paid the same as similarly qualified men, half the families now living in poverty would not be poor.

Given economic realities, the cost of raising a child frightens some women into having abortions. But statistics show that the majority of abortions are not performed on poor women but on middle-class women who feel that a child might threaten a career or financial gain; or, in the case of young, unmarried women, might bring shame on a family.

It is a confusing and difficult time to be a woman, facing new possibilities and at the same time some of the old limitations. There were few options open to our mothers and grandmothers, and certainly undeniable strides have been made for women. Many of us in my generation have chosen careers, delayed getting married or having children, and rejoiced in the opportunities that have been opened up to us at great sacrifice by many of our sisters.

But it is never easy being a "transition generation." More and more I hear women talking about how they no longer believe they can "have it all." Juggling career and family demands has taken its toll and forced many women to reevaluate what is most important to them.

Most women I know struggle with some ambivalence about biological realities—mothers caught between the immense joy of childbearing and the equally immense upheaval and disruption of it; the rest of us trying to take in stride the regular reminders that our bodies are preparing (whether or not we are) to conceive; all of us plagued at times with the painfulness and vulnerability of being women and reveling at other times in womanhood's unique gifts and strengths. Sometimes the burden feels painfully unfair, and other times the joy is overwhelming.

We live with our fears in this dangerous age when an estimated one in three pregnancies ends in miscarriage and cancers that strike women are on the rise. We have faced anguish and losses in our families and communities—molar pregnancies thought to be linked to chemical exposure, birth defects and breast cancer, fears about what we're doing to our environment and how future generations will pay.

Facing the possibility of cancer a few years ago—with weeks of tests and waiting for biopsy results—brought my own deeply embedded fears to the surface. Feelings of powerlessness and self-doubt overtook me, leaving traces long after I had received reassuring news of the results.

There are not many signposts or anchors in this time. We want to claim our strength even as we live in constant vulnerability. Our biology makes us nurturers, but we don't want to be only nurturers. We are trying to break out of prescribed roles, but we confront—as do the men we know—ingrained socialization at many points. We want to change the world, and we want to love our children. And it almost never feels like there's enough time or space.

The political right wing has added to our vulnerability by launching an assault against feminism. Couched in "pro-family" rhetoric, its agenda would reverse much of the progress that women have made in the last several decades. Pro-family has been used to justify, among other things, increasing militarism in the name of protecting all that has been the basis of traditional American family life, including Mom confined to the kitchen with her apple pie.

It is indeed not an easy time and place to be a woman. But it seems there never was such a time or place. On every continent, in every age, women have suffered as a result of being designated inferior, sexually impure, and needing to be put under male control.

Footbinding of young girls was carried out for a thousand years in China, leaving women grotesquely crippled and forced into total dependence by a lack of mobility. Female infanticide was also practiced and still continues in some areas today.

In India, the rite of suttee was created to spare widows from temptations to impurity by forcing them to burn themselves on their husbands' funeral pyres. Widespread throughout Africa is the painful ritual of female genital mutilation, thought to "purify" a woman from sexual sensitivity.

In Europe, chastity belts were used on women when their husbands were away, causing great discomfort and often infection. From the fifteenth to the seventeenth centuries, witch hunts were carried out across the continent. The primary accusation leveled against the victims, usually unmarried or widowed women, was sexual impurity. Many were publicly stripped, raped, tortured, and burned or hanged.

Witch hunts were carried out to a lesser extent in the United States. Wife beating was common in the early American colonies, which modeled their statutes after British common law. The common expression "rule of thumb" dates back to the law—considered merciful—that a husband could beat his wife with a stick no thicker than his thumb.

The inferiority of women was considered part of natural law, and their dependence on men was ensured by legislation that denied women the essentials of a stable life—education, property, employment options, and participation in the political process through the vote. When slavery was instituted in the United States, the laws governing the rights of slaves were modeled after those governing women.

Today many women, especially women of color, are victims of forced sterilization, part of an effort to control minority populations. The U.S. government, with the active support of many of the biggest U.S. corporations, is the largest contributor to sterilization programs both domestically and around the world. In this country, black, Hispanic, and Native American women have been the targets of sterilization abuse.

Religion, unfortunately, offers women no haven of dignity and equality. Religion has, in fact, undergirded patriarchal power and justified the subjugation of women in almost every society. A common thread in every major world faith—Hinduism, Buddhism, Judaism, Christianity, and Islam—is the definition of woman as the blighted and inferior sex.

It was several years ago, when I was the scheduled preacher in church and the lectionary included the story of King David and Bathsheba, that my anguish over the Christian faith's record on women became most acute. I was struck most deeply not by what was recorded in the story but by what was missing.

Recorded in the eleventh and twelfth chapters of 2 Samuel, the account is the story of a king who lusts after a woman. The king takes her, and she conceives. Trapped in a desperate situation by his lust, David arranges an unexpected furlough for Uriah, Bathsheba's soldier-husband.

But Uriah cannot be persuaded by the king to go to his wife and indulge in the comforts of home while the other soldiers suffer the discomforts of war. David tries Plan B: he fills Uriah with wine. But still the soldier refuses to go to his wife. Backed into a corner, David arranges Uriah's death in battle. And in what seems to be a bit of divine understatement, the Scripture tells us, "The thing that David did displeased the Lord."

Eventually David takes Bathsheba as his wife, and she gives birth to their son. But, as a punishment to the king, the Lord takes the life of the son. The story has gone down in history as "David's great sin." It has never occurred to the biblical historians to call it "Bathsheba's great loss."

With the exception of a brief notation that Bathsheba mourned the deaths of her husband and son, the thoughts and feelings, dreams and hopes, fears and strengths of Bathsheba appear nowhere in the story. Set in the middle of a scenario of military intrigue and victory is the very personal tragedy of a woman who is powerless to affect her own situation.

She is given no identification apart from being the daughter of a particular man and the wife of another. The only attribute assigned to her is a physical beauty that arouses the lust of the king, who uses his power to violate her and her marriage vow and then arranges the death of her husband.

We will never know what resistance or willingness Bathsheba offered to the king's demand. Perhaps she, too, was plagued with guilt and shame. But more likely, she felt herself a very personal victim of the passions, power, and prowess of a king.

What ambivalence must she have felt toward the child she bore, loving it as part of her own flesh and despising it for the sign it was of her shame and pain. Did she have dreams for herself, for her baby? Did the day come when she whispered to herself, "I want it to be a son; I want this child to have a life full of choices and not a life full of pain."

As she went through the agony of childbirth, did she not wish that this boy were a son of her poor, fallen soldier instead of a king? While the king fasted for the life of his son and the elders rushed to his side, what quiet sorrow did she feel in her soul? What hatred for the sinner? Did she not cradle that dying child and cry out for its life? In the frenzy of mourning, did she not feel utterly alone with her grief?

I picture a heart torn in two. I picture a woman pondering in that broken heart, "No one can touch the pain of a woman who never even had herself and now has lost everything."

Bathsheba's marginalization from her own story might not have felt so weighty in my reading of the account if hers was an isolated case. But any serious reading of the biblical account shows the overwhelming loss of women's history in its pages. One of the difficult struggles we women face as Christians is coming to terms with the fact that the record of our faith largely excludes us. We can search out and claim the Deborahs and Esthers and Priscillas who are profiles of wisdom, courage, and faith, but they seem all too rare in a history whose shapers are men.

The Old Testament is a disturbing record that for the most part portrays women as property, pawns, and prostitutes; cursed if they are "barren"; cyclically unclean; identified only as wives of important men, mothers of important sons. We are often unnamed, as in the case of God's blessing after the great flood: "God blessed Noah and his sons, and said to them, 'Be fruitful and multiply, and fill the earth' " (Gen. 9:1). We have no idea of the names of the wives who had no small part in this effort to be fruitful.

Hebrew law assigned women the status of property. A Genesis account of Lot's capture shows Abraham as rescuer of Lot, along with "his goods, and the women and the people" (Gen. 14:16), offering women a ranking somewhere between possessions and persons. Wives are listed in the Tenth Commandment among those possessions that are not to be coveted.

In the patriarchal Hebrew culture, lineage was traced through the male line, and even God was claimed as the "God of Abraham, Isaac, and Jacob," with no mention of Sarah, Rebekah, and Rachel. The contributions of these women to faith history are largely written out of the biblical account.

Rachel and her sister Leah were used as pawns in a ploy by their father to trick Jacob into marrying both of them, with Laban, the father, substituting plain Leah for beautiful Rachel on Jacob's wedding night. The two sisters, like most of the women in the Old Testament, are peripheral to the biblical account except in their capacity to bear sons. Rachel anguished over her inability to conceive and finally turned over her maid, Bilhah, to Jacob so that he could have sons through her (Gen. 30:1–8). This script was previously played out by Sarah and her maid, Hagar, who bore a son for Abraham (Gen. 16:1–6).

The desire for plentiful male offspring created a culture in which men were free to have several wives, and situations such as Bilhah's and Hagar's were considered acceptable. We find only a few brief glimpses at the insecurity, shame, and anguish such situations must have caused for women.

Among the most difficult of the biblical texts to read are those that center on the outright abuse of women. Immediately following the David and Bathsheba account is the story of Tamar, a daughter of David who was the object of her brother Amnon's lust. Amnon feigned illness and called for Tamar to bring him some cakes. Then, despite her pleadings and resistance, he overpowered and raped her. Another brother, Absalom, warned her to keep the incident quiet for Amnon's sake. We know nothing more of Tamar except that she "dwelt, a desolate woman, in her brother Absalom's house" (2 Sam. 13:20).

The nineteenth chapter of Genesis records the sojourn of two men in the home of Lot. The men of the city of Sodom surrounded Lot's home and demanded to see the two visitors, desiring them for homosexual rape. Lot condemned them for their wickedness and then offered to the crowd his two virgin daughters in place of the two men. Fortunately, the daughters were saved from such a fate.

A disturbing underlying assumption of the story is that homosexual rape is more sinful than heterosexual rape, that the violation of young women is not as serious an offense as the violation of men. Such a double standard surfaced in more subtle ways in Hebrew law as well. Adultery was considered a most serious offense because it was seen as a violation of a man's property rights, and a significant part of Tamar's desolation resulted from her being considered "damaged property" after her rape.

Women went from the homes of their fathers to the homes of their husbands. Women on their own had no rights and no stable means of survival. Widows and their children were the most vulnerable class in Hebrew culture, and the phrase *widows and orphans* appears throughout the Scriptures as the paradigmatic example of oppression and powerlessness. The word *fatherless* is often substituted for *orphans*, bringing home the point that children without a male parent had no secure means of survival.

The treatment of widows and their children was often reprehensible. According to Scripture, the proud and wicked "slay the widow . . . and murder the fatherless" (Ps. 94:6); they "feed on the barren childless woman, and do no good to the widow" (Job 24:21). The princes "do not defend the fatherless, and the widow's cause does not come to them" (Isa. 1:23); they "have been bent on shedding blood. . . . The fatherless and the widow are wronged" (Ezek. 22:6–7). Cast off from the normal protections of the society and excluded from economic stability, the widows and their children were defenseless against the violence and exploitation of the wicked and powerful.

The Book of Ruth is the story of two women who undergo a radical change in social status when they become widows. Left with no option but to glean for food in the fields, Ruth and her mother-in-law, Naomi, survived by their own resourcefulness and love for one another. But ultimately they recognized that long-term survival depended on the protections of a stable relationship with a man. Ruth made known the obligation to marry her that fell to her husband's next of kin, Boaz. Boaz, who had already offered her protection in the fields from molesting men, agreed and took her as his wife.

Concubinage was acceptable under Hebrew law. It created a class of women who faced the vulnerability of living with a man under a virtual sexual slave-master relationship, without the legal protections and securities of marriage. An unnamed concubine of Bethlehem was not as fortunate as Lot's daughters in Sodom.

When men in a foreign city demanded her master, their host offered the concubine as well as his own young daughter in the master's place. "Ravish them and do with them what seems good to you," said the host to the crowd of men, "but against this man do not do so vile a thing." The master "seized his concubine, and put her out to them; and they all knew her, and abused her all night until the morning" (Judg. 19:24–25). At dawn, the men let her go, and she fell down at the door of the host's house, where she died.

Such unspeakable violence is possible only in a culture in which women have been so objectified as to be considered less than human. The roots of the dehumanization go deep.

The creation story itself has been misused to justify the subjugation of women. The mutuality and partnership between

Adam and Eve in Genesis 1 has given way to a theological preference for the subordination in Genesis 2.

Women have come to be viewed as an afterthought, a secondary and inferior version of the species. Adam's judgment in the garden goes largely unquestioned, while Eve has been saddled with having given evil a toehold in the world. Such a view has served through the centuries to equate women with temptation, deception, and manipulation.

With such a view predominating in Hebrew culture, it is no surprise that patriarchal assumptions carry over into the New Testament. We don't find the brutal subjugation that seems to be a foundational pattern in the Old Testament, but we are still faced with a biblical record whose primary players are men.

The narrative revolves around Jesus, the circle of twelve men closest to him, then Paul and the other missionaries who established the early church. The chronicle of events is authored by men who offer us a Word that is at the same time inspired by God and limited by the perspective of the vessels of that Word.

Women continue to be essentially negligible, uncounted in the census or in situations such as when Jesus fed the crowd with seven loaves and a few fish: "Those who ate were four thousand men, besides women and children" (Matt. 15:38). And words addressed to particular conflicts in specific historical situations, especially Paul's words about the role of women in a few of the early churches, have been distorted into broad theological principles about the second-class status of women in the faith.

The clear leadership of women in the early church and Paul's support of them is overlooked. His word about women's submission to their husbands is wrenched from its context of mutuality. It is interesting that those who would quote these passages from the Epistles to justify male domination of women would not quote adjacent passages to condone slavery. To do either is to distort the message of liberation that is at the heart of the Scriptures.

Some would still saddle us with narrow images of Eve as temptress and Mary as puritanical paradox of virginity and motherhood. But the women of the Bible are much more than the stereotypes.

The first proponents of civil disobedience in the biblical record were the Hebrew midwives Shiphrah and Puah, who disobeyed Pharaoh's order to kill the newborn sons of Israel. Sarah trusted God for a child and a home, and Miriam, a prophetess, sang a song of victory. Deborah was a judge over Israel; Esther was a queen who pleaded for and saved the lives of her people, while Vashti refused to be paraded around as a sex object for the pleasure of the king and his friends. Priscilla was an articulate church leader who risked her life to save Paul's.

And long before the wilderness beckoned or the lame were deposited at Jesus' feet or the cross was in sight, Mary knew what was coming. It was the women, Mary and Elizabeth, who understood first, while Joseph tried to distance himself from the scandal and Zechariah was struck silent for his unbelief.

By the night of Jesus' birth, with the truth fully revealed to him, Joseph had accepted his supporting role. The shepherds and the kings were mere spectators. At the heart of the drama was a woman—a woman who had heard God's call and given her life to the awesome and frightening miracle chosen for her.

It was Mary who had seen and proclaimed a world where the poor were exalted and the hungry were fed. And she began to feel stirrings of her own liberation from the painful realities of being Jewish, poor, and female.

Those oppressions by race, class, and sex divided the world long before and are still the fundamental divisions today. But the Scriptures offer us a word of promise: "For as many of you as were baptized into Christ have put on Christ. There is neither Jew nor Greek, there is neither slave nor free, there is neither male nor female; for you are all one in Christ Jesus" (Gal. 3:27–28).

The passage was a baptismal formula in the early church. It

was offered as a proclamation that the convert to Christ was being initiated into a new social order in which there was no place for divisions based on race, class, or sex.

Each pair of attributes in the verse implied an assumed "superior" and an "inferior." The apostle Paul often gave exhortation to correct the Jews' perception that they were more faithful than the Gentiles; it was clearly better to be free than a slave; and Jewish males gave regular thanks in a traditional Jewish prayer for not being born female. The passage holds the kernel of equality and unity.

But there is much more for us as women to celebrate in our faith history. Women were not only the most significant people at the beginning of Jesus' life but also the ones who stayed closest to him in his death. While the disciples huddled in fear during events surrounding the Crucifixion, the women kept vigil at the cross.

And they were the first witnesses to the risen Christ. They carried the news to the disciples. The revelation of the Resurrection to Mary Magdalene and the others was particularly astounding in a society in which the testimony of women was considered unreliable and inadmissible in court.

Throughout his life, Jesus' response to women was one of compassion and inclusion, a rare posture in his day. He was not afraid to be seen in public with the most marginalized "sinners"—prostitutes, adultresses, and a woman who had been "unclean" for many years with a flow of blood. He revealed himself as the Messiah to the Samaritan woman at the well, invited Mary of Bethany to sit with him and learn, welcomed Mary Magdalene into his circle of friends, and received an anointing of rich ointment before his death, rebuking his disciples for criticizing the woman who lavished such care on him.

But Jesus received much more. Healing began for my friend, the victim of incest, one morning at the Communion table. As the bread was consecrated, the words "This is my body broken for you; eat this, and remember" opened the floodgate of memories that started her on the path.

She began to see that shame was not the same as guilt, that she had nothing to be forgiven for regarding the violations of her body. And she knew that the broken body being offered to her—the one that had been stripped and beaten—had carried her pain to the cross.

One Easter morning another friend shared with me a nightmare she had had the night before. In the dream she was on a stage. In one corner she was raped, then thrown to another corner and raped again. The violations happened repeatedly, and she woke up sobbing and fearful. She felt deep reassurance when she identified what the dream was about. She was experiencing the stations of the cross.

The horror began to melt as she understood that Jesus too was a victim in her rape two years earlier. She felt Jesus' bearing of her suffering in a way she never had before. Through the scars, Resurrection was breaking through.

As women, we have this gift of vulnerability and strength to offer the world. Despite the pain and uncertainty, this can also be a marvelous time to be a woman.

There is much to learn about ourselves, much support we can offer one another. And this support will be the basis of political change that can move us toward a society in which both women and men participate equally and with freedom from prescribed roles; where singleness can be celebrated as a life choice; where the future is protected by making the shared care of children a priority.

It is too easy these days for people to talk about the disintegration of the family and moral values and pin the blame on the changing role of women. Mobility, technology, materialism, alienation from authority structures, and many other factors have set the tone of the times. We must forge an alternative that provides stability for the family as well as freedom for all its members, or we can expect the society to heed our conservative brothers and sisters and retrench itself in old patterns that limit women.

New understandings and creativity are being infused into the society as women assume responsibility in areas which we have previously avoided or been shut out of. Part-time vocations, flexible work hours, and creative care of children are opening new possibilities and must be pursued further as we also work for economic justice for women. Relationships and communities of faith based on mutuality are crucial in these times.

So is recovering our history. Faced with such overwhelming evidence of our assumed inferiority in our faith tradition, we need to find creative ways to see the good news behind the hurt and pain.

We can start by recovering God's original intention for humanity. God's plan, recorded in Genesis 1, included partnership between man and woman. Subjugation was part of the Fall, part of the arrangement created by sin (Gen. 3:16).

The creation narrative makes plain that we were created "in the image of God . . . male and female" (Gen. 1:27). We women bear the mark of God, too. It is rather astounding that God who comes to us as rock and refuge and fortress and shepherd and light is banned in most of our churches from coming in any female guise. The biblical images of God as a mother who nurses Israel and a mother hen gathering her brood are rarely appealed to in most churches.

Reaction against pagan fertility goddesses centuries ago set the stage for a rejection of God as Mother. Until we affirm that the creative principle is both male and female, that women as well as men share in the image of God, we limit not only women but also God.

As we look toward our future, we must look to the past as well, at the women who, against all odds, powerfully contributed to history. We must also write the stories like Bathsheba's into the pages of faith history, receiving an invitation to understand our own pain through theirs and to stand in solidarity with women past and present.

Perhaps most important, with the knowledge that other women have gone courageously before us, we can refuse to be the victims of history and claim our right to be its shapers. The record of faith is not yet closed. It is being constantly written by people who attempt to live their lives in faithfulness to God. It is our responsibility to see that our half of the story gets written.

11. The Road to Jalapa

The sun paused for a moment on the edge of the Honduran mountains that ring the tiny town. A broad-leafed banana tree, the centerpiece of the community peace garden, formed a striking silhouette against the bright colors of the sky. A pig wandered through the market, now empty, where a few hours earlier onions were spread out over the ground and fresh rolls sold for pennies a bag.

From the church tower next to the garden, a bell rang loudly, and the voices of children giving glory to Mary drifted out of the church's windows. A rooster crowed—they crow at all times of the day and night here—and a few dogs barked as the sun became half a disk on the western horizon.

Someone who had visited this tiny corner of the earth before me told me that Jalapa is "at the end of the world." It was meant as a compliment to the dusty, little Nicaraguan town that exudes character and warmth to the peaceful stranger who comes to its isolated streets.

There is one telephone in Jalapa (it works most of the time), and transportation is mostly by foot, horse, or oxcart. Time seems to hide itself here. The community is called together to the church or the town's park by a sound truck that roams the streets announcing the day's events: a town meeting, a children's rally, a funeral.

When the sun finally slips behind the mountains, stars pop out by the millions in Jalapa's sky. At night one can occasionally hear the call of a child, the clopping of a horse down a dusty street, or, if you're in the right part of town, the seemingly misplaced North American rock music filtering out of Sandra's Place. A report of gunfire now and then from the mountains reminds the visitor that all is not at peace in Jalapa.

Jalapa may seem like the end of the world to a foreigner's eye, but it is the center of the world for the people of the town and the surrounding valley, the agricultural hub of northern Nicaragua. Ironically, by virtue of its isolation, Jalapa has become the focus of attention from unwelcome intruders.

The story of Jalapa begins at the start of the century, when the U.S. government forced out Nicaragua's president and established a puppet regime, safeguarding the interests of U.S. mining and fruit companies, as well as ensuring Nicaragua's strategic importance for U.S. military campaigns. To enforce U.S. control, the marines occupied the country from 1911 to 1933.

In the late 1920s and early 1930s, a small man emerged with great prominence among the people of Nicaragua, a beloved leader committed to improving the plight of the poor, particularly through literacy training. His name was Augusto César Sandino. He was a nationalist determined to free his people from the iron grip of U.S. imperialism, fighting the marines until President Franklin D. Roosevelt finally withdrew them.

Before the marines departed, however, the United States established a National Guard in Nicaragua, and the marines handpicked Anastasio Somoza García to head it. In February 1934, after sharing dinner at Somoza's home, Sandino was murdered on his way out by Somoza's men, an action that had been cleared with the U.S. ambassador.

Thus began the Somoza dynasty, one of the most brutal in history. Inheriting the throne in 1967, Anastasio Somoza Debayle, the third and last Somoza to rule Nicaragua, created a country of extreme poverty while amassing a personal fortune worth half a billion dollars. His holdings included half of the arable land of Nicaragua and 40 percent of its industry. He cleared the way for U.S. companies to appropriate Nicaragua's land and exploit its labor.

Nicaraguans have not forgotten the days of that reign. A drive through the countryside takes one to infamous points of Somoza history: the buildings where people were tortured, the hill where Somoza took people to massacre them, the mass grave by the lake where 200 bodies were discovered, the former Boy Scout headquarters high on a hill that Somoza used as a base from which to bomb and nearly destroy the city of Masaya, the town where National Guardsmen roped a grandmother onto the front of their truck so that no one would try to shoot at them.

For years the reign of brutality and terror backed by U.S. power and money felt unshakable. But as reprisals against the opposition grew more barbaric and systematic, the opposition grew as well. Finally, in July 1979, the king was dethroned. The triumph came through an armed struggle as well as a strong nonviolent campaign that included marches, general strikes, and a common tactic of constructing barriers to stop the advance of the National Guard by piling up "Somoza bricks"; Somoza owned the factory that made the bricks and sold them at exorbitant prices to the people to pave their roads.

Sandino's spirit had reemerged to bring Somoza's downfall. The peasant leader's nationalist philosophy became the foundation of the revolution that challenged Somoza's power, and the broad-based front—composed of groups of peasants, workers, women, and students—was named in his honor: the Sandinista Front for National Liberation.

Among the front's supporters was the grass-roots Catholic church. In the wake of Vatican II and their bishops' "preferential option for the poor," many Catholics became ardent participants in the liberation struggle.

U.S. president Jimmy Carter's foreign policy of concern for human rights contributed to a climate that helped topple Somoza, but it did not erase decades of U.S. collaboration with the terrorist regime. The fall of Somoza was widely viewed in Washington as a serious blow to U.S. hegemony in Central America.

As they assumed power in Nicaragua, the Sandinistas reversed the decades-long priority of catering to the appetites of a small elite and exhibited a deep commitment to improving life for the country's majority. They made vast strides in health care, bringing a rapid drop in infant mortality and virtually eradicating the plague of polio from Nicaragua. They built parks and opened up theaters and galleries, formerly patronized only by Somoza and his friends, for community projects.

Perhaps their greatest accomplishment, in keeping with the spirit of Sandino, was a major literacy campaign—called by Nicaraguans "the second victory." From Nicaragua's cities 100,000 young students spread out through the countryside, where they lived with campesino families and taught them to read. In the six months following the Sandinista victory, illiteracy plummeted from 58 percent to 12 percent.

There was a great deal of palpable hope in the country. People lived free of the fear that marked the Somoza years, and everyone knew—some people, for the first time—that there was food for them to eat and a chance for a bright future for their children.

But there were problems, too. As in every revolutionary situation, there were many strong and varying opinions about the shape of the country's future. The Sandinistas' inheritance of a bankrupt economy and a $1.5 billion national debt posed a major challenge. And their own inexperience and insensitivity led to early conflicts with the minority Miskito Indian population.

But perhaps the greatest challenge was what to do with the National Guard. Unlike most revolutions, this one carried out no mass reprisals or executions. In a gesture of good will, the new government released 3,000 members of the National Guard; others were put on trial and given prison sentences if found guilty.

The Sandinistas' commitment from the beginning was to reintegrate these men back into the society, and their efforts received commendation from the Red Cross and international human rights groups. A plaque on the outside wall of a prison-farm dormitory states, "The past is behind us; we speak of the future."

I often wonder how the Sandinistas feel now about their generous gesture to free a large segment of the National Guard. That decision, probably more than any other, set the course of their future.

Most of the National Guard members fled to the border area in Honduras. The United States, like a bully who had lost a prize and saw an opportunity to take it back, capitalized on the situation. Channeling strategy and equipment and vast sums of money their way, the U.S. transformed the ragtag troops into a force that could pose a formidable threat to the Sandinista government. Using the same methods of terror they had employed under Somoza, the counterrevolutionaries, or contras, launched raids into Nicaragua.

The war in Nicaragua also required a propaganda war at home. The contras were "freedom fighters"—the "equivalent of our founding fathers," who were valiantly fighting to free their people from the "totalitarian dungeon" that was Nicaragua under the Sandinistas, according to President Ronald Reagan and his administration. But the people of Nicaragua were experiencing a far different reality.

Located just six kilometers from the border on a peninsula of land that juts into Honduras, Jalapa was an ideal early target for the contras in their effort to capture a town and set up an independent territory with a provisional government. Contra activity began in Jalapa in March 1982. The first evidence: numbers of people found beheaded outside their homes.

By December 1983, when I was there, four major attempts to take Jalapa had been launched; all had failed. Bands of contra marauders were roaming the hills spreading terror, kept relatively comfortable in their state-of-the-art camping gear supplied by the CIA. Unable to prevail militarily, the contras' slogan at that time was, "We cannot win, but we can kill."

It was a very long road that had brought me to tiny, isolated Jalapa. My first step on the path was taken almost four years before, in March 1980.

I will never forget the shock and grief on Jim's face the afternoon he came to tell me that Archbishop Oscar Romero of El Salvador had just been assassinated. Romero had been celebrating Mass at the funeral of a friend, in the small chapel of the hospital where he ministered to the cancer-ridden poor. As he raised the chalice, proclaiming that it was Christ's blood shed for the salvation of his people, a gunman stepped forward and fired.

I soon learned that Romero was only the most visible of countless victims of the military's stranglehold on El Salvador. The killings were occurring at the rate of ten or eleven a day, and "I'm happy you've lived to see another day" became a common morning greeting among the country's peasants. Thousands of people packed into San Salvador's cathedral each Sunday to hear the beloved archbishop preach a word of hope in a time of terror.

Romero had let no victim of the military's brutal repression go unhonored. He closed each sermon with a litany of the dead, reading names and circumstances of those who had been killed the previous week. At such readings, it is a custom in Latin America for people to shout "¡Presente!" after each name, affirming the presence of those who have died in the cause for which they still struggle.

Among his last words—at the conclusion of his final sermon—Romero offered a defiant challenge to the troops of the National Guard, the army, and the police: "I beseech you, I beg you, I command you in the name of God: Stop the repression!"

It was no surprise that Romero did not live long after boldly uttering those words. The target of frequent threats on his life, Romero was prepared to face his own death, stating a few days before he was assassinated: "If I am killed, I will rise again in the people of El Salvador."

The injustice that Romero denounced and the violence that claimed his life took root in El Salvador a century before. In March 1880, a coffee boom suppressed communal land ownership and paved the way for the concentration of ownership among a small elite. Rural peasants were evicted from their land and put to work on large estates. A police force was created to enforce the reorganization.

A hundred years later, 2 percent of El Salvador's population owned 60 percent of its land, and 90 percent of El Salvador's people earned less than $100 per year. The country was suffering the greatest repression in Latin America, according to observers—worse even than at the height of General Augusto Pinochet's terror in Chile in 1973. Systematic and premeditated brutality was aimed at eliminating popular leadership and terrorizing the entire society with fear of murder, mutilation, rape, and torture. Among the victims that year were four U.S. missionary women.

And the United States just kept throwing military aid El Salvador's way. Despite Romero's pleas against the aid before his death and overwhelming evidence of widespread repression by the military, the U.S. government—fearing "another Nicaragua"—stayed its long course of throwing military solutions at political and economic problems.

I had missed out by a few years on the political education about America that I might have gotten from Vietnam. But Central America became my Vietnam, a window through which I saw U.S. policies and priorities at work. It was a disturbing view.

The United States initiated Guatemala's most recent chapter in a long, dark history of repression in 1954. Democratically elected Guatemalan president Jacobo Arbenz had begun a radical land-reform program, targeting the U.S.-owned United Fruit Company (now United Brands), which had vast landholdings and dominated Guatemala's agricultural system.

Branding Arbenz a Communist, United Fruit executives enlisted the help of the CIA to engineer and finance a right-wing coup. It was CIA aircraft that bombed Guatemala City and a U.S. embassy plane that flew in Colonel Castillo Armas, the new military dictator. Armas began his reign with a bloodbath that left 8,000 campesinos dead in the first two months.

Knowing their interests would be protected, almost 200 U.S.-based multinational corporations flocked to Guatemala after the coup. They joined the elite landholding minority in consigning Guatemala's indigenous majority to a desperate life, with 81 percent of their children suffering from malnutrition and more than half dying before they reached the age of five.

The injustice was brutally enforced by Guatemalan police trained by U.S. personnel. As in El Salvador, an insurgency developed in response, and its violence has also claimed civilian victims. But by far the vast majority of the repression issues from the government side of the conflict.

Impoverished Honduras has also been drawn into the U.S. web of military arrogance. Palmerola Air Base, just north of Honduras's capital of Tegucigalpa, has become the center of U.S. military operations in the region—and the town at its gates a hell for young women kidnapped from all over the country and sold into prostitution to service U.S. soldiers.

U.S. militarization of Honduras and support for the contras based there has been at the expense of developing democratic institutions and has led to internal protest and strife. The Honduran military has begun to respond in fashion similar to its neighbors—torture, arbitrary imprisonment, and disappearances of people are on the increase.

Central America is a picturesque land of kaleidoscopic colors—lush green rain forests and deep blue lakes, dark volcanoes and bright Indian weavings. But today, red seems to predominate. It is in the eyes of those who see only Communism behind the struggles of the people for survival. It is in the streets, in the blood of the peasants whose lives have been lost in the struggle for justice.

It is not hard to understand why a courageous and faithful voice in the midst of the madness—the voice of Archbishop Oscar Romero—became the articulation of the cries of a whole region. When that voice was silenced, many of us in the United States began to find our own voices.

On Easter eve of 1980, twelve days after Archbishop Romero

was killed, a group of people gathered in Lafayette Park in Washington, D.C., across from the White House. Spotlights shone brightly on the imposing building on Pennsylvania Avenue. Across the street in the park, soft light glowed from thin candles clutched by those of us clustered there. It illuminated only simple faith on worn and somber faces, many of them from El Salvador. El Salvador—"The Savior"—a land being crucified.

Tragic testimonies were offered—about an eight-year-old boy who saved his own life by covering himself with the corpses of his family during a massacre; about babies being tossed into the air and caught on the points of soldiers' bayonets. I remembered a picture of a sobbing mother picking through skulls at a mass grave, hoping not to find her disappeared son's: "This one cannot be him—he had a gold filling in that tooth."

We shared the Eucharist, sang hymns, offered prayers in Spanish and English. And then a litany of the sorrow of a decade was read. For each year, the names of Christians killed in El Salvador were raised, a brief description of their death given, the name repeated, and a response from the people offered.

The sorrow took its toll as the list wore on, and the responses became more hushed. Then, a final name was offered.

"Archbishop Oscar Romero. Killed just twelve days ago in San Salvador, El Salvador, while celebrating the Mass. Archbishop Oscar Romero."

"¡Presente!" The people thundered their response amid many tears. But across the street, in the imposing building that shared responsibility for the suffering, no one seemed to be listening. That night I felt that my life had just changed again. I knew that the death of a man I had never met was somehow going to transform my life's journey and my faith.

The people of Central America are walking through a river of grief that empties into an ocean of martyrs. But still they courageously persist in their efforts to transform their lands. The violent repression, rather than creating a paralyzing fear, has thrust them back into the arms of God and the Bible's promises of justice.

The plan of control by terror is simply not working. The formulas of repression have not accounted for faith, which Central America's Christians are proving again and again cannot be killed by even the most sophisticated designs of systematic murder.

All over Central America, Christians have been coming together in small groupings known as base Christian communities, joining the movement that has swept through Latin America. Sprinkled like leaven throughout the continent, these communities offer hope and empowerment as people come together to pray and reflect on the Word of God for their situation. By their outspoken courage and undaunted pursuit of justice, they have brought even greater repression upon themselves.

I felt a great deal of despair as I learned more and more about the suffering in Central America and my country's role in it. For decades we have controlled the region's resources and treated its people like beggars in our backyard.

In the middle of the last century, U.S. mercenary William Walker conquered Nicaragua and declared himself its president in the name of "Manifest Destiny" and on behalf of railroad robber-baron Cornelius Vanderbilt. Not much has changed in 130 years—except that Manifest Destiny has evolved into "our sphere of influence."

I was disturbed at all the hypocritical rhetoric that placed America at the top of the list of the world's great and righteous nations. It seemed plain that if our country would indeed choose to put its moral weight on the side of justice, a great deal would change in the world. Instead we touted our freedom—and our commitment to helping others gain or keep theirs—while depriving the very people we were supposedly protecting of the right to land, health, and even life.

But the people of Central America themselves drew me back

to hope. Theirs was invincible in the midst of the most tragic of circumstances. They were daily living Christ's Passion, but their eyes seemed always on Resurrection. They were deepening my conversion to Christ.

I was particularly touched by the poetry of Julia Esquivel. The editor of the ecumenical Guatemalan church magazine *Diálogo*, Esquivel had discovered her name on a death list and went into exile outside the country. I was gripped by her poem "We Dream Awake."

> . . . What won't let us sleep
> what won't let us rest
> what won't stop pulsing away
> here within
> is the silent warm weeping
> of the Indian women without their husbands,
> the tragic gaze of the children
> engraved deep down in our memory. . . .
>
> Six gone just now . . .
> and nine in Rabinal,
> And two and two and two,
> and ten and a hundred and a thousand . . .
> a whole army
> witness to our pain,
> to our fear,
> to our courage,
> to our hope!
>
> What won't let us sleep
> is that we've been threatened with Resurrection!
> Because every evening,
> tired by now from the endless
> counting since 1954,
> we still go on loving life
> and we won't accept their death.
>
> We've been threatened with Resurrection
> because we've touched their lifeless bodies
> and their souls have penetrated our own,
> now doubly strengthened.

Because in this Marathon of hope,
there are always replacements
to carry on the strength
until we reach that goal
beyond death. . . .

Be with us in this vigil
and you'll learn what it means to dream
you'll know then
how wonderful it is
to live threatened with Resurrection!

To dream, awake
to watch, asleep
to live, dying
and to know yourself already
Risen!

It was a privilege to meet briefly this small and humble, yet so courageous, woman. She told me a story that I would never forget—about soldiers cutting out the fetus from a pregnant friend, then putting her decapitated husband's head in her womb and sewing it back up. "We struggle against the devil incarnate," she said. "But we are people of profound faith."

A few months later I had the honor of having Julia to my home for breakfast. We were both trying to do better with the other's language, so she spoke to me in English and I to her in Spanish, promising to correct one another's mistakes. She began, "You are our voice. We cannot speak for ourselves. We have been silenced. You must keep writing. Do you plan to visit Guatemala?"

I told her about my deep desire to go to Central America but also about the warnings I had been given about going. "I wish I had been smarter about signing my name to so many articles against the repression there," I told her.

She smiled and said, "Yes, I made the same mistake."

As we talked, black smoke suddenly began pouring out of the toaster. I pulled out two pieces of bread, burnt to a char.

"Perfect!" she exclaimed with a smile that filled her face with beautiful wrinkles. "It's exactly the way I like it." I apologized, declaring that she didn't have to eat burnt toast just to make me feel better about my competence as a breakfast cook.

"No," she explained, "it is good for my throat." And just to prove it, she pulled out a small box filled with carbon tablets that she took for a bronchial condition.

She hardly allowed me the time to tell her how deeply my life had been changed by her courage and faith and that of her people. She instead wanted me to know, "When I heard of your community, I could not believe it. Not in this country. It gives me such hope. I had to come and see it."

I will never forget that morning. There was something so poignant about Julia's kindness and faith, about her being able to suffer so much and still make the most of a burnt piece of toast.

In those days it was easy for me to feel obsessed with anger and shame about America's doings in Central America, to walk around as if I alone were carrying the burden of the tragedy there. Julia lifted the burden and invited me back not only to hope but also to joy and gratitude.

I never really let go of my fervent hope to go to Central America. In December 1982 Jim and I were invited by Nicaragua's Evangelical Committee for Aid and Development (CEPAD) to be part of a delegation of U.S. evangelical church leaders and journalists to that country.

Just days before we left for Nicaragua, *Newsweek* magazine exposed the fact that a $19 million covert operation was being carried out by the CIA against the Nicaraguan government. At that time, *contra* was not yet a household word.

During our ten days in Nicaragua, we met with evangelical pastors, students, and U.S. missionaries who had fled from the contras in the border area; the U.S. ambassador, a member of the Catholic hierarchy, and an editor of the opposition newspaper *La Prensa*; a Miskito leader and Sandinista officials, including President Daniel Ortega and Foreign Minister Miguel D'Escoto. We saw evidence both of the tremendous strides of the revolution and its mistakes as well as of its broad and deep support among the people. We also saw traces of fear—fear that the United States was going to rob Nicaragua of its newly won and precious freedom.

Less than a year later, the United States invaded the small nation of Grenada. Friends in Nicaragua alerted us of the sweeping fear in their country that Nicaragua might be next. U.S. rhetoric, rapidly escalating support for the contras, and an unswerving determination on the part of the Reagan administration to destabilize Nicaragua gave our friends' fears a solid foundation.

That same month, October 1983, a number of U.S. people of faith concerned about Nicaragua gathered for a retreat in Philadelphia. Some had been on a different delegation several months before which had arrived at Nicaragua's northern border just after a contra attack. People in the area believed that the attack had been halted because of the presence of the U.S. citizens. With that in mind, we had gathered to talk about a grass-roots effort that would maintain a permanent, prayerful, nonviolent presence on the border between Nicaragua and Honduras.

As Nicaraguan casualties had mounted and U.S. policy stayed its course despite the unpopularity of the contra war among the American people, the time seemed right for a permanent confrontation between U.S. military power and the power of conscience—a confrontation led by Americans willing to share in the suffering that was being inflicted on others in our name.

What was born that weekend was Witness for Peace. We imagined teams from all over the United States taking two-week intervals at the border, engaging in times of prayerful witness as well as in reconstruction work, repairing some of the damage our government was inflicting on Nicaragua.

With the help of a more permanent long-term team, they would document atrocities committed by the contras and gather eyewitness testimonies. The returning teams would bring back a regular flow of information to the United States, speaking publicly about what they had seen and working to counter the propaganda war and to change U.S. policy.

We saw Witness for Peace as an act of intercession on behalf of the people of Nicaragua, offered with bodies as well as voices, and as an act of confession for the sins of our nation. And we hoped that its presence would provide some practical protection for our sisters and brothers on the border.

There was a great deal of excitement among us that weekend as we saw a dream take concrete form. We had no idea whether what we were hatching would be received as good news by anyone else. But we felt clear that it was our responsibility—in response to the fervent plea of Nicaraguan Christians—to offer a type of U.S. intervention in Nicaragua with an entirely different spirit and intent from the Reagan administration's aggression.

We were later astounded by the response when we announced our plan. Witness for Peace immediately received support from church denominations, religious orders, and peace organizations. When he heard about it, one Mennonite professor described Witness for Peace as "one of the most kingdomlike initiatives since the Underground Railroad." We were tremendously encouraged.

When it came time to put together the first two-week team to go to Nicaragua in December, several of us felt that if we were going to be sending people into war zones, we should take that risk ourselves first. Both Jim and I signed up for the first team.

We didn't know then that, several years later, Witness for Peace would still be going strong, with almost 4,000 people in five years sent to Nicaragua and almost always a backlog of teams ready to go. Nor could we have known that, at a time when a U.S. invasion felt imminent, one of our teams, armed only with a Bible and a bullhorn, would go out in a small fishing boat into Corinto Harbor—where earlier the U.S. had violated international law by mining its waters—to try to turn away a U.S. naval frigate that was trespassing in Nicaraguan territorial waters. Nor did we have any idea that another Witness for Peace team would be kidnapped by the contras on the San Juan River on Nicaragua's Costa Rican border. We simply had a dream and a plan and a commitment to give ourselves to it, whatever might come. We were headed for Jalapa.

We were scheduled to leave on Friday, December 2, 1983. But the night before, we received word, with apologies, that our flight to Managua, Nicaragua's capital, had been canceled. As it turned out, President Daniel Ortega had to fly to Ecuador for some high-level talks. And since Nicaragua has no air force—and no presidential "Air Force 1" to carry him to such meetings—he and his entourage had to borrow one of Nicaragua's two commercial airliners. The irony didn't escape us that this is the nation that is supposedly a military threat to the entire free world.

An extra flight was scheduled on Sunday to accommodate Friday's passengers, and we arrived in Nicaragua two days late—on the day that the Sandinistas set a date for elections in 1985, declared a general amnesty for all contras outside Nicaragua, and set free 300 Miskito Indians who had been imprisoned in Managua following the killing of Sandinista soldiers by Miskitos two years earlier.

We spent Monday in Managua with friends at CEPAD. On Tuesday we arose well before dawn to begin our journey to Jalapa in a bus belonging to the Baptist College in Managua. Nicaraguan Christians were our hosts and contacts throughout our journey, and we steadfastly maintained political independence both from the Sandinistas and any partisan U.S. politics. Faith in a God of justice and opposition to the contra war united us.

We stopped for breakfast in the town of Estelí, then pushed north toward Jalapa and got as far as Ocotal, a town thirteen kilometers from the Honduran border and about sixty kilometers west of Jalapa. Local military officials there told us that we could not continue on: The contras had taken over a section of the road to Jalapa, and combat was taking place in an effort to reclaim it.

The town of Ocotal was under alert, and we held our first vigil there that night. We began with a procession through three of Ocotal's barrios, and by the time we arrived at the town park, we had with us a crowd of 400 people.

In the park we had an ecumenical service of song and prayer. David Gracie, an Episcopal chaplain at Temple University in Philadelphia, unfurled an American flag that had been given to us by a supportive U.S. congresswoman. He talked about his shame at what the U.S. government was doing against Nicaragua and explained that we were there to remember and uphold the best of the American tradition, which claims a commitment to justice and freedom.

We spent that night at the Baptist church, which we shared with refugees who had fled their scattered mountain homes during attacks by the contras. Their presence, as well as the deep trenches dug in front of Ocotal's homes, reminded us that we were in a war zone. We heard gunshots that night and slept close to our "crash packs," small bags packed with our most essential items—passports, flashlights, water purification tablets, and antimalarial medication—that were easy to grab in case we needed to flee on sudden notice.

I remember feeling very vulnerable that night, knowing that we were making our way through a war zone armed only with gifts and prayers. I had with me letters from members of my community and family, including a rainbow painted by my young nephews and labeled "for God's promise of safekeeping."

I felt assurance in knowing that people in many places were praying for us. Members of a sister community had given us a candle to light every night, as a reminder that identical candles were burning for us at their community and at the center of a continuous prayer vigil at Sojourners. A member of our worshiping congregation at Sojourners had given me a beautiful African necklace made of myrrh to carry to Jalapa as a reminder of her prayers and then give away. And the children back home had hung a map in the kitchen of one of our community households and were tracing our route as we traveled. I had warm thoughts of many people that night in a place very far from home.

By morning, the water that had been turned off throughout the town the night before because of a severe shortage was not yet back on. We awoke early with Jalapa on our minds and washed our faces in a rain barrel outside the church. The refugee women already had firewood in their dome-shaped clay oven and were slapping out tortillas. They had fled with little more than the clothes on their backs, but they offered us coffee and tortillas, one of many examples we found in Nicaragua of profound graciousness and generosity in spite of extremely meager resources.

The road to Jalapa was narrow, rutted, and steep, with the first leg through dense underbrush. It was easy to see why so many vehicles had been ambushed along this way. We got word at a military checkpoint of an expected contra attack and pushed on rapidly through clouds of dust.

An open truck carrying some soldiers and a family caught up behind us. I could see a mother holding an infant drinking from a bottle, and I thought how hard the dust must have been on them and how vulnerable they were. For us, this was a journey into a war zone; for them, it was home.

From time to time we saw groups of young soldiers along the road, carrying their day's rations of rice and red beans. The youngest of the soldiers in the militia, we learned, was eleven—the oldest eighty.

It was a great sadness to see how militarized this society had become in order to protect itself from the U.S.-backed contras, even putting guns into the hands of children. And money that earlier would have been poured into health care and literacy was being diverted to defense.

But at least one thing was certain: If indeed the Sandinistas were as unpopular and totalitarian as my government proclaimed them to be, they certainly would not have armed the population so broadly. In the truly repressive countries, such as El Salvador and Guatemala, the governments were trying to keep arms from the people. Here in the frontier it was very clear: The people were mobilized to protect their revolution.

About halfway to Jalapa the road opened out onto expansive fields of coffee, beans, and rice. Ambush was less likely on this part of the journey, but the Honduran mountains were visible, and the road within mortar range.

Women pounded laundry against rocks in the streams that flowed over the road and that sometimes made passage difficult for the bus, as did the cows that wandered in our path. Scattered on both sides of us were small homes with orange clay-tile roofs. We saw an occasional homemade cross along the route, marking the site where someone had been killed.

A large cemetery marked the edge of Jalapa, row upon row of homemade crosses. A sign at the entrance to the town listed the names of Jalapa's martyrs fallen in battle or by contra attack. We offered a prayer of gratitude for our safe arrival.

That evening, as a light rain fell, we held our first vigil in Jalapa in the town's park. People from the town joined us, and one woman gave us each a gift: a warm piece of cooked squash with a sweet topping, served on broad leaves.

When we explained that we were the first of many teams that would continue to come to Jalapa as long as the war went on, one of the townspeople exclaimed, "This is the kind of U.S. invasion we like!" Their prayers in this war zone were marked with gratitude. One mother prayed, "Thank you for the rice, the beans, the coffee. Protect the harvest. Protect the children." And one of our team members added, "May there be a harvest of peace."

Activity began in Jalapa as soon as the sun appeared. Our first morning there, a bright green parrot hanging upside down from a branch of a dead tree argued in Spanish with a radio for dominance of the dawn.

We began our first day by asking the proprietor of our *pensión* where we should go for shelter in case of an attack on the town. She nodded toward boards covering a large hole in her porch floor. Three of her children were swinging over the boards in a hammock, laughing and playing with dolls.

More than 600 families in the area had been made refugees by the contra raids. Some had temporarily resettled in old tobacco barns; others were building more permanent shelter in places like La Estancia, a resettlement community a few kilometers from Jalapa.

At La Estancia we met fifteen-day-old Martita and her mother, who had fled on foot from their home in the mountains just days before delivering her beautiful daughter. Her husband was fighting with the militia and had not yet seen his baby. Another mother told how armed contras had come to her home and killed all her sons.

It has been said that to understand Nicaragua, one must talk with the mothers. Through their tears of grief we found the most profound understanding. Some of them had established the Gallery of the Heroes and Martyrs, a house across from the church in Jalapa that displayed pictures and stories of their slain children.

One of the mothers asked, "Why should the United States attack us now? Before we had to live like animals. The first thing the new government gave us was not arms but hospitals and a chance to read." Another added, "The rich can still stay here, and the government is giving amnesty to those who fight against it—what other government would do this?" And still another, "We want peace. We don't want blood. But we must defend ourselves."

Mostly they spoke about their children. "It is incomparable suffering for a mother to lose a child," said one. "We feel the loss of a child in our own flesh."

We were in Jalapa during the *Purísima*, the celebration of Mary, and the bond of mother and child was particularly poignant. This festival, accompanied with processions and singing, is as important in Nicaragua as Christmas. It is a celebration, but also a remembrance that Mary bore Jesus and gave him up to death, a Passion with which the mothers of Nicaragua readily identify.

Perhaps the most agonizing of the stories we were told came from a mother who had lived in Teotecacinte, located right on the Honduran border about fifteen kilometers northeast of Jalapa. This loving mother had put one of her daughter's favorite dolls on a small chair in the family's recently dug underground shelter so that if an attack came, the little girl would find some comfort there.

The mother was preparing a meal when she got word of a contra raid. She sent her daughter to the shelter and planned to follow as soon as she had tended to the fire. But the girl thought of her puppy and went off in search of it. When the mother got outside, her daughter was dead. She quickly carried her body to the shelter, and it wasn't until she got inside that she realized that her daughter had been decapitated by a mortar. Like so many of the others, this woman broke into weeping as she finished her story.

We heard unending stories about the atrocities committed by the contras: bodies dismembered, tongues cut out, eyes removed, spikes through limbs, facial skin cut and rolled back over the heads of victims, and gang rapes of women both young and old. It is difficult to write about such things, even more difficult to listen as the stories were related. But it is a hell for the people who must endure the horrors, and it must be told that the U.S. administration that denounced terrorism in so many places was sponsoring such terrorism against the civilians of Nicaragua.

I remembered the plea of one mother: "Please ask your government to stop. If they had any degree of mercy, they would end this war. If they could hear the mothers, then maybe they would stop."

Half of the population of Nicaragua is under fifteen years of age. It seemed that we met most of the children of Jalapa—the exuberant ones and the serious ones, the ones who saw us as a curiosity and gathered around with endless questions, the sad ones who had been made orphans by the war, and the unforgettable little boy with long sticks for crutches who had lost his left leg to a contra land mine.

And there were the very astute and sophisticated ones, like fourteen-year-old Isaac, who, upon hearing of Witness for Peace, decided to form a "peace corps" of Nicaraguan teenagers to go to the United States and pray for peace. He extended an invitation to the children of the United States to come visit Nicaragua: "So that we can express solidarity with one another, let us have an exchange of children for peace." When we asked Isaac what he wants for his children when he has them, he replied, "I want my children not to be marginal."

At the close of our day at La Estancia, we held a Eucharist. The priest began, "I would like to invite the future of the community to come and gather around the table." The children came forward to the simple table which held bread and wine and a brilliant red-and-yellow orchid.

But one child hung back. He was a small thirteen-year-old who had captured our attention throughout our visit, perhaps because he looked so innocent and was carrying an automatic rifle almost as tall as he was. We had asked Agenor earlier how he felt about carrying a gun, and he had answered proudly, "I'm glad that I can protect my family."

Now, when the children were summoned forward, he was like thirteen-year-olds everywhere. He hesitated, not sure whether he was a child or an adult. Finally he came to stand at the edge of the circle of children. As I watched him standing there, looking down at the ground and swinging one foot in the dust, I thought what a terrible weight that gun was for him—a weight put on his back by a belligerent U.S. policy that was robbing parents of their children and children of their childhood.

On Friday morning we got up in the dark to meet a truck carrying workers to the bean fields. December was a peak harvest month in Nicaragua. It was also a time of heightened contra activity, both because it was more difficult for the Nicaraguan people to keep defense forces high when people were needed for the harvest and because abductions and assassinations were much easier when workers were scattered throughout the fields.

Because of the war, only half of the rice crop had gotten planted the year before, and losses between December 1982 and July 1983 amounted to more than $100 million in land, homes, storage barns, and crops. Crops had sometimes been brought in under a rain of bullets.

We headed toward Teotecacinte, site of the worst suffering in the last major contra attack in the Jalapa area. When we had told the proprietor and others at our pensión of our plan, they said repeatedly, *"Peligrosa"* (dangerous), and tried to convince us to stay closer to Jalapa.

At the edge of Teotecacinte, we were told that the bean harvesting had been temporarily halted. A group of teenagers had become separated from their work brigade, and the safety of the twenty-six youths was the preoccupation of the town that morning.

As we spoke, we could hear and see a plane flying over the Honduran mountains just ahead of us. Commercial planes arrived in Nicaragua only three times a week, so the sound of a plane usually signaled a reconnaissance or bomber plane from Honduras and sent an anxious stir through the town.

We held a short vigil as close to the border as we could and then returned to Jalapa. We were relieved to learn later that the lost teenagers had been found unharmed.

Our last night in Jalapa, a young man who worked with the local Sandinista government in the town spoke about the situation in Nicaragua.

It will be a long struggle. Our children and their children will engage in the struggle.

We encounter the question every day that this may be the day of our death. In the long road our people have traversed toward the luminous reality of liberation, many people have been left dead on the road. And many more will be left in the future.

But confronting the power of death every day we also confront the reality of definitive liberation with joy and hope. Our people are full of sadness for the death of their brothers and sisters. But we all hope, because it is the future we are building.

He ended by saying what many other Nicaraguans had told us—that if the United States invaded Nicaragua, the outcome would not be like that in Grenada two months before. The U.S. would have to fight an entire population determined to preserve their revolution: "The people are capable of giving to the last drop of blood."

In the years since, I have often thought back to that young man's words. Like so many others we had met, he had a vision that meant no death was in vain; an understanding that though peace may not come in his lifetime, he was contributing to the struggle that might bring peace to his children or their children.

I have often tried to remember his idealism as the reports out of Nicaragua have worsened over the years. The tremendous mobilization for defense has wreaked havoc on an already-struggling economy, and people have become disillusioned as many basic goods have fallen in short supply. Tightened press censorship, expulsion of priests and diplomats, curtailing of opposition, and states of emergency are increasingly disturbing signs from Nicaragua.

I often wonder what Nicaragua would look like now if the United States had given the Sandinistas a chance to live up to their best ideals. The tragedy is that we will never know. Terrorism and economic embargo from the United States have put constant pressure on Nicaragua to become a fulfillment of U.S. prophecy: a controlled society dependent on the Soviet Union for economic and military support.

To their credit, the Sandinistas have endured more admirably and graciously, in my opinion, than anyone might have been expected to under the total U.S. assault. And I am convinced that, at heart, they have a deep love for their people and a true desire to create a just society.

Before leaving Nicaragua, I remember feeling a twinge of pride that I was mastering the hard theological command that had so dumbfounded Jesus' disciples: "Love your enemies." I had ventured right into the land of America's enemies and offered my friendship.

But of course I had discovered what I had expected to discover—that these so-called enemies of the United States were not my enemies at all. They were, in fact, very loving and forgiving and generous people, with a deep faith in God.

In Nicaragua I eventually discovered the true meaning—and the challenge—of Jesus' command for me. It was Ronald Reagan I could not love—and William Casey, and Caspar Weinberger, and all the others implicated in Nicaragua's suffering. Seeing the victims firsthand had escalated my anger, and I prayed to be as forgiving as the Nicaraguans we met.

On the day that we were to leave Jalapa, the road was again closed, but we were told that it might be open in two hours. That gave me time for one last walk through Jalapa. I headed toward the entrance of the town. Since the day we had arrived in this little out-of-the-way place, I had wanted to walk through its cemetery, perhaps because in Nicaragua death is so prevalent and the sacrifice of those who have given up their lives for freedom is so well remembered and drawn upon for strength.

The sun was just up, and the mist hung low on the simple crosses stuck in the thick grass. The mist brought to mind the image of the "cloud of witnesses," and I felt quite literally surrounded by them in this quiet place. There was an enveloping stillness—and then a giggle. A young girl carrying a water jar appeared, and then another and another behind her.

They were sisters, they explained, with eleven children in their family. "I'll go get the rest," the oldest one said, and she skipped off. They came like a parade, each with a jar, the youngest, a three-year-old, with a small tin can.

There's a well in the center of the cemetery, I learned. And the children begin every day carrying the water the family will need for that day. A well of life in the center of so much death. And before me, the future of the community, which draws life from both the well and the cemetery crosses; which understands the struggle.

My musings were interrupted by the sight of our bus turning the bend by the sign of the martyrs. The road was open, and we were on our way home. I had left the myrrh necklace with María, one of the mothers who ran the gallery of martyrs and the giver of the sweet squash our first night in Jalapa. I was carrying home with me a handmade card from her with a fervent plea for peace in the world.

Because transportation was infrequent on the road, a young mother asked if she could get a ride with us as far as Estelí, where she was going to visit her twelve-year-old son in the hospital. As the bus started up, she looked lovingly at the seven-month-old son on her lap and then asked one member of our team if she would take Ricardo back with her to the United States.

"But wouldn't it be hard for you to be separated from him?" she asked in response.

"Yes, but I will follow," the mother answered. "I will come as soon as I can."

"But there are problems in the United States, too."

Ricardo's mother began to weep softly. "But at least there is no war. Please take him to safety. I don't want him to grow up in a war."

We stopped at a military checkpoint and were told that there was mortar fire on the road ahead of us. It was too late to turn back, and we were instructed to drive as fast as we possibly could to Ocotal. We couldn't imagine how Gonzalo, our driver, could drive any faster on the narrow, winding road, but we took off again in a large cloud of dust.

Ricardo's mother became quite carsick, and one of our team put a comforting arm around her. Another cradled tiny Ricardo while the bus bumped on.

I thought of the words that had most traveled through my thoughts in our time in Jalapa: *fragility* and *vulnerability*. We saw it in the revolution. We saw it in the children.

As we pulled safely into Ocotal and whispered prayers of gratitude, the faces flashed again through my mind: Martita and Isaac and the little boy on homemade crutches, the young ones with guns, the orphans, the laughing children in the cemetery. They are the ones who ask not to be marginal; who ask simply to have a future. We owe them at least that much.

12. No Neutral Ground

She had fashioned for herself a big hairbow out of a discarded plastic bag. The bag swathed her head and came to a knot with two points spread out to form the makeshift bow. She was only four, too shy to pose for a picture at close range. She lives in a shack in Crossroads, where government control and destitution make it impossible for little girls to dream of silk or satin bows.

Her friends can be found all across South Africa. They piece together bits of paper and plastic and string to make kites. They create crude push toys out of fragments of wire stuck through tin cans. They fashion a childhood from the bits and pieces of life that are left to them.

In Crossroads they are fortunate to reach the age of four. Diarrhea, dehydration, and the severe malnutrition known as *kwashiorkor* claim the lives of many children in this squatter camp outside Cape Town. In desperate times, sand is mixed with cornmeal to make a meal stretch further.

At the medical clinic, intake forms for children read "Siblings: alive_____, dead_____." Beyond the camp is a vast graveyard. Graves the size of children are dug in large numbers in ominous expectation.

On the edge of Crossroads is the KTC satellite camp. Entire portions of this camp were recently razed by the government. For weeks the fires raged and the bulldozers ravaged and the children cried. Razor wire now encircles the area, and military blockades control the flow of people in and out.

Razor wire and rifles, petrol bombs and *casspirs* (huge armored personnel carriers), and the whips known as *sjamboks*— all are part of the landscape for the children of apartheid. Childhood ends almost before it begins in black South Africa.

The children raise fists in defiant determination as soon as they are old enough to understand the struggle, an understanding that comes early. By school age they are organizers and participants in school "stay-aways," commemorating and protesting such events as the massacres of children by government forces in Sharpeville in 1960 and Soweto in 1976.

Ask a ten-year-old in Mamelodi, the black township near Pretoria, if he'll see apartheid end in his lifetime. Without hesitation he'll say "yes," and then add thoughtfully, "but maybe toward the end of it."

Then put this question to him: "Do you think your children will grow up without apartheid?"

His answer is clear: "I will see to it."

Their energy has threatened the ruling powers of South Africa, who have targeted them in massive numbers for detention and torture. But there is no quashing that energy, which erupts most powerfully when they join together in a celebratory, defiant mass stomping called *toi-toi*, singing the freedom songs as they sway together, sending energy like a bolt of electricity surging through any crowd.

As they moved in a mighty current down the aisles, young people from the black townships riveted the attention of 3,000 people packed into St. George's Cathedral in Cape Town on March 13, 1988. They had slipped through police roadblocks set up to keep them away during this service of worship.

One worshiper beamed a smile and whispered, "I knew they would get through." The message on their exuberant young faces was, "We are here. And things are going to change."

It was our first day in South Africa. Jim and I had come at the long-standing invitation of Rev. Allan Boesak. For years we had hoped and prayed to come to this land of such pain and promise, but we could not find a way. Then, unexpectedly, a way opened up for us.

Upon our arrival in Cape Town, we received word that we were to meet up with Allan the next day at a rally to launch the newly formed Committee to Defend Democracy. Just two and a half weeks before, on February 24, the South African government effectively banned seventeen organizations that had been leading the struggle against apartheid. Among these were the 2-million-member United Democratic Front and the nation's largest labor federation, the Congress of South African Trade Unions.

Into the breach stepped South Africa's church leaders. On February 29, in an unprecedented display of church unity, 25 church leaders, along with 500 clergy and laity, marched to the Parliament in Cape Town with a petition demanding the restoration of the right of peaceful protest. Their action was met with water cannons and arrests. It triggered a church-state conflict that dominated the attention of the country for weeks and set the stage for a new era in the church's struggle against apartheid.

The leaders quickly formed the Committee to Defend Democracy and planned the rally to launch it for March 13. But within an hour of our receiving word about the rally, we were told that it had been banned, along with the three-day-old organization itself. A worship service at the cathedral for the same hour was scheduled in its place.

Despite government efforts to obstruct communication, word of the service traveled quickly and broadly. People crowded into every available space in the large cathedral—in the aisles, the choir lofts, behind and in front of the pulpit. Outside, the riot police were assembling.

As he preached to the overflowing cathedral, Archbishop Desmond Tutu proclaimed to South Africa's white rulers, "You are not God, you are mortals. It is God whom we worship, and God cannot be mocked. You have already lost. Come and join the winning side!"

Rev. Allan Boesak arose in his bright red-and-black robe and thundered, "The battle is on! But Jesus Christ is Lord!" Preaching from 1 Kings 19, he boldly declared that God's message to

South Africa's State President P. W. Botha today is the same as that delivered by Elijah to King Ahab and Queen Jezebel: "Your days are over!"

To thunderous applause and acclamation, he concluded his sermon by addressing the brutal enforcers of apartheid. "The government of South Africa has signed its own death warrant. No government can take on God and survive. And that is the good news for the people of South Africa, and the bad news for you!"

As the service ended, the cathedral priests were sent out first to meet the riot police in order to discourage any violence toward the congregation. We were swept up in a surge of chanting township youth who surrounded the preachers and escorted them outside. Nine-year-old Allan Boesak, Jr., rode high on his father's shoulders above the crush of the crowd.

The service at St. George's was a dramatic baptism into our forty-day sojourn in South Africa. Our home base for that time was the Boesak home outside Cape Town. It was a place of abundant joy and life in the midst of tremendous threat.

Two nights before we arrived, a large brick had come flying through the living room window, sending shattered glass in all directions. A death threat against Allan followed over the phone.

Allan, Jr., and his twelve-year-old sister, Pulane, had decided to sleep on the floor of the large walk-in closet in their parents' bedroom for a few nights. At their own initiative and insistence, a few theology students came each evening and kept watch through the night outside the house, armed only with the thermos of coffee the family gave them.

Our first evening in the Boesak home, we relished a dinner of spicy curry, deeply grateful for the graciousness of Allan and Dorothy and their four children. After dinner, Allan, Jr., slowly read the day's psalm—Psalm 20—from the lectionary: "The Lord answer you in the day of trouble! The name of God protect you! . . . Some boast of chariots, and some of horses; but we boast of the name of the Lord our God. They will collapse and fall; but we shall rise and stand upright."

I remember vividly the faces around the table that night as we all listened to the promises of God in a difficult time. Those faces—and many others—are the clearest images I keep of South Africa. They are a multitude of shades. One might consider the variety a gift. But in South Africa, the color of a face is a stamp for the future, the overriding factor determining one's existence.

In Crossroads that first week Jim and I first saw the row upon row of tiny corrugated-iron shacks that we would see everywhere we traveled—and the ubiquitous razor wire that, I surmised after six weeks there, South Africa has in enough abundance to circle the globe. Beyond the "Not Open to the General Public" sign is an islolated island of human misery, caught in the crossfire between a cruel government, a corrupt local administration, brutal right-wing vigilantes, and the militant hope of the squatter camp's youths.

Crossroads came into being when women moved from the homelands, or bantustans—the barren areas designated by South Africa's regime for the nation's blacks—to be closer to Cape Town, where a few of their husbands had found jobs. The women formed the core of resistance when the government tried to force the families back to the homelands. They won that round of the long battle to be a "permanent" squatter camp.

Not far from Crossroads are rows of primitive migrant hostels. It is illegal for wives with their children to live in these dark and decrepit shelters with their migrant-worker husbands. Many stay in the homelands and see their husbands and fathers only a few weeks out of every year.

But some wives choose to live here illegally rather than suffer separation, crowding in, three families to a small room. Police frequently come to check on people in the hostels. When you ask the women here how many people live in a room, they reply, "Three men."

The next week in East London, we were hosted by a pastor and his family in Buffalo Flats, a so-called colored area outside the city. Rev. Eddie Leeux warned us as we entered his home that a video camera was aimed at the house twenty-four hours a day, and conversations in the front rooms could be monitored by police living across the street and next door.

He began talking about his detention, interrupting the story at one point to get a shoebox full of small pieces of toilet paper upon which he had kept a diary during his fifty-five days in prison. He had smuggled the paper out in the sleeves of a jacket he sent home to his wife, Lizzie, sending word without any explanation that she was not under any circumstances to wash the jacket until he got home.

Eddie was detained on Father's Day, June 15, 1986. His children had just finished giving him his Father's Day present and Lizzie had walked toward the kitchen to start breakfast, when the men with guns appeared in the doorway. As his father was being taken away, Eddie's youngest son, Zebedee, threw himself on a heap of laundry and wept. One of the arresting officers had the audacity to complain that Eddie was keeping him from spending Father's Day with his children.

Eddie's crimes included preaching against apartheid and using his car to transport dead and wounded people out of Duncan Village when the township exploded in riots in 1985. Eddie remembers that the bells at his church rang that Sunday morning as he passed by on his way to prison.

In characteristic fashion, the arresting authorities gave Lizzie no information about where her husband was taken, and her tireless efforts to find him took her to many dead ends. The security police did all they could to break Eddie emotionally and convince him that his family had forgotten him. He reached such despair that at one point he wrote in his journal, "I can still see the hand of God, but I am beyond his reach."

"In this country," said Lizzie, "if you don't have a strong faith in God, you go right down." Young Zebedee was also a source of strength. "Papa said before he went away that you must never cry and let them know that they have hurt you," he told his mother. Every day after school he asked her, "How are you? Did you cry today?"

As Eddie and Lizzie finished telling us their story, he quoted the bishop of Port Elizabeth: "This country is mortally wounded. It is bleeding to death. And no one is allowed to heal the wound." But, as Jim and I were discovering everywhere we went, some people keep trying.

Every afternoon at 3:30 a truck comes to the dump near Buffalo Flats. About 1,000 kids—orphans and runaways, blacks and Indians and so-called coloreds—live in the bush surrounding the dump. The oldest are teenagers, the youngest their infant sons and daughters—children of children.

Sustenance comes just after 3:30, when the children scavenge through the day's garbage. Nutrition is scarce, and chemicals and gasoline often get dumped over the "edible" stuff, slowly eating away at the young stomachs that swallow the tainted garbage.

A kid came one day to Reggie Naidoo, a young Indian seminarian with dark, intense eyes, asking him for food. He recounted the day he first took a carload of bread to the dump: the kids, eyes as vacant as their stomachs, surrounded his car and rocked it wildly. Naidoo has been taking food there ever since.

Reggie Naidoo wants to build a "Child Safety Home" that will house 250 kids—as a start. He has offers of free mattresses and donated labor from architects and plumbers. But his dream goes unrealized. He won't build a home in a particular racial area that will exclude others; government officials refuse to allow a nonracial children's home. They don't seem to be bothered about a nonracial dump.

Eddie Leeux served as a pastor for five years in the black township of King William's Town on the outskirts of East London. He asked one evening if we would like to go there to see the home of Steve Biko, the well-known antiapartheid student leader and proponent of "black consciousness" who was tortured and brutally murdered in 1977 while in police custody.

It was a rare privilege to be going to the home of this man whose courageous witness had deeply influenced us. It was even more of a privilege—and a complete surprise—when we walked in on a group of older women dressed in the purple garb of the Anglican Mothers Prayer Union and Eddie led us over to one and said, "I'd like you to meet Mrs. Biko, Steve's mother."

Alice Biko is a gracious and faithful woman who talked proudly about her beloved son. She related both the anguish and hope that have been part of being the mother of Steve Biko. Her house was frequently searched, and she lived every day, she said, with "the fear of a mother whose son could be shot at any time." One morning he left and never came back. She phoned everywhere, trying to find him.

She eventually received a call from the security police, assuring her that her son was fine. Two weeks later they called to tell her he was dead. She said of the agony they forced her son to endure and the anguish with which she still must live, "I am a bit bitter, but I must forgive."

In one of her last conversations with her son, she told him how difficult it was to be always worried about him being arrested and put in jail, how she never slept at night until she knew he was home. She related to us that he had responded by reminding her that Jesus had come to redeem his people and set them free.

"Are you Jesus?" she had asked impatiently.

Steve gently answered her, "No, I'm not. But I'm going to do the same job." After that, she said, she never asked him any more questions.

She told us that she now understands so much more about what he was saying to her then. He had once said to her, in words not unlike Jesus' to Mary, "I am not your son only; I have many mothers. And you have many children." He gave his life so that those many mothers and their children might not suffer.

Alice Biko finished her poignant reflections with thoughts about the week we were about to enter—Holy Week. "It seems as if during Lent," she said, "the suffering of Jesus becomes very acute. It is not unlike the suffering my son went through."

As we were about to leave, Jim told her how deeply his life had been affected by her son and thanked her for giving Steve Biko to the world. She reached over, took his hand, and said, "You are my son, too."

We got up early the next day for our long journey with Eddie through the rural areas surrounding East London. At the border of the Transkei, an independent homeland, we stopped to get transit visas.

The homeland is an integral piece of the South African government's failed plan of "grand apartheid"—a scheme that would have all of South Africa's blacks cornered in independent states on the most arid and unproductive land, leaving the best of South Africa for the whites, where blacks would be entitled to be "guest laborers."

The Transkei's rolling green hills, dotted with thatched-roof *rondavels*, are deceptively beautiful. The land is barren, good only for grazing herds. In the northern homelands, the barrenness is more stark—long stretches of sandy, dusty land lacking vegetation, shacks and huts built hastily on soft earth.

We left the Transkei and made our way north to the town of Lady Grey. We drove under a canopy of low-hanging trees as we approached the stream at the entrance to the tiny village. Playing children parted and waved as we drove through, sending a spray of water in all directions.

The members of a poor church in this isolated rural area are struggling to survive. A four-acre plot of land that lies not far from their church is overgrown with weeds. They have a dream to grow vegetables there to feed their families.

While we were visiting Lady Grey, the new pastor of the church was miles away in Port Elizabeth, trying to get government permission to acquire the land and transform the weed plot into a community garden. Though no whites were anywhere in the area, word came back that the weed plot was in an area designated white; no blacks could own it.

The children smiled and waved again as we left Lady Grey. And I sent up a quick prayer for children who live under a government that will not surrender four acres of weeds—"white" weeds—so that they might eat.

Jim and I went the next day to Duncan Village. Like other black townships, this one is totally isolated and totally controlled.

Military eyes peer constantly from the tower that rises above Duncan Village. The eyes are aided at night by powerful floodlights that can search out "suspicious activity" in any corner. We arrived in early afternoon and, under the tower's watchful eye, were greeted by a young man active in the struggle.

We walked unhindered for almost an hour, with Tommy pointing out overcrowded homes and fetid latrines and encouraging us to take pictures to carry out of the country with us for the world to see. We were told a story about police nailing shut the windows and doors of a home, tossing in a petrol bomb, and then watching a young girl who managed to escape burn to death.

To any township folk who raised eyebrows at whites in a black area—a rarity in South Africa, except for army personnel and police—Tommy smiled and said simply, "Comrades." We were greeted warmly by adults and thronged by children as we made our way through row after row of identical, boxlike, four-room houses.

It was one of the South African Police's omnipresent yellow vehicles that first stopped and questioned us. Fifteen minutes later a casspir appeared on the horizon and made its way toward us. Eight members of the South African Defense Forces, wearing khaki fatigues and pointing rifles, jumped out and surrounded us, ordering us to the military "strong point."

We were escorted at gunpoint in the direction of the tower,

taken past the rows of barbed wire that surround the military headquarters, and ushered into an interrogation room. A soldier told us we were being detained, pending arrival of a member of the Special Branch, South Africa's security police.

I kept my eyes on Tommy. The worst that could happen to us was a hasty, premature departure from South Africa, but Tommy could face far worse. Though his demeanor became immediately subdued, a glint of courageous pride remained in his eyes.

The security police officer spoke rapidly in Afrikaans to the other police and army personnel. He checked our passports and airline tickets and then asked us brusquely if we didn't know it was illegal under the current state of emergency to take pictures in a black area. We had been informed only that it was illegal to take pictures of police or military activity—and told by several people in the struggle that keeping up with this government's constantly changing body of regulations would be a full-time job.

He mentioned how much foreigners like to come to the townships and then take "unnecessary propaganda" about his country overseas. He accused us of "creating a rumble among the people" and added, "For all we know, you might be ANC"— a reference to the banned African National Congress, labeled Communist and perceived by the South African government as apartheid's worst enemy.

After his interrogation of us, he turned to Tommy, shaking his finger and ejecting stern and threatening warnings. "Didn't you just get out?" he said, referring to Tommy's recent release from ten months in detention. He finished with a promise that Tommy would be back in detention before long if he didn't give up his subversive activities.

Tommy's only response was to reach calmly into his back pocket, remove his pocket New Testament, and, putting it in front of the officer's face, say simply, "I am a Christian." A brief moment of silence descended as the arrogance of evil met the quiet power of the gospel.

In the end, the police decided against keeping Tommy or sending us home or confiscating our film. Instead they gave us an immediate escort out of Duncan Village. We took Tommy out with us, making sure he had a place to hide for a few months from the security police.

"Why did you do it?" Jim asked him on the way out. "Why would you take the risk of taking around a couple of white Americans you never even met before?"

Tommy talked about nonracialism at the core of the new South Africa he and his friends are building, about how important it is that people in the townships see whites who are with them in the struggle. "We are not fighting against whites; we are fighting against injustice," he said. He offered his observation that the police and even State President P. W. Botha are workers oppressed by the system.

He spoke of his detention, when he and many of his friends were rounded up as "threats to public safety," kept in cold cells, fed cornmeal infested with worms, and denied access to a doctor. Like many others we met, he was reluctant to talk about his torture.

"Our solidarity grew there," he said. As in every other jail in South Africa, the police strategy to thwart resistance was turned on its head. After participating in hunger strikes and hours of political discussion, young people came out more politicized and determined than ever to rid their country of apartheid.

"We are just going forward," said Tommy with determination written on his face. "It's not the time to be afraid."

Jim had been asked to preach in Eddie's church the next day, Palm Sunday. We had been warned that there would be police informers in the congregation.

The text for Sunday was the account of Jesus' setting his face for Jerusalem, knowing that persecution and death awaited him there. In South Africa, there was no need to elaborate on the story. The churches were making the same choice, walking into a confrontation with the powers that was bringing down on them an unprecedented level of persecution.

One of the great tragedies of apartheid is that it was conceived by the Dutch Reformed church, of which P. W. Botha is a member. It was first implemented around the Communion table in the nineteenth century, according to Allan Boesak, when white Christians said, "We will no longer drink with these slaves and former slaves out of one cup and share the one bread in the one church." Here, in the central expression of the unity of the body of Christ, racial separation was pioneered.

On Tuesday of Holy Week, church leaders and clergy came together in a strategy session in Bishopscourt, outside Cape Town, at the residence of Archbishop Tutu. There was discussion about whether the congregations were ready to follow the church leaders, but a feeling of unity emerged that the time was right for beginning a massive campaign of nonviolent resistance on the local and regional levels.

There was great energy and courage in the room that day. I remembered words Allan had spoken to us earlier when we commented on the joyful spirit in the Boesak home. He had said that if you live in fear, "you die a thousand deaths before you die." As we returned to Cape Town, we passed by Pollsmoor Prison, where African National Congress leader Nelson Mandela and others are serving life terms, sentences imposed on them almost twenty-five years before.

The next day on the way to Lavendar Hill, a large township outside Cape Town, we saw police surrounding a school bus and emptying it of its young students at gunpoint. Such sights were becoming very familiar.

The tenements of Lavendar Hill all bear names of streets from District 6. The residents used to live in District 6, a thriving, multiracial neighborhood of Cape Town that was destroyed when the Group Areas Act was enacted and the area was declared white.

The huge tenements make up one of the most densely populated areas in South Africa. Women have to get up before dawn to secure space on a washline. There are 45,000 families on a waiting list for the small flats in the broad, three-story brick buildings. Meanwhile, homes in white areas stand empty.

Unemployment is above 65 percent and rising every year in Lavendar Hill. Gangs with names like the Mafia, the Mongrels, and the Young Americans—borrowed from American TV—have taken control of the streets, with the largest gang boasting 800 members.

We talked with Jan de Waal, who had helped to start the New World Center in Lavendar Hill. The center is used almost round-the-clock for day care, community meals, afterschool programs, church activities, and meetings dealing with community and political issues.

De Waal talked about the tremendous indoctrination whites are subjected to. Those who join the antiapartheid struggle experience painful rejection from family and friends, and few choose to pay the cost. De Waal is losing the sight in his right eye, the result of being struck by a police baton during a protest march.

Just beyond Lavendar Hill is a place called Vrygrond, meaning "free ground"—ironic, since residents have to pay rent for space to construct a miserable, little shack. The shacks can be no larger than four meters by four meters here—government regulation.

Miriam came out of her shack when she saw us coming. She had just gotten word that sixty families in an adjacent area were going to be pushed out that night, their homes bulldozed. In a gesture of generosity beyond her means, she had offered to take three women and their children into her already overcrowded, tiny corrugated-iron shack. The rest would have to build shacks behind the sand dunes and tear them down by morning before the police saw them.

Bulldozing squatter areas is one of the government's strategies for making life in South Africa so intolerable for blacks that they will move to the homelands. New legislation introduced while we were in the country would fine illegal squatters up to 10,000 rand (about $5,000) or sentence them to five years in prison.

Unemployment here is 90 percent. "Most people don't even know if they'll have a piece of bread tonight," said Miriam. She and others in Vrygrond used to have monthly meetings with people from other squatter camps to try to organize for change, but the government banned the meetings.

"If only Botha could come and walk here . . ." Her voice trailed off, leaving her thought unfinished. She didn't want to accept that Botha and his friends were plotting her suffering. Her spirit of generosity made her incapable of believing that anyone would have an approach to life different from hers.

"This is our South Africa, too," she said. "That is the sadness—God created it for all of us."

Miriam knew it was only a matter of time before the police would come and raze her home again. She had been pushed out from numerous places. "The government never tells us where we can go," she said. "But this time we are not moving. This is our dead end. They can lock us all up if they want to. And they will—the children too."

A woman with nothing was having even that taken away from her. "I see a very dark future—very, very dark," she said. "It's not only me—I think the majority of us sees it that way."

There is no home for black South Africans. Or rest. They are exiles and sojourners in the land of their birth, always on the move, always under threat of being pushed to yet another distant, barren corner of earth.

Vrygrond, like all black areas, lies out of view of white society. On the other side of the main road, a two-minute drive away, is Marina de Gama. Sprawling homes painted dazzling white, draped with bougainvillea and roses, cluster around a human-made lake, with moorings for boats outside every door. There are no restrictions here on the size of homes.

It has often been easy for a self-righteous world to point a finger at South Africa as an evil aberration. But in Vrygrond and Marina de Gama, the Third World and the First stand side by side, a microcosm of the economic order that rules the globe. The racism and greed and violence that tear this country apart are, in the extreme, the same barriers that divide the rest of us.

We had asked Miriam before we left her if she had any hope for her children. I had been conditioned from asking this question in food lines and jail cells at home and war zones in Nicaragua to expect a statement of steadfast faith in a God who loves the poor. The despair was evident in her eyes as she said, "No . . . no, I have no hope."

At the Good Friday service in the church which Allan Boesak serves as pastor, my attention became riveted on a young girl in the first row. She sat on the edge of the pew, a simple white bow fixed between the tight cornrows that covered her head. Her small legs, crossed at the ankles, occasionally swung gently; her unseeing eyes wandered in all directions.

Her fingers kept returning to the red rose pinned to her plain, blue dress. She stroked the soft petals, occasionally pulling one off and putting it to her face, smiling as she breathed its sweet fragrance.

She and her friends from a school for the blind outside Cape Town were the featured choir for the Good Friday service. At the appropriate moment, teachers from the school brusquely grabbed the arms of the children in blue uniforms with flowers and herded them to the front of the church, where they sang a few songs and then returned to their seats. Her fingers returned to her rose.

When she prayed, her head bowed and her tiny hands came together in perfect form, fingers extended, just as she had been taught. By the time the preacher from America got up to speak, her head began to nod with weariness.

I wondered if it would be frightening to her to be gathered up and held by a stranger she couldn't see. Her only response to my going over to hold her was to sigh and fall asleep quickly in my arms.

Jim focused his sermon on Jesus' cry from the cross, "My God, my God, why have you forsaken me?" He reminded the congregation that despite God's faithfulness to the very end, the gut-wrenching cry of God's son was real, the feeling overpowering. I heard it echo in my soul for the sake of this land.

Jim held forth a resounding promise: "If the South African government puts the church of Jesus Christ on the cross, it will be overthrown by the Resurrection!" The words had the powerful ring of theological truth, and a rush of affirmation surged through the congregation.

But I could not see it. All I could see for this land was an unending Good Friday; I did not yet have eyes to see the Resurrection. I wondered if the child in my arms ever would.

I led her back to her seat for the closing hymn. Now she had only to wait for someone to grab her arm and take her home. She sat quietly with her head down, her small legs swinging, a stem without petals pinned to her plain, blue dress.

She could not see an older, more confident schoolmate rush to the front of the church. With some assistance, the teenager groped her way toward Allan Boesak, whom she had dreamed of meeting some day.

She asked to touch his face. She gently ran her fingers over every feature and then touched his hair. As joyful pride spread over her face, she said, "It's true; you're not white."

"What made you think I'm white?" Allan asked.

"I thought anyone who's so famous must be white."

She wanted to meet "the preacher" as well. She was led to Jim. She touched his face and hair, commenting with quiet surprise, "I never heard a white man talk that way."

In South Africa, even the blind are not allowed to be color blind.

On Easter Sunday, April 3, Allan preached to the memory of Martin Luther King, Jr., who had been martyred twenty years earlier on April 4. Allan draws strength from King and his witness to the power of nonviolence. In a sober moment of reflecting on the threats against his own life, Allan quoted King: "There are some things so dear and so precious and so eternally true that they are worth dying for. And if you are not willing to die for those things, then you are really not fit to live."

Now, on Easter morning, he was boldly proclaiming the hope of the Resurrection. I envied his hope. I still felt caught at Good Friday.

In Johannesburg, Jim and I waited one afternoon in front of our hotel for Rev. Beyers Naudé, South Africa's best known white dissident. Naudé, who was in the inner circle of Afrikaner power and widely considered a likely choice for prime minister of South Africa some day, rejected his white privilege and joined the black freedom struggle. Naudé was late, as it turned out, because of circumstances related to the recent detention of his secretary.

While we were waiting, a young white South African woman, overhearing our conversation and detecting our American accents, asked us how we liked South Africa. Jim told her that we didn't like apartheid.

"Well, there's not much apartheid left," she said. "They can go to our cinemas and our restaurants and even our hotels."

"But black people can't vote," Jim responded.

"But that's all," she said. "And most of them can't read or write anyway. They refuse to get educated. They boycott their schools and sometimes burn them down."

"Do you think that Archbishop Tutu ought to be allowed to vote?" Jim asked her.

"Look what happened in Rhodesia," was her only response. "The blacks took it over and called it Zimbabwe!"

Beyers Naudé, who has paid such a great cost for his long years of opposition to apartheid, later spoke sadly about such expressions of racism and ignorance among South Africa's whites. He was not optimistic about white involvement in the struggle. "You must be willing to risk your income, your security, and your very life. You have to be prepared to be ostracized by your own people and walk by faith with God. Until they come to that point, whites will be unwilling."

Banning, which Naudé suffered under for seven years, is a particularly sinister tactic employed by the South African government. A banning order prohibits a person from attending public gatherings, being published or quoted, or being in the company of more than one person at a time.

Soweto—a sprawling township, home to 2 million people and larger than neighboring Johannesburg—is a prominent sign of the pain and promise that are South Africa. We were honored to share lunch there in the home of Rev. Frank Chikane, general secretary of the South African Council of Churches, and his family.

Chikane has been detained five times since 1977. Within an hour of his first detention he couldn't walk, so brutal was the torture. During one detention, his interrogator/torturer was a deacon from the white congregation of his denomination. Their home still shows evidence of having been petrol-bombed in 1985.

Mothers are revered in South Africa, and like several other people we met, Chikane proudly took us to meet his. She received us graciously in the small home, with pounded earth floors and bare cement walls like most in Soweto, where Chikane had grown up. The homes here have large, crude, hand-painted numbers distinguishing them—the work of the police, who got tired of mothers rubbing out less visible numbers to protect their children from police searches.

Mrs. Chikane has one son under public government attack, another on the run from police, and another in exile—and she is very proud of all of them. At about four in the morning the previous Sunday, the police had come to this home in search of Frank's younger brother, the president of the Soweto

Student Congress. The first time they had come with the army. They deployed soldiers around the house and trained bright searchlights on it.

Sitting in that small dark home, one easily imagines the vulnerability and terror that children in this society must feel. Since the state of emergency was imposed on June 12, 1986, the government had detained 30,000 people—10,000 of them children under the age of sixteen.

If ever a country was run like a "totalitarian dungeon," this is it. And yet the U.S. government, while boycotting and attempting to destabilize Nicaragua, carries out a policy of "constructive engagement" with this terrorist state.

We returned to Soweto for a "tea party" ("meetings" are illegal) for detainees and their families. The Detainees' Parents Support Committee is one of the organizations that was restricted by the government on February 24, but the gathering went on anyway.

With riot police just outside the door, the young people toi-toied and sang freedom songs, rocking Soweto with hope. They ended the meeting with a moving dramatization of township life.

Most of the children in the drama looked to be eight or nine years old, the oldest fourteen. Their drama centered on a black policeman who had been brutalizing township people and then asked to be forgiven and received into the struggle.

The young man whose home he had approached at first slammed the door in his face and sent him away. But then he paused and said, "But wait, Jesus tells us that we must turn the other cheek and forgive those who persecute us, even our enemies."

This young man went after him and found a crowd about to "necklace" the traitor by lighting a gasoline-filled tire around his neck. The man intervened, called him "brother," and invited the others to welcome him into the struggle.

In the final scene, the former policeman was shot by riot

police during a protest and died in the arms of his new comrades. They gathered around him and, with heads bowed and arms raised, prayed for South Africa. "Lord, we are tired of the bullets," prayed one. "Please give us peace and freedom," implored another. They ended by reciting together the Lord's Prayer.

There was a hush—and many tear-filled eyes—as the children finished their drama. Then people began slowly to clap, and cheer, and finally to burst into singing more freedom songs.

I thought of the challenge and invitation that the young people of the South African Council of Churches offer to people interested in joining their work: "If you have come to help me, you are wasting your time. But if you have come because your liberation is bound up with mine, then let us work together."

Their mothers, who courageously formed the support committee in response to the detention of their children, provide the leadership for the tea parties. Several mothers offered their testimonies in Xhosa, the gentle clicks of the tribal language rolling rhythmically off their tongues.

I noticed as they spoke that interjected throughout were words uttered in English. Words like *banning, detention, terrorism, state of emergency*, and *unemployment*. I began to keep a list.

I mentioned the list to Mncedisi, our interpreter, as we left Soweto. "Yes," he explained, "we have no root in our language for words such as these."

We were back again in Soweto for Sunday services at the Anglican church, dominated by a beautiful, simple crucifix. The service concluded with all the children toi-toiing past the bishop as he offered them his blessing.

He greeted us after the service and said, "You know, the government is even against the trains in this country now." We looked puzzled, and he explained. "When the trains start up they go, 'Boessssak, Boessssak, Boessssak,' " he said, hissing out the *s*'s; and then, pitching his voice high at the end like a whistle, he said, "And when they get moving, they go, 'Tutu, Tutu, Tutu.' " He laughed heartily at his joke, and we joined him.

I thought of another joke someone had told us. Archbishop Tutu, the story goes, was having a conversation with someone from Zambia about that country's decision to appoint a minister of naval affairs. When Tutu questioned why this landlocked African nation would need such a minister, the Zambian replied, "Why not? You have a minister of justice, don't you?"

We were on our way after church to meet Albertina Sisulu, whose home has an open door for everyone from Soweto's children fleeing the police to sympathetic American strangers in awe of her courage and humility. Those keeping watch on that door will never understand what greatness is inside.

Sisulu was a leader in a famous march against the extension of "passes" to women. The passes, instituted to control the black population and restrict its movement, were an early symbol of the evil of apartheid. The government made a mistake when it tried to force women to carry them.

Organized by the just-formed Federation of South African Women, in August 1956 some 20,000 women marched to Pretoria in protest. At that march the women sang a defiant chant that has become a cornerstone of the women's movement in South Africa: "You have struck the women; you have struck the rock."

Sisulu has been harassed, tried for treason, imprisoned, placed under house arrest for ten years, and banned for seventeen—the longest banning order ever handed out in South Africa. Her husband, Walter Sisulu, was sentenced to life imprisonment in the same trial that put Nelson Mandela behind bars. Two of her sons were in jail, and three other children in exile.

Through decades of suffering, she has served her people as a nurse and midwife. She has been granted the high honor of being named one of the three presidents of the United Democratic Front. And she was given a recent "honor" by the other side as well: So threatening is her strength to the defenders of apartheid, the South African government singled her out and gave her individual restrictions when it banned the seventeen organizations in late February 1988.

Albertina Sisulu has ushered countless new lives into the world, each one likely, in time, to join the struggle for freedom. Her own children have followed her dauntless example. She has been midwife and mother to a movement, with an impact that spans generations.

When you ask her what helps her bear her tremendous burden of suffering, she smiles warmly and says, "I wouldn't be alive if I weren't staying with God. He's a wonderful man. He's the only man who takes care of me."

Black South African women are exiles among the exiles. Raised in a culture that forces their dependence on men, oppressed by a government that wrenches that dependence from them, they are often compelled to survive by their own strength and resources.

With children on their backs, they work the fields and weave bright tapestries. In the homelands they herd sheep and offer pineapples with hollow reeds stuck into their juicy cores for sale by the side of the road. They wander from home to home in the suburbs, looking for "chare," light housework that earns some enough money to feed their children.

Too many must watch helplessly as their children die of malnutrition. And far too many are forced to wander from police station to prison in search of husbands and children snatched from them in the night.

But more and more, women are claiming their strength and joining a movement begun by their sisters generations ago. The weekend of April 16, on the anniversary of the establishment of the Federation of South African Women (FEDSAW), a massive women's cultural festival took place in Cape Town. Preparations for the festival had gone on for weeks, with meeting locations kept secret to avoid government interference in the wake of the February bannings.

The huge event was opened by Helen Joseph, who more than three decades before was elected the first secretary of FEDSAW. People parted to make way as the white-haired "Mother of the Struggle" was brought in her wheelchair to the stage. With her fist raised and a radiant smile on her face, she brought the gathering to its feet in a resounding ovation for this eighty-three-year-old stalwart of the struggle.

Like Beyers Naudé, Helen Joseph has paid the price for opening herself to be transformed by the strength and hope of the black community. The first person to be put under house arrest in South Africa (a restriction that lasted ten years), she has through many years steadfastly held forth a vision of a nonracial South Africa—and of the crucial role women play in the freedom struggle.

I asked her later what women can contribute to the struggle. "Everything!" she exclaimed with a broad smile and a characteristic twinkle in her eye. "Their lives, their courage, their discipline, their gifts, their determination. The spirit of women cannot be crushed. That's what I have learned over the years."

The struggle may indeed require everything of many people. As Frank Chikane expressed it: "For us to go over into victory, we will have to go through the cross. . . . To choose Christ is to choose death for the sake of justice against evil." He and Desmond Tutu and Allan Boesak all talked about the pain of being pastors in a situation in which they are encouraging their people for the sake of the gospel to go the streets, knowing that many will die there. "We find ourselves in a situation," said Chikane, "where we cannot do otherwise but offer ourselves for sacrifice."

Allan Boesak described the situation as he sees it. "There is no neutral ground anymore. We have arrived at the time of the apocalypse." Like many others, he expressed his belief that the tremendous repression against the people is a sign that the government is losing its grip, that white desperation and panic are growing beyond all bounds.

He is more deeply convinced than ever that the church needs

to cling to nonviolence in its witness. The government claims that its state of emergency is aimed at stopping unrest, but in fact the enforcers of apartheid are doing all that they can to foment violent unrest—jailing experienced and disciplined leaders, brutalizing children, sowing suspicion among people. They want the battle on terms they know they can win.

"Apartheid will not exist for one minute without the awesome violence that is needed to maintain the system," said Allan. "And I think they are trying to get the churches to believe that that is what is left for us as well. . . . But if you choose violence from a strategic point of view, you make it so easy for them, because violence is just about the only thing they know how to do well."

But for Allan the commitment to nonviolence is much more than a strategic option; it is a matter of following the example of Christ. Allan believes that the very soul of the people is at stake: "Because the government is so incredibly violent and brutal, I fear also for the brutalization of the soul of our people. We will become just like them if we're not careful."

But the nonviolence he advocates is neither judgmental nor passive. "We all have been knee-deep in blood," he said. And people who talk of nonviolence in such a brutal situation "must be willing to wade into that river of blood and fight alongside others without weapons that will kill."

I remembered as he said these words a story that he had told us one evening while he was tending the fire under the *potjie-kos*, an oxtail stew that took most of the day to cook in an old iron pot. Allan's father had died when Allan was seven years old, and his mother, a seamstress, struggled to raise eight children on her own. But she was—and is—an extremely faithful woman who believes God's promises.

When Allan was twelve, she had ordered some bricks for fixing up the very old and dilapidated house they had bought. When she counted the bricks, she discovered that the man who delivered them had cheated her. He refused to listen to her. But finally this very small and humble woman simply said,

"The God I believe in is the protector of the widow and the fatherless. And somehow you're going to know that."

A week later the man came and delivered the rest of the bricks. He explained that he had been building some houses, and two of them had mysteriously caught on fire. He interpreted it as a sign from heaven.

The incident left a deep impression on Allan. He says, "So when today I say, 'God is the God of the poor and the widow and the fatherless—and he calls them to stand where he stands, namely for justice and against injustice'—people say, 'Oooh, that's liberation theology.' And I say, 'It may be liberation theology; but that's what I learned at home.' "

Desmond Tutu told us the story of a man he met when he was praying with people in the village of Mogopa one night. This man's house was going to be demolished the next day. Clinics, churches, and shops had already been destroyed. And people were going to be moved at the point of a gun. In the middle of the night, as the people of the village prayed together, this man prayed, "God, thank you for loving us."

Such stories of simple and profound faith that deeply touched me in South Africa. But often I wrestled with despair, struggling to find the internal resources to keep the evil that was so pervasive in this country at bay. The thought of how many people were going to lose their lives before this country changed—some of them, perhaps, friends we had come to love—often brought a convulsion of tears.

But there was one constant for me, one pervasive ring of hope. That was the singing of "Nkosi Sikelel'i Afrika" (God bless Africa), the African national anthem. Old people sang it at the end of the Soweto church service, and young athletes before a sports celebration; children belted it out at the detainees' meeting, and women sang it with pride at the beginning of their first national festival in Cape Town. It is always sung with dignity and strength, and chills run up and down the spine at the swelling affirmation that this is God's land, to be shared by all.

It is a sad and beautiful land, as I was reminded one evening—one of our last in South Africa—as the sun was beginning to set over a black township. Domestics and laborers, weary from a day's work in the city, were making their way home in the last moments of daylight. A stream of women, water jugs balanced on their heads, some with babies on their backs, moved slowly out from the central spigot over the township's rutted roads in the encroaching cool of the evening. Children left their play and moved inside, and dogs seemed to take the sun's disappearance as a signal to commence barking.

At the entrance to the township, spread out on a table, were rows of sheep's heads, blood still running from their necks and the look of terror from the slaughter still on their faces. Women tending fires cut pieces of meat from the carcasses and skewered them for sale.

A family that could not afford the mutton bought scores of the sheep's legs. Scraping the hair from the legs, they cooked the pile of bones with scant meat over a fire for their evening meal.

At dusk the air got heavy with smoke and a pungent odor from the cooking fires and the paraffin lamps that came to life, one by one, up and down the rows of tiny houses. I thought of the homeless people we had seen in downtown Johannesburg gathered around a fire in a barrel, and the children in the bush surrounding East London taking turns stoking a small blaze for warmth. I remembered those children's bellies, swollen from hunger, and the dazed look on the faces of their parents, who had been routed by the police from their dilapidated, makeshift homes in the middle of the night and returned to find nothing but smoldering ashes.

A comrade was taking us through the township, speaking of the struggle, of the land and the freedom that have been stolen from his people. As he spoke, I thought back to the glimpses of this land's beauty that we had been privileged to behold— its vast expanses of beaches, pounding surf, plains populated with ostrich herds, and mountains poking through clouds. A sliver of a crescent moon resting one night on the edge of Cape Town's famous Table Mountain urged a stream of tears from me, so tragic is it that some South Africans have robbed the glory of this land from others. What a strong nation this would be if all its wealth and beauty were shared.

As we walked toward our friend's home, the sky turned blood-red. We stopped, speechless, in awe of the red expanse that formed a brilliant canopy over South Africa. After a moment, he said, "But they cannot take the sky from us."

It is the only claim that black South Africans still have on their home, where they cannot vote or own land or even be sure of a four-by-four-meter shack to live in.

This is an absurdly tragic nation—where tallies of recent flood victims included only the white ones; and where, at a famous natural wonder, an extra hole was blasted into the cave's wall so that blacks would have a separate entrance. It is a land in which it is illegal for husbands and wives to live together, and where, for the sake of "public safety," people are shot in the streets. A land that has the audacity to ban human beings and attach racial labels to pieces of earth, to tear-gas church congregations and torture children, to declare candles lit in solidarity and hope a threat to the state.

"Ten years of Botha, forty years of apartheid, and a lifetime of suffering," sadly proclaims a popular poster. And, according to many, the suffering has just begun.

Frank Chikane says of the young people: "They understand that you cannot get closer to liberation without bringing out the viciousness of the system. The pain is an indication of the closeness to our day of liberation." That is the hope that permeates the dark corners of South Africa.

Their confidence comes from the assurance that this triumph was already won many years ago on a cross. And they are willing to follow the one who won it—even to their own deaths.

While assessing the sides in the battle that escalates day by day, Allan Boesak confidently summed up the hope. "We are more certain of our victory than they can ever be of their endurance." Without a doubt, South Africans will pursue that victory—until South Africa is a home for all.

13. The Way Home

I met five-year-old Kyle a few years ago just before Christmas. Kyle loved the Christmas story, and he had learned it by heart that year. He delighted in telling the story of Jesus' birth to his parents.

Like most parents, Kyle's were proud of his accomplishment and anxious to have him share it the first time a guest came to their home. Kyle started out strong. But he started to falter just when he hit his favorite part, when the angels appeared to the shepherds and shouted, "Glory to God in the highest, and on earth, peace." He remembered the "Glory to God" part, but he couldn't remember what came next.

His mother offered a gentle note of encouragement. "Come on, Kyle, think hard."

He started out again: "And the angels appeared to the shepherds and said, 'Glory to God in the highest . . .' " He hesitated a moment, and then his face brightened. "Glory to God in the highest . . . and I'll huff and I'll puff and I'll blow your house down."

That story is one of my favorites to tell. Scripture tells us that what is hidden from the wise has been revealed to babes. Beneath a child's confusion is a truth that goes to the heart of the difference between God's intentions for the world and the sad reality that we have made of it.

We see so little of the peace on earth that was announced on that cold night to simple shepherds. But the world is rampant with huffing and puffing.

In my neighborhood, the preying wolf of real estate speculation is breathing right outside the door of many homes, wrenching the inner cities house by house from the poor of our nation, who have nowhere left to go. A decade after a D.C. defense lawyer predicted the odds of stopping gentrification, the streets resound with the truth of his words.

Increasingly, families are among those who are showing up at overnight shelters for the homeless, made "urban refugees" by the tide of gentrification. It is an inevitable result of free enterprise, we are told. And unfortunately its defenders are right: Whenever housing is a profit-making commodity rather than a right, some will have their homes blown down around them. We face a wolf in capitalism's clothing.

A mile and a half from the White House, 300 families are served in the food line at the Sojourners Neighborhood Center on Saturday mornings. Some people get up before dawn to wait in line for a bag of groceries. Many say it has made a change in their lives—they no longer have to choose between paying the rent and feeding their children.

Downtown, they get different treatment. "Cheese will be given out to any person who can prove need at twelve locations throughout the city," said the radio one morning just past dawn when I had dropped Nicole off at the hospital for her nurse's aide training. The dangling phrase hit me like a five-pound brick of cheddar. For indeed the poor are forced to jump through at least a dozen government-bureaucracy hoops to prove that they are "deserving." And then they must smile and say "cheese" for their survival.

More and more young women in our neighborhood—some still children themselves—are joining the welfare rolls, raising their children on their own without the support of the men who fathered them or the resources that could help them break out of the cycle of poverty that began with their mothers and their mothers' mothers. And more and more of their children are not living to see their first birthdays.

Six years ago our day-care center in Clifton Terrace was forced to close—the federal government raised the rent beyond our capacity; and many of the mothers, who needed day care for their children when they received job training through a federal program, no longer needed it when the program was gutted under Reagan budget cuts.

Meanwhile, Clifton Terrace has become a den for illegal drug dealers. In the summer of 1987 the situation reached such a crisis that police set up an around-the-clock mobile arrest unit right outside the front door.

With the increasingly lucrative drug trade have come escalating crime and violence that have made my neighborhood a war zone and turned Washington, D.C., into the "murder capital" of the nation. A murder a day took place in 1988, with ninety-four more in the first two months of 1989. Police now carry semi-automatic weapons to try to match the lethal force of the drug dealers. Just a month ago, in an apartment building down the street, a multiple murder took place. Among the victims was an elderly woman who came regularly through our food line. The killers were crazed on drugs when they seized and then murdered their hostages.

Another killer stalks this neighborhood. The AIDS epidemic claims more and more victims every day. While adequate research dollars have yet to be devoted to the crisis, its sufferers die painful and often isolated deaths.

Perhaps nowhere is there a clearer view of the chasm between rich and poor than in our capital city. There are two Washingtons—the powerful one that shapes the world, and the powerless one that is marked by homelessness and hunger and the second highest infant mortality rate in the nation. This "other Washington" is plagued by the many problems that run rampant in all the places where jobs and money and power and hope are scarce.

Whole segments of our population are getting the message that they are marginal, expendable, abandoned. They are being pushed to the corners that no one else wants, and to the limits of their endurance.

They are a minority in the United States, but globally they are the majority. The same forces that push people out of inner-city Washington, D.C., are pushing peasants off their land in the so-called Third World to make room for U.S. military bases and the coffee, sugar, and bananas that will keep affluent Americans content.

The cycle of eviction, homelessness, and refugeeism has become a global epidemic. The whole world spins in the gale-force winds of those who huff and puff and blow away homes at will. Concentrated power and wealth, apathy and racism, have converged to create this mighty wind.

The statistics have not changed since I was in East Harlem. Two-thirds of the world's people are still hungry. Conservative estimates have it that forty million people on our planet die each year of starvation and hunger-related illnesses; some calculations place the figure at twice that. Every thirteen seconds a child dies of hunger on this globe that has enough to feed everyone, if we saw to it that what we have is shared. But, as one neighbor put it, "The rich keep getting richer, and the poor keep getting nothin'."

Never has the breach between rich and poor been wider. And never has there been such a vast array of places created to keep the poor separate and out of our view. We have put them in ghettos and institutions, on homelands and reservations, in barrios and cells and camps of all varieties.

At its heart, we suffer not from a geographic or sociological problem but from a moral one. The price of our alienation is immeasurable suffering for most of the world. Surely this is a price too high to pay simply to guarantee a few of us our affluence and security.

Our imbalance of resources has created a so-called balance of terror. So deep is our alienation from one another, so obsessive our desire to protect what we have, that we have armed the globe with the nuclear capacity to destroy it all. We have threatened to make us all expendable.

What can we do? How can we possibly feel at home in this world?

Most days we don't talk about the fear, about this sense that the world is about to blow. The children are more honest about it, and their fears help us to see the fear in ourselves.

We fear nuclear war and all the tragedies short of it, the poisons we are dumping in the earth and the plagues they cause. We fear death, but maybe even more we fear life in a world controlled by those who believe that the solution to every crisis is to deploy either missiles or marines.

The fear is understandable. But we must go back to the first words of the angels on that cold night—the greeting that came before "Glory to God." "Be not afraid" was the angels' introduction to the quaking shepherds.

It was a message that was delivered to every one of the characters in the Christmas drama: to Mary when she received word that she was to be the mother of Jesus, to Joseph when he wanted to forsake their marriage plans, and to the wise men when they had to reroute their journey to avoid Herod.

And that message echoes today from the corners of the earth where there is the most reason to be afraid. It is here that we must look for answers: at the margins, where people intimately know the good news that Jesus brought.

Scott Wright and Yvonne Dilling, who each worked for several years in Salvadoran refugee camps in Honduras, related stories of Christmas there. The week before Christmas, four National Guard members came to the home of a young lay catechist, bound him by the thumbs, and began to take him away. When he tried to escape, they opened up with machine-gun fire. Later, his pregnant wife and five children gathered around the coffin, as a single candle burned in the darkness.

In another part of the camp, a group of women surrounded an infant and sang to him in a dark tent, lit only by the light of a candle. Between the verses of the song, the anguished cries of his mother filled the air. She had fed her son through the night from an eyedropper, trying to coax some nourishment into his starving body.

The child lay in the center of them, his eyes and mouth open. He did not cry. One of the mothers marked the sign of the cross on the child's forehead while he looked at them fervently, as if expecting an answer to a question he could not ask. Then the singing stopped. The child was dead.

These were the events that preceded Christmas. But when Christmas Eve came, the camps burst into joyful celebration. Women baked sweet cinnamon bread in an adobe oven, while men butchered hogs for the making of special pork tamales. The children made figurines for the Nativity scene out of clay from the riverbed, adding local touches to the usual characters: pigs, an armadillo, and baby Jesus sleeping in a hammock rather than a manger. They painted beans and kernels of corn in bright colors and strung them into garlands, decorating a tree branch with these, ornaments they made from small medicine boxes, and figures they had shaped from the tin foil that wraps margarine sticks.

The children dressed as shepherds and passed from tent to tent, recounting the journey of José and María in search of shelter. "This Christmas we will celebrate as they did," said one mother, "looking for a place where our children can be born."

This story is their story. They know the special love of a savior who was also a refugee, and a mother who fled with her child to escape Herod's slaughter of the innocents.

Yvonne tells the story of a refugee woman who once asked her why she always looked so sad and burdened. Yvonne talked about the grief she felt over all the suffering she was witnessing and her commitment to give all of herself to the struggle of the refugees. This woman gently confronted her: "Only people who expect to go back to North America in a year work the way you do. You cannot be serious about our struggle unless you play and celebrate and do those things that make it possible to give a lifetime to it."

Each time the refugees were displaced and had to build a new camp, they immediately formed three committees: a construction committee, an education committee, and the *comité de alegría*—"the committee of joy." Celebration was as basic to the life of the refugees as digging latrines and teaching their children to read.

In times such as these, despair can threaten to take up residence in our hearts. But those who suffer most remind us of how tragic and arrogant it would be for us to lose hope on behalf of people who have not lost theirs.

I will never forget the evening that friends active in our neighborhood tenants union took suitcases downtown and marched in on a city council debate over rent control, making the point that if rent control didn't pass in D.C., many of them would be packing their bags. We lost that round of the battle. Afterward, when I asked some of the people involved how they felt about their thwarted effort, one spoke up immediately, "We'll get it next time." And another added, "You know, it says in the Bible, 'It came to pass.' It doesn't say, 'It came to stay.' "

The people in my neighborhood have shown me how to be faithful in these times. Every Saturday morning before our food line opens up, Mary Glover offers the same prayer—always the same, but never redundant. It is one I will always carry with me.

We thank you, Lord, for our lying down last night and our rising up this morning. We thank you that the walls of our room were not the walls of our grave, that our bed was not our cooling board nor our bedclothes our winding-sheet. We thank you for the feet that are coming through this line for food today and the hands that are giving it out. We know, Lord, that you're coming through this line today, so help us to treat you right. Yes, Lord, help us to treat you right. We thank you, Lord.

Mary Glover's infection of praise is contagious, and it doesn't take long after hearing her prayer for me to put my own troubles into perspective. She begins each and every day by thanking God for waking her up and giving her another day to serve her Lord. She has so little, and she is thankful for so much. I have so much and am never thankful enough.

Naomi Scott, who lives just around the corner, shared in our

Monday night neighborhood Bible study about the fire several years ago that swept through her apartment building, a result of landlord negligence. She was severely burned and had to spend six months in the hospital two different times. She hovered for a while near death. She lost several fingers on both hands. She says of the experience, "I just thank God that I can still play the piano." And play she does—all the hymns and gospel favorites at our neighborhood gatherings.

We have marvelous companions on this journey. And one for whom I am especially thankful is Art Brown, the professor who dared to take a group of college kids into East Harlem and helped start me on the road.

I always thought that the late-night political and theological conversations with Art that had been such a formative part of my experience in East Harlem and back at college would continue into our future. But on November 6, 1978, everything changed. A massive stroke claimed Art's speech and crippled the right side of his body.

As Art slowly healed, he kept a diary, painstakingly recorded with his functional left hand. He pleaded on paper, "Plug up the holes in my brain, please. . . . They're killing me. . . . They're making an awful draft." The anguish was profound as Art started over again like a child, practicing simple arithmetic in his diary and wrestling with emotions that often seemed out of control. When he spoke, his sentences often hung in midair, unfinished.

The helplessness was the most devastating thing for us both. On my first visit after the stroke, I held his hand and offered a prayer for him before leaving. After my "Amen," he began the Lord's Prayer; it was the only thing his battered brain remembered from beginning to end. When we finished, he wept and said, "All I have left is faith. I cry to God that I can live a righteous life."

On my second visit a year later, Art invited me to read his now-copious journals. I pored over them late into the night. Two years after his stroke, he had written, "What a treasure trove I have stored up in my smashed brain." He was right. Where intellect had died, wit, warmth, and poetry burst forth.

Of his continuing struggle with speech, he reflected, "As the voice of the female cricket speaks, so speak I unto thee, O Lord, for the female cricket makes no sound when it speaks." And of his suffering, he wrote, "A snowflake is a tiny thing compared to the sky. Pain is as nothing when measured to the tune of everything else in the universe."

His journals contained his reflections on whales and cobwebs, on unicorns and solar eclipses. And he made the observation that "it's unfair to children to call owls wise."

Most hopeful to me was his sense of humor, his capacity to laugh at himself and his predicament, what he called "struggling from tears to cheers." He wrote about "mailslotitis," his inability to mail a letter without the use of his right hand to hold the slot open. Reflecting after an operation, when to laugh pulled at his stitches and was painful, he wrote, "If you can't laugh, *be* one." With the dramatic change in his life, he asked, "Who am I? Who am I? Who am I? I really don't know the answer to all three of those questions."

His brain put forth remarkable puns and plays on words. On a hopeful day he recorded, "The worst of my stroke of bad luck is over." And on a sadder day, he wrote, "Pealing bells and peeling onions are not the same thing at all. But both can make you weep. Take away our crying and you deprive us of our humanity." Later he penned, "Tears are the telescope through which sometimes we see God."

I will never forget a visit I made to see Art just before Christmas one year. He produced a large piece of white paper, on which was drawn a small face surrounded by bold red strokes that swept in two large arcs toward the top of the page. The words he had crayoned at the bottom read, "The late Aunt Minnie encased in a lobster claw."

I knew he had lived the last two decades of his then sixty-four years in Maine, where lobsters are abundant, but still I was mystified at why he would choose to encase Aunt Minnie in one of their claws. When I asked him about it, he grinned and explained, "Well, I was trying to draw a Christmas angel—but it didn't come out quite right."

"Look at this one," he said as he held up a drawing labeled, "Hey, lady, you got eggs in a nest growing in your hair, in case you haven't noticed!" He explained that he had gotten a bit carried away with her bouffant hairstyle and had to add the nest to justify all the hair. On these recent visits, we have laughed together more than we have cried.

I have never seen such a longing in anyone, so evident in Art's eyes, for God, for healing, for understanding—above all, for God. When all else is stripped away, faith remains. Art is learning childlike faith and total dependence on God, and by example invites me to follow. As he articulated it in his journal, "I want to spend the rest of my life playing 'Follow the Leader' with Christ."

In Art's struggle, he has taught me what it means to persevere. The only way it works is with faith and humor. I'm beginning to see that that lesson is more important than all that I could have gleaned from him in a lifetime of late-night conversations.

Follow the Leader isn't always easy. We aren't always successful or graceful or articulate. But, with a grain of faith and a dose of humor, we can keep up—and hang in—making the best of what we've been given. And if a Christmas angel looks more like Aunt Minnie in the clutches of a killer lobster, so be it.

I thank God for all these witnesses who have taught me the virtues that are necessary for the walk of faith. Joy, hope, gratitude, perseverance, humor, and prayer are the keys to survival on this road. And I need to keep surrounding myself with the people for whom they are second nature.

I have come to believe that I was not so far wrong back at the age of fourteen when I thought that the world would change if we could just see and feel one another's pain. I still believe it is the first step on the journey.

And we have the Word of God in which to keep our feet firmly planted as we walk. Every time I visited Mrs. Latham in the housing project in New Haven, she was sitting with her Bible open in her lap. One day I asked her why she read the book so much, and she put her hand on it and said, "I've got a feeling someday real soon the Good Lord's gonna show himself to me real plain. But until he does, I'm gonna keep looking for him in here." She had devoted her life to looking for God, walked that journey from a farm in North Carolina to a housing project in New Haven, and said as I left that day, "Keep in mind that standing fast in the Lord is not the same as standing still in the Lord."

This Word of God and its promises are our weapons in the battle for justice. It unites the struggle against apartheid in South Africa with the struggle against racism in this country, last century's movement to abolish slavery with this century's movement to abolish nuclear weapons, the refugees fleeing Central America with those who welcome them here.

During the trial of Jack Elder—charged with transporting "illegal aliens" because he had given a ride to refugees while helping them to safety—Rev. Donovan Cook, a Seattle pastor active in the sanctuary movement, was a witness on Elder's behalf. He gave a compelling testimony, with frequent references to Scripture.

The judge responded something like this: "You are talking about feeding and clothing and visiting needy people. Of course the Bible talks about those things. But the Bible says nothing about transporting them."

Cook looked squarely at the judge and responded, "Let us recall for a moment a very familiar story. The Good Samaritan found a wounded man in the road. He bound up his wounds, put him on his beast, and *transported* him to the nearest place of shelter."

The Word of God is all we need in this journey—the Word of God and companions to encourage us and point the way.

That Word has already come and made a home among us.

The wonderful mystery of incarnation is God's good gift to a world drowning in its own tears. God chose to come within our reach.

And the Son rejected worldly power, rejected even the privileges that would have been the rightful claim of the Son of God, rejected it all and lived among the marginal and unwanted ones, making them the honored people of God. It was the ultimate act of reconciliation.

"In Christ God was reconciling the world to himself . . . and entrusting to us the message of reconciliation," says 2 Corinthians 5:19. And, the Scripture continues, we are invited to be "ambassadors" of this "ministry of reconciliation" that Christ initiated. We have been entrusted with this message—and this responsibility.

Eras of Christian history have been marked by prevailing theologies addressed to particular historical situations. Emphasis has been placed at various times and places on salvation, conversion, or grace; on pietism, evangelism, mission, or liberation. I would assert that what we most need today is a theology of reconciliation—a faith that acknowledges Christ's redeeming grace, the social burden of the gospel, and the promise of a new unity in the body of Christ which cuts across all lines of division. At this juncture in history, we must heal the divisions and learn to live together, or none of us will live at all.

But now in Christ Jesus you who were once far off have been brought near in the blood of Christ. For he is our peace, who has made us both one, and has broken down the dividing wall of hostility, by abolishing in his flesh the law of commandments and ordinances, that he might create in himself one new person in place of two, so making peace, and might reconcile us both to God in one body through the cross, thereby bringing the hostility to an end. And he came and preached peace to you who were far off and peace to those who were near; for through him we both have access in one Spirit to God. (Eph. 2:13–18)

This is the promise for our age. This—and a very old baptismal formula that says there is no longer Jew or Greek, slave or free, male or female . . . black or white, rich or poor, Russian or American, young or old, born or unborn—or any of the other distinctions that have been used to divide the globe.

Jesus has abolished them all, inviting us away from the legalized and institutionalized and nationalized barriers that separate us, into a new world where compassion reigns rather than law. All those divisions were nailed to the cross. And the dividing wall came crashing down at the Crucifixion with a fall that must have rivaled Jericho's. We need only to live in the promise.

But the Scripture continues:

So then you are no longer strangers and sojourners, but you are fellow citizens with the saints and members of the household of God, built upon the foundation of the apostles and prophets, Christ Jesus himself being the cornerstone, in whom the whole structure is joined together and grows into a holy temple in the Lord; in whom you also are built into it for a dwelling place of God in the Spirit. (Eph. 2:19–22)

As I learned on a bus to Boston many years ago, God is our dwelling place, a refuge for all generations. And we are invited to be a dwelling place for God's Spirit—and a home for Jesus. "Abide in me, and I in you" is Jesus' invitation and promise.

But the way of Jesus is scandalous to this age, as it was in his own. Mary was the first to risk the scandal. Can we?

From time to time I think of that day thirty years ago when I chose Jesus as my shepherd and felt chosen by him. Soon after that day, I committed to memory the Twenty-third Psalm: "The Lord is my shepherd, I shall not want." For a long time I walked around with a confusion about why I shouldn't want him; I had wanted this shepherd from the day I turned five—maybe even before.

That psalm has become a mainstay through many difficult and joyous times. Friends and I recited its comfort before Millie's heart surgery and my biopsy; Jim and I prayed its strength in Nicaragua and South Africa; and at our request, my father-in-law read its promises at our wedding.

I laugh now when I remember the confusion that I felt as a child about its meaning. But I also admit that there have been moments when I haven't wanted this shepherd, when the journey has felt too hard and I would just as soon be abandoned to my own wanderings. And sometimes, like the people of Jesus' time, I really would prefer a hero who would come riding in on a military steed and dash all the injustice and set everything right.

But that was never the strategy. The strategy was the cross. It wasn't fair. Even Jesus knew that. Near the end, he made one final plea to God to spare him the pain and the scandal. "If it be possible, let this cup pass from me."

We are invited into the breach, which is where Jesus made his home. This world cannot be a home for any of us until it is a home for all of us. Until it is a home for little María and her twin brothers, who came into my life on that windswept, bitter night years ago and taught me about vulnerability. Until the poor are no longer cradled in mangers and hammocks and dishwasher cribs.

That dream will come at a great cost. It is the cost of playing Follow the Leader with Christ.

It requires turning away from what is, toward something not yet seen. As long as those of us with privilege and power keep moving up, or even sit still, nothing will change. There are lines that must be crossed and walls that must be torn down if we are to celebrate the humanity of all of us and make the earth a home for everyone. For such a task, we need the strength and courage of one another.

I have shared my journey in the hopes that it may offer some small encouragement to those who read these pages. It is written as a gift of thanks to the many saints who have shown me the way, whose lives have been shaped by the needs of the poor, lived in peace, and reconciled by the cross.

It is for those who feel compelled by the widening chasms

and deepening alienation to look for new answers; who are unwilling to accept that this is the best we can do. It is an invitation to all who are open to discovering, and willing to walk, the gospel journey. For each of us there is a rich and joyful pilgrimage, a way to Jesus; which is, finally, the way home.